CHILDREN'S DREAMS:
FROM FREUD'S OBSERVATIONS
TO MODERN DREAM RESEARCH

CHILDREN'S DREAMS: FROM FREUD'S OBSERVATIONS TO MODERN DREAM RESEARCH

Claudio Colace

KARNAC

First published in 2010 by
Karnac Books Ltd
118 Finchley Road, London NW3 5HT

British Library Cataloguing in Publication Data

A C.I.P. for this book is available from the British Library

ISBN 978 1 85575 636 6

Edited, designed and produced by The Studio Publishing Services Ltd,
www.publishingservicesuk.co.uk
e-mail: studio@publishingservicesuk.co.uk

www.karnacbooks.com

CONTENTS

ACKNOWLEDGEMENTS

Permission to use copyrighted material:

Extracts from the *Standard Edition of Complete Psychological Works of Sigmund Freud* reproduced by permission of Paterson Marsh Ltd, London.

This book describes the results of the studies on children's dreams I conducted in the decade 1989–1999. For various reasons, the analysis of the most important part of extensive materials collected and the writing of this book took a very long time. During this period, various people have contributed to the achievement of my studies and, indirectly, to the possibility of my producing this book.

I would like to thank Professor Cristiano Violani (University of Rome, "La Sapienza") for his continuous guidance in terms of methodology and scientific rigour that were of great help to me in taking my first steps in research on sleep and dreams. I remember having to wait for a long time before he could receive me, but I also remember the valuable suggestions that I brought home with me after I left his room. Besides, his genuine "dislike" of the psychoanalytic theory of dreams helped me to remain neutral in the opinion I was forming myself about it.

The most important part of the studies reported in this book started during my PhD in Psychology at the Department of Psychology of the University of Bologna , during which I always could rely on the authoritative guidance of my tutor, Professor Marino Bosinelli, to whom I feel most grateful. With his competence and sensibility, and his knowledge of the aspects of the psychoanalytic theory of dreams (a rare thing in the academic world), he made a major contribution to solving the various theoretical and methodological doubts that came to my mind while planning my studies.

A big thanks goes to Dr Bruna Tuci (a psychologist working with issues related to development age) who has proactively participated in the researches on children's dreams, taking care of the relationships with school managers, teachers, and parents, and who carried out part of the interviews with the children and of the analyses of the materials collected.

I also would like to thank all those colleagues, Dr Rita Ferendeles, Giorgio Celani, Silvia Gasparini, Anna Testa, and Bruna Tuci again, who helped in my research on children's dreams based on the use of questionnaires distributed in the schools and completed by parents. Their co-operation made it possible to implement a study on a sizeable sample of children in various cities of central and northern Italy.

I found one particular difficulty in my studies, which was obtaining an appropriate enough measure of the indicators of development of the superego functions of personality. In this regard, I remember with pleasure the profitable conversations had with Professor Anna Silvia Bombi, (University of Rome "La Sapienza"), who made available her great competence about the psychology of development age and was of great help to me in the design of projective test stories aimed at evaluating the development of the ability to experience a sense of guilt.

I will not forget the kind patience and availability of the managers and teachers of all the schools in which our research took place. I thank all those mothers who, with dedication and patience, together with their children, allowed the research on children's dreams to be carried out in their homes.

My special thanks go to my wife, Monnalisa Angiletti, who always encouraged me in the writing of this book, even when other job commitments made this achievement seem unlikely and distant to me.

I would like to thank Professor Vincenzo Natale (University of Bologna), who found the time for a critical reading of the first version of this book and provided me with valuable indications on how to improve it.

This book was originally written in Italian. My effort in translating it into English would not have even begun without the certainty of counting on the supervision by Dr Alessandra Maugeri, whom I would like to thank for the commitment and the patience shown.

This book is dedicated to my beloved parents
Luciana Carboni and Antonio Colace

ABOUT THE AUTHOR

Claudio Colace is Executive Psychologist in the Operational Unit of Psychology (AUSL Viterbo) in the National Health Service in Italy. He achieved an MD in Psychology at the University of Rome "La Sapienza" and a PhD in Psychology at University of Bologna, Italy. After training in sleep research at the Sleep Laboratory of the University of Rome "La Sapienza", he conducted studies on children's dreams, dream bizarreness, and on dreaming in addiction. He is member of the Italian Society of Sleep Research and of The International Neuropsychoanalysis Society.

His major research interests are the dreaming in a psychoanalytic perspective, particularly, the empirical study of dream reports in young children; the study of dreaming in drug addiction.

He has published in *Neuro-psychoanalysis*, *The American Journal on Addictions*, *Alcohol and Drug Review*, *Sleep and Hypnosis*, *Sleep Research*, *Sleep*, and *Psichiatria dell'infanzia e dell'adolescenza*.

Introduction: Freud's dream theory and modern dream research

This book aims to represent a study on the actuality and empirical value of Freud's dream theory through the analysis of a specific part of it, that is, the hypotheses about children's dreams. The main assumption that this book will try to support is that Freud's dream theory has systematic properties that allow it to be tested empirically. Moreover, some empirical data provided here will enable a first empirical judgement about the main hypothesis formulated by Freud on children's dreams.

Except for some recent scientific contributions (Solms, 1995, 1997, 2000) that have led us to reconsider sizeable parts of Freud's dream theory and revived the dream debate (Boag, 2006a,b; Domhoff, 2001, 2005; Hobson, 2000, 2004, 2005, 2006; Solms, 2004, 2006), we must say that the aforementioned thesis on empirical properties of Freud's dream theory is rejected by a good part of the scientific community (e.g., Domhoff, 2001, 2005; Hobson, 1988, 2002; Hobson, Pace-Schott, & Stickgold, 2000a; Vogel, 2000). To understand the reasons that have brought us to this situation, I believe a review, however rough, of the vicissitudes of Freud's dream theory in the history of modern dream research may be useful. I believe four main trends may be identified.

A first trend, present from the beginnings of modern dream research (Aserinky & Kleitman, 1953) up to the end of the 1960s, is represented by an attempt to integrate Freudian concepts with the data coming from psycho-physiological research on REM sleep and dreaming. This is due to the fact that, in those years, many sleep and dream researchers had received psychoanalytic training and/or influence (on this matter, see Foulkes, 1996). Various studies were conducted based on hypotheses derived directly from psychoanalytic dream theory. Dement (1960), for example, developed a research paradigm on REM sleep deprivation to evaluate Freud's hypothesis of dream as a "safety valve", and Foulkes and Rechtschaffen (1964) studied the possible role of repression in dream recall. In this period, various reviews of scientific literature also appeared that tried to compare new research data with psychoanalytic dream theory (e.g., Altschuler, 1966; Trosman, 1963). However, the studies of this period frequently failed to reach clear results regarding the hypotheses analysed, I believe because these lack an appropriate study of that part of the Freudian model that is supposed to be tested and the research's hypotheses formulated cannot actually evaluate the original psychoanalytic hypotheses. There are, indeed, very well conducted studies, but they are rare. Bokert (1968), for example, studies in a systematic way the effects of the biological drive frustration on REM dream contents. While potentially rich in experimental implications for the psychoanalytic model, no attempt to replicate this study was ever made. I have recently reviewed the literature on the effects of biological drive frustration on dream contents and could not find a replication of Bokert's study (Colace, 2009a). In conclusion, in this phase, although dream research is directed towards neuro-physiological options, we may observe that there is still an attempt to conjugate new findings with the Freudian dream model. In this period, the psychoanalytic model probably had its peak influence. However, already towards the end of the 1960s, there was a spread of sleep laboratories distant from the psychoanalytic background, and the interest in the psychological component of the psycho-physiological dream research started to wane (see Foulkes, 1996).

A second trend developed in the early 1970s and remains in several present-day researchers. It consisted of a gradual and final consecration of the physiological–neurobiological component in the study of dream processes to the detriment of the psychological–motivational one. This period saw the strengthening of a process that had started with the discovery of REM sleep (Aserinky & Kleitman, 1953): the implications of this discovery for the Freudian dream model at once appeared important. The cyclical and automatic character of REM sleep and dreams led to consideration of dreaming as an event caused by neuro-physiological factors rather than by affective–motivational causes, as psychoanalysis had suggested. Besides this, the studies on animals (REM sleep is present in different species) in the following years opened the way to investigations on the possible neuro–biological mechanisms of REM sleep (and of dream) as well as on its possible neuro–anatomical location (Jouvet, 1962; Jouvet & Delorme, 1965; Moruzzi & Magoun, 1949). These tests, conducted especially in France and in Italy, in the span of a few years, led to another discovery that gave a new blow to the Freudian model. In particular, the data from the study on the sleep of cats showed that REM sleep and dream was activated by brainstem structures and that forebrain activity (i.e., ideational, cognitive centre) is not necessary to activate such a phase of sleep and therefore dreaming; this was in contrast with the Freudian hypothesis about dream being a valid psychological phenomena with an ideational–motivational meaning. These data gave rise to the development of various neuro–biological theories on dream, and the Freudian dream model became a more and more burdensome heritage. This trend ultimately led to the formulation, in 1977, of a new theoretical dream model: the "activation–synthesis" hypothesis, which suggested that dreams are the result of random neural subcortical activation during REM sleep state synthesized by the forebrain (Hobson & McCarley, 1977). The "activation–synthesis" model, as Foulkes noticed (1996) was publicized and promoted very effectively, thus becoming popular. Although accompanied by various criticisms, it dominated the scene until the early 1990s. In *The Dreaming Brain* (Hobson, 1988), the leading author of the model provided a complete version of his theory, together with an extensive criticism and refusal of every aspect of Freud's dream theory. Hobson's underlying assumption was that the Freudian theoretical model of dream would be unproductive from a heuristic and scientific standpoint, as long as its hypotheses could not be empirically tested (Hobson, 1988, 2002, 2004, 2005, 2006). However, these conclusions were based neither on an epistemological analysis of the model, such as, for instance, that formuled by Popper (1959, 1963), nor on empirical data coming from a direct testing of the psychoanalytic dream hypotheses (i.e., dream bizarreness, disguise–censorship model) (Colace, 1997a, 1997b, 2003).

A third trend developed when dream, towards the end of the 1970s, became the subject of cognitive psychology (Antrobus, 1977, 1978; Foulkes, 1978, 1985). The cognitive approach expressly abandoned the study of the motivational aspects of dreams, which inevitably involved a true lack of interest in the theory that, more than any other, had believed in the role of motivations in dream processes: that is, psychoanalysis. For example, the activation of dreams, which in psychoanalysis remains peculiarly motivational, according to the cognitive approach was reduced to a diffused activation in the memory systems. Cognitive dream models, besides, privileged the study of dream production processes rather than the study of dream contents and meaning, thus avoiding any interpretation intent. Leading advocates of this approach were psychologists who, while affirming the status of mental phenomena of dreams and rejecting Hobson's reductionism, eventually neglected the motivational part of dreaming processes (i.e., why do we dream). In conclusion, after psychiatrists and neurophysiologists, psychologists also took no interest in the psychoanalytic dream model in the end, the former because they believed that this model was not scientific, the latter more for a choice of field of investigation, rather than due to the existence of empirical data contrary to the model (Foulkes, 1993a). We must say, however, that the cognitive approach also pursued certain objective ones that, just a few years later, proved helpful for a revaluation of the Freud's dream theory, in the first place, the revisiting of the rigid equation REM sleep = dream. In those years, the cognitive approach capitalized the empirical evidence that, through the years, had shown that dreams are not exclusive to REM sleep and that NREM dreams are similar to REM dreams under various aspects (e.g., Bosinelli & Molinari, 1968; Foulkes, 1962; Foulkes & Vogel, 1965; Goodenough, Lewis, Shapiro, Jaret, & Sleser, 1965) (for a review on this matter see: *Behavioral and Brain Sciences* [2000],volume 23). In the second place, the formulation of models of dream production processes, regardless of the different phases of sleep that also included the production of waking fantasies and that in more general terms freed the dream production model from strict ties to the neuro–physiological conditions of sleep (Antrobus, 1978; Foulkes, 1985). This trend was supported by new empirical data from some Italian researchers that convincingly showed that dream production processes were unique both for REM and NREM sleep (e.g., Cavallero, Cicogna, Natale, Occhionero, & Zito, 1992; Cicogna, Cavallero, & Bosinelli, 1991; Cicogna, Natale, Occhionero, & Bosinelli, 2000; Zito, Cicogna, & Cavallero, 1992). In any case, towards the end of the 1980s, while Hobson's neuro-biological model dominated and the psychologists of dream decided to abandon the study of the motivational aspects of dream, very few authors continued to pay attention to Freud's dream model. In this climate, one clearly against the mainstream trend was Rosalind Cartwright, who, with her interesting studies on the influence of emotional aspects on dreaming, dealt with aspects considered decidedly "out" in the scientific community (e.g., Cartwright, 1991; Cartwright, Lloyd, Knight, & Trenholme, 1984).

A fourth trend, still existing, started in the first half of the 1990s and was characterized by a partial revaluation of the Freud's dream theory. This new position was affected by certain lines of research coming from different areas of investigation, such as: (a) the rehabilitation in cognitive psychology of certain Freudian mental constructions (e.g., the unconscious), including the role of motivation and emotions in the cognitive processes (see Erdelyi, 1985); (b) the development and use of the new techniques of visualization of images of brain activity (neuroimaging) by means of PET (position emitting tomography) and NMR (nuclear magnetic resonance). As these techniques facilitated the study of the neuroanatomic bases of emotions and of primary motivations ("affective neuroscience"), they allowed neurosciences to investigate very complex matters that so far had been dealt with only by psychoanalysis (e.g., Panksepp, 1998; for review see Solms & Turnbull (2002); (c) the neuroimaging techniques that, for the first time, made it possible to directly observe the brain activity of sleeping subjects, to map active and inactive areas and, hence, those areas that appeared most involved in the dream production process (Braun et al., 1997; Maquet et al., 1996); (d) the neuropsychology of dreams that allow one to observe the consequences of a trauma suffered by a given brain area on dreaming processes (e.g., cessation of dreaming) and to draw several conclusions on the role that this area has in normal dreaming processes (Doricchi & Violani, 1992; Solms, 1995, 1997; Yu, 2007a,b).

The neuro–psychological studies culminated in the formulation of a new theoretical model of dream by Solms (1995, 1997). This author reported the results of observations of dreaming in subjects with brain damage, together with a review of the pre-existing neurological literature. The data shown by Solms brought into discussion some "certainties" of the previous models, that is, he shows that: (a) dreaming can be initiated by the forebrain mechanism, regardless of REM state, (b) the neuro–anatomic bases that seem to be most involved in the dream production process are those that "affective neuroscience" has identified as involved in the instigation of goal-seeking behaviours and appetitive interactions with the world (i.e., the mesocortical dopaminergic system situated in the ventral tegmental area) (Panksepp, 1998). It has been suggested that these appetitive states may be considered as something that recalls the Freudian concept of "libido" with reference to the consequential mental activation deriving from our bodily needs. Modern neuropsychoanalysis tends to use the term "appetitive drives" in lieu of "libido drives" (Solms & Turnbull, 2002).

Solms' clinical–anatomical observations developed two important issues. In the first place, if—as the data seem to suggest—motivations have a crucial role in the generation of dreams, this is certainly a new challenge to the psychodynamic model that had produced so many observations in this respect. In the second place, and regardless of any consideration about Freud's dream model, dream research needs to regain ground in the study of the motivational bases of the dreaming processes, generally neglected in the past. Nowadays, these trends are on their way up. There are frequent debates among those who aim to revalue Freud's model and those who have always challenged it (Hobson, 2004, 2006; Domhoff, 2005; Solms, 2004, 2006). Attention is being given to the possible role of motivations in dream processes, as one can learn from a mere glance at the titles of recent scientific papers in which such terms as "motivation" and "emotion" appear (e.g., Colace, 2004a; Peterson, Henke, & Hayes, 2002; Smith et al., 2004). Last but not least, such an authoritative dream researcher as Antrobus has openly admitted that the motivational character of dreaming "has not been well-studied" in the past years (Antrobus, 2001, p. 2). In this trend, a profitable path might be the study of the motivational bases of dreams, where a more scientifically grounded comparison between neurosciences on the one hand and psychoanalysis on the other might be started. An important contribution to this aspect may come from the recent neuro–psychoanalytical approach. Neuro–psychoanalysis, of which a first international convention was held in London in 2000, was born from the co-operation between neuroscientists and psychoanalysts and studies the neuro–anatomical correlations of the psychological processes described by psychoanalysis (see Solms & Turnbull, 2002).

*   *   *

When I began an empirical insight study of Freud's dream model (Colace, 1991; Colace & Violani, 1993; Colace, Violani, & Solano, 1993), I was in the midst of the above-described "Hobsonian era" and the dominant position within the academic community was the rejection of Freud's dream model due to its supposed scant eligibility for empirical testability. In those years, the debate on the scientific status of psychoanalysis in general was also a hot one (Canestrari & Ricci Bitti, 1993; Conte & Dazzi, 1988; Fisher & Greenberg, 1979). With regard to this, I happened to read, to my great satisfaction, the works of Grünbaum. An authoritative philosopher of science, known for his radical criticism of psychoanalysis and for his generally negative judgement on it, Grünbaum had always contested that the psychoanalytic model, to the contrary of what Eysenk (1953) and Popper (1959, 1963) affirmed, can be submitted to an empirical control (Grünbaum, 1984). According to Grünbaum, psychoanalysis contains cause–effect aetiologic hypotheses that allow for statistical predictions (i.e., causally necessary but non-causally sufficient) that have "a high degree of empirical falsifiability" (Grünbaum, 1984, p. 110), that can indeed be empirically tested. Through the study of Freud's dream model, I have reached the conclusion that Grünbaum's assumptions may apply widely to this. In my opinion, the study of Freud's dream model suggests that several parts of it are formulated in a manner that is systematic enough to enable their empirical verification (Colace 1997a, 1997b; Colace,

Violani, & Solano, 1993). A considerable part of the Freudian dream theory that lends itself well to direct empirical control and that can show the groundlessness of the opinions about its ineligibility for empirical testing are Freud's hypotheses on children's dreams. This is the main reason that encouraged me to conduct studies on children's dreams. Besides, as I will point out later in these pages, the theses on children's dreams represent a "reliable test bench" for the verification of some more general assumptions of the Freudian dream model. I must say that there were hardly any data on child dreaming available in literature for the evaluation of Freud's hypotheses; in fact, those few authors that had studied children's dreams had not specifically dealt with these hypotheses (e.g., Foulkes, 1982). Therefore, the only way to test the hypotheses in question was to conduct new studies with programmes that included certain research hypotheses derived directly from psychoanalytic ones.

In the decade 1989–1999, I performed four studies on children's dreams with the purpose of verifying systematically certain Freudian hypotheses on the matter, in particular those related to the progressive presence of bizarreness in children's dreams and to the role played in this by the development of the superego functions, and the hypothesis of dreams as direct wish-fulfilment. In parallel with the start of these studies, I began a detailed analysis and a close examination of the Freudian references on child dreaming in order to have better guidance in the formulation of my research hypotheses. This allowed me to achieve a systematization of Freud's observations. Therefore, before describing the essential results of my research, I will attempt to provide an exhaustive description of Freud's observations with respect to child dreams, highlighting the clarity and the systematic character of his hypothesis, that make this eligible for an empirical test. I have developed this first part of the work with Rapaport's words always in mind: in fact, in 1960, he suggested that an empirical control, safe from dangerous misunderstandings of the psychoanalytic assumptions, could be performed only after a systematic formulation of the general theory of psychoanalysis (of which dreams are a material part). Other authors whom I have taken as reference are Andersson (1962) and Erdelyi (1985), who have contributed so much to the theoretical arrangement of Freud's works.

This book is composed of two parts. In the first part, I try to provide a systematic description of Freud's observations on child dreaming and an evaluation of their eligibility for empirical testability. For this purpose, I will review those writings in which Freud directly or indirectly dealt with children's dreams. This part is composed of four chapters. In the first chapter, I report a chronological and reasoned list of Freudian references on children's dreams in order to give an overview of the evolution of Freud's interest in the matter. In the second chapter, I try to emphasize how Freud considered studying children's dreams useful for understanding dreams in general. Therefore, I describe his method of collecting dreams and the samples used. The third chapter describes the general characteristics of children's dreams identified by Freud, and the fourth chapter deals with the evaluation of the eligibility of Freud's theses on child dreaming for empirical testing, after analysing the issue of empirical testability of psychoanalysis as a whole, and of its theory of dreams.

The second part of the book deals with the main results obtained from four studies on children's dreams that I carried out. Of the four studies, two were conducted in a school setting (Studies I and II), one in home setting (Study III), and another one was based on a questionnaire (Questionnaire on Dreaming in Developmental Age [QDEA]) completed by parents (Study IV). The vast amount of material collected in these studies was only partially analysed and published. While the results of the first study conducted in schools and those of the questionnaire study have been previously published in some technical journals (Colace, 2006a; Colace & Violani, 1993; Colace, Violani, & Solano, 1993; Colace et al., 2000), the results of the study II and III were partially described in my Ph.D. dissertation (Colace, 1997a) and partially published only in abstract form (Colace, 1998b; Colace & Tuci, 1996a; Colace, Tuci, & Ferendeles, 1997; Colace, Tuci & Ferendeles, 2000). The results I am presenting here do not cover the general contents of the dreams, nor other (however interesting) aspects of child dreaming (e.g., self-representation in dreams, children's conceptions about dreams), which would require another volume;[1] on the contrary, this book only deals specifically with the findings related to Freudian theses. In particular, I will describe how children's dreams relate to three key matters covered by Freud: (a) the formal aspect of children's dreams, i.e., length, narrative complexity, and, particularly, dream bizarreness compared to age, (b) the relationship between dream bizarreness and development of the superego functions, and (c) the issue of direct wish-fulfilment dreams. The second part of this book comprises seven chapters. Chapter Five describes the general and methodological aspects of the research on children's dreams. Chapter Six presents the methodology of my four studies on children's dreams. Chapter Seven presents the formal characteristics of children's dreams (length, narrative sequence, dream bizarreness). Chapter Eight reports the findings about the relationships between dream bizarreness and development of superego functions. Chapter Nine deals with the hypothesis of children's dreams as wish-fulfilment dreams, and Chapter Ten presents a longitudinal observation of dreams of a little girl between four and five years of age. The final chapter tries to evaluate the implications of the results on studies of children's dreams on certain aspects of current dream research and theory.

Note

1. Other analyses carried out previously pertain to: dream bizarreness and indices of the superegoic functions (Study I), Colace & Violani, 1993; Colace, Violani & Solano, 1993; (Study II), Colace, 1997a; dream bizarreness and age of children (Study I), Colace & Violani, 1993; Colace, Doricchi, Di Loreto & Violani, 1993; Colace, Violani, & Solano, 1993; (Study II), Colace, 1997a; Colace & Tuci, 1996a,b; (Study III), Colace, Tuci, & Ferendeles, 1997; (Study IV), Colace, 2006a; self-representation in dreams (Studies I, II, III), Colace, Tuci, & Ferendeles, 2000; Colace, Violani, & Tuci, 1995; (Study IV), Colace, 2006a; general dream contents (Study I), Colace & Tuci, 1995; (Study II) Colace, 2006b; (Study IV), Colace, 2006a; wish-fulfilment (Studies II, III, IV), Colace, 1998b,c, 2005; and the relationships between dreaming, sleep characteristics, and television-watching habits of children (Study IV), Colace, Dichiacchio, & Violani, 2004, 2006a,b.

PART I

AN ATTEMPT TO SYSTEMATICALLY DESCRIBE FREUD'S OBSERVATIONS ON CHILDREN'S DREAMS

CHAPTER ONE

An overview of Freud's writings on children's dreams

In this first part of book, I try to give a systematic description of the observations and hypotheses developed by Freud on children's dreams in the early twentieth century. To this end, I have reviewed all the available material on the matter, comparing and organizing it by main subjects, taking for reference the complete psychological works by Freud, as translated into Italian and published with the title *Opere di S. Freud* by Boringhieri. The Italian edition includes the same works and critical apparatus as the *Standard Edition of Complete Psychological Works by Sigmund Freud* (Hogarth Press, 1953–1974). In reporting the quotes from Freud taken from the *Standard Edition*, I have been helped by using the comparison table between the paging of the Italian edition and that of the *Standard Edition* present in the Italian version of Freud's works (Boringhieri Editore, Torino, 1966–1980, volume 12).

In this chapter, I present a chronological and reasoned list of all works in which Freud deals with child dreams in order to provide the reader with an overview of Freud's interest in this subject. We will see that while in certain years there are only brief notes on and/or references to children's dreams, in other years Freud produced longer and more elaborate writings.

The references below are the sources of my attempt to give a systematic description of Freud's ideas on this subject.

1897

In a letter sent on 31 October to Wilhelm Fliess, Freud reported a dream had by his daughter Anna (eighteen months). She pronounced a few words while sleeping: "Stwawberries, high berries, scwambled eggs, pudding". This was Freud's first mention of children's dreams (Freud, 1985, p. 276).

1899

In a letter sent on 6 August to Wilhelm Fliess, Freud asked his friend whether he could include a dream had by Fliess's son Robert among "hunger dreams of children" together with the dream had by his daughter Anna. Freud reflected here on the fact that in dreams children show a tendency to exaggerate (*ibid.*, p. 365).

In a subsequent letter of 27 August, Freud informed Fliess that Robert's dream would not be included among hunger dreams, but in another excerpt dealing with the "egoism in dreams" (*ibid.*, p. 368). (These three letters are the only sources of information considered, apart from the *Complete Psychological Works of Sigmund Freud*.)

1900

Freud dealt with children's dreams in *The Interpretation of Dreams* (1900a). This work lacks a specific chapter on the subject, which is mainly dealt with in the third chapter, "A dream is the fulfilment of a wish", and mentioned in other parts of the work. Eleven child dreams and six child-age dreams reported by adults are given as example. Among the topics treated are: the utility of studying child dreams in order to understand dreaming; the thesis of dreams as a wish-fulfilment; the scarce presence of distortion in children's dreams and the reason for this; the types of wishes appearing in child dreams; the dreams and the psychic system of children; dreams aroused by hunger and "childish" dreams in adults. In later years, in the numerous revisions of his principal work, Freud introduced some notes and additions on children's dreams: I have organized these by chronological order (see below), separate from the original version of *The Interpretation of Dreams*, in order to highlight the evolution of Freud's knowledge on children's dreams.

1901

Freud treated children's dreams in a specific paragraph of his short work *On Dreams* (Freud, 1901a). Here, he reported seven examples of dreams, six of which are the same as those that had already appeared in *The Interpretation of Dreams*. Freud tried to draw a picture of what may be considered the general characteristics of children's dreams. He classified these dreams with respect to the relation between latent and manifest content, to degree of distortion, and to quantity of dream-work. Child dreams are distinguished from adult dreams in their intelligible (i.e., not strange) form and in the direct way in which the wish is fulfilled. Greater space is given to the issue of connections with daytime experiences and to the nature of wishes fulfilled in these dreams. Freud also dealt with childish dreams in adults. He used for the first time the subject of childish dreams to criticize medical theories on dreaming (dreams as dissociated brain activity during sleep).

1905

In *Jokes and Their Relation to the Unconscious* (Freud, 1905), Chapter VI, "The relation of jokes to dreams and to the unconscious", Freud dealt briefly about children's dreams and stated that, in children, dreams can be aroused by any wish that may remain from the awake state.

1909

In *Analysis of a Phobia in a Five-Year-Old Boy* (1909b), Freud described three dreams had by little Hans at three different ages and showing differences in terms of dream distortion.

In an addendum to *The Interpretation of Dreams*, Freud described a dream had in childhood which showed a strange content, defined "a very peculiar dream" (p. 413).

1910

On the occasion of the *Five Lectures on Psycho-analysis* (1910a), held between 6 and 10 September 1909 at Clark University, USA, Freud spoke about children's dreams. In the third lecture, "Psychic determinism, dreams, and parapraxes", about the interpretation of dreams, Freud expressed the concept that not all dreams are apparently incomprehensible, confused, or with contents alien to the dreamer, and that evidence of this might actually be seen in the dreams of young children. Freud then suggested that understanding children's dreams does not require an interpretation technique, but merely information on what the child had experienced the day before.

In *Leonardo da Vinci and a Memory of his Childhood* (1910c), Freud mentioned the existence of "flying dreams" in children (p. 126).

1911

In 1911, Freud added a word and two footnotes to *The Interpretation of Dreams* with respect to children's dreams.

On page 127, he limited the general assumption that the dreams of children are pure wish-fulfilment by adding the word "frequently" (Freud, 1900a, p. 127, fn. 1).

In the first footnote (*ibid.*, p. 130, fn. 2), Freud seemed to suggest that "sexual instinctual forces, in infantile form", being very important in the psychic system of children, may be sources for dreams.

In the second footnote (*ibid.*, p. 131, fn. 1), he added more specific notes to the general assumption that young children have simple and transparent forms of dreams. Therefore, as an example of more complex dreams, he reported those had by little Hans and those mentioned in the work by Jung (1910).

1912

In a note, *Request for Examples of Childhood Dreams* (1912), published in *Zentralblatt für Psychoanalyse*, volume 2, p. 680, in the column "Offener Sprechsaal" (Open Forum) (quoted in Freud, 1918b, p. 4), Freud invited his colleagues to take note of dreams that their patients recalled having had in childhood and that might appear to refer to having witnessed sexual intercourse.

1913

In the note *Children's Dreams With a Special Significance* (1913), published in *Internationale Zeitschrift für ärztliche Psychoanalyse*, volume 1, p. 79 (quoted in Freud, 1918b, p. 4), making reference to the previous note of 1912, Freud thanked those colleagues who had sent material. However, he postponed any opinion on the matter to the moment at which he would have further information available.

In *The Occurrence in Dreams of Material From Fairy Tales* Freud (1913d) described the "wolf-dream" of a young man (Freud, 1918b) as an anxiety dream dating back to childhood. Freud noticed that elements from fairy-tales may reappear and develop in dreams.

1914

In a footnote added to *The Interpretation of Dreams* (1900a, p. 131, fn. 1), Freud quoted ten studies performed by other authors on children's dreams published between 1909 and 1913. Among these, the study by Wiggam (1909) suggested that children's dreams show a tendency to wish-fulfilment.

1916–1917

In *Introductory Lectures on Psycho-Analysis* (1916–1917), Freud dedicated an entire lecture (VIII) to children's dreams. He reported four examples of child dreams that had already appeared in his previous works. Freud described the method used to collect and understand children's dreams and their characteristics. This work is different from the previous ones because, based on the analysis of children's dreams, it provides a systematic list of what Freud defined as conclusions on dreams in general that he hoped would prove "decisive and universally valid" (*ibid.*, p. 126). The differences among children's dreams by age are described in more detail. Children's dreams ("intelligible, completely valid mental acts", p. 127) are used to reject medical theories on dreams. The subject of childish dreams in adults is also dealt with. In other brief parts of lectures XIV and XXIII Freud underlined the utility of studying children's dreams to understand dream functions and, in general, to understand adult dreams.

1918

Freud quoted children's dreams in the introduction of his work *From the History of an Infantile Neurosis* (Freud, 1918b), underlining the significant theoretical importance that these dreams may have in understanding adult dreams. Several dreams appear in the description of this clinical case, mostly of a complex nature, that dated back to the childhood of the patient.

1919

In 1919 two paragraphs, an addendum and a footnote were inserted in *The Interpretation of Dreams* concerning children's dreams.

In two paragraphs entitled "Dreams of castration in children" (Freud, 1900a, p. 366) and "The feeling of reality and the representation of repetition" (*ibid.*, p. 372), Freud showed the presence of symbolism in child dreams.

In an addendum (*ibid.*, p. 522) referring to the wolf-man case, Freud explained the utility of studying dreams occurring in infancy to understand the development and the neurosis of the dreamer.

Finally, in a footnote (*ibid.*, p. 461, fn. 1), he reported a dream had by his grandson at twenty months of age, regarding affections in dreams.

1925

In *An Autobiographical Study*, Freud (1925d) quoted the dreams of children, considering them as a "convenient test" (p. 46) of the fact that dreams are not always generated by sexual desires. Child dreams are explained according to the characteristics of the psychic systems of children (absence of the repressions).

Likewise, in the same period, in a addendum to *The Interpretation of Dreams* (Freud, 1900a, pp. 160–161, fn. 1), Freud reported "the variety of the wishes whose fulfilments are to be found in children's dreams", together with dreams of hunger and dreams stimulated by other vital needs, to reject the critics of psychoanalysis, according to whom "all dreams have a sexual content".

In another addendum to *The Interpretation of Dreams* (*ibid.*, p. 127, fn. 1), Freud underlined that certain distorted dreams, requiring interpretation, may even appear in children aged four or five.

In the work *Some Additional Notes on Dream Interpretation as a Whole*, in the part entitled "The limits to the possibility of interpretation" (1925d), Freud deduced from children's dreams that any dream, in principle, can be interpreted.

We may notice from this overview that Freud kept children's dreams in mind in the evolution of his thought for several years, at least up to 1925 (Table 1.1). The 1897 and 1899 letters to his friend Fliess point out that Freud had referred to children's dreams since the beginning of the construction of his theory on dreams.

Table 1.1.   List of works in which Freud dealt with child dreams.

The Interpretation of Dreams	1900a
On Dreams	1901a
Jokes and Their Relation to the Unconscious	1905c
Analysis of a Phobia in A Five-year-old Boy	1909b
Five Lectures on Psycho-analysis	1910a
Leonardo da Vinci and a Memory of his Childhood	1910c
Request for Examples of Childhood Dreams	1912
Children's Dreams With a Special Significance	1913
The Occurrence in Dreams of Material From Fairy Tales	1913d
Introductory Lectures on Psycho-Analysis	1916–1917
From the History of an Infantile Neurosis	1918b
An Autobiographical Study	1925d
Some Additional Notes on Dream-interpretation as a Whole	1925i

The interest in children's dreams would build up during the years. In *Introductory Lectures on Psycho-Analysis*, in 1916, Freud focused more on the subject than he had in *The Interpretation Of Dreams*.

Originally, Freud's ideas on children's dreams were based on the dreams of his own children and, moreover, on children not suffering from psychopathologies. Later on, clinical cases of infantile neurosis and his investigations of child personality and sexuality led him to partially review his theories, as is shown by the notes added to *The Interpretation of Dreams* in 1911.

In 1914, Freud listed a series of studies by other authors on children's dreams, unfortunately without providing details.

From 1914 on, when Freud described the clinical case of the wolf-man (published later in 1918), Freud suggested another main function of children's dreams, apart from being useful in understanding adult dreams: he suggested that these dreams may be of clinical interest in psychopathology, in order to understand the development of the patients and their neuroses. This concept was re-asserted in 1919, and in 1925, in his *Autobiographical Study*, Freud returned to the subject of child dreams as evidence of the validity of his theory of dreams.

CHAPTER TWO

How Freud studied children's dreams: method and samples

Freud's interest in child dreams

What are the reasons that led Freud to include children's dreams in the development of his dream theory? Children's dreams represented for Freud a theoretical exemplification and, at the same time, easy evidence of his hypotheses on dreaming in general. Through children's dreams, Freud described a series of characteristics (e.g., the dream as wish-fulfilment) that he tried to apply in general to adult dreams.

> From these children's dreams, we can draw conclusions with great ease and certainty on the essential nature of dreams in general, and we can hope that those conclusions will prove decisive and universally valid. [Freud, 1916–1917, p. 126]

> LADIES AND GENTLEMEN, – The study of dreams of children has taught us the origin, the essential nature and the function of dreams. [*ibid.*, p. 136]

> But consider what a large amount of light has been thrown on things by our examination of children's dreams, and with scarcely

any effort: the functions of dreams as the guardians of sleep; their origin from two concurrent purposes, one of which, the desire for sleep, remains constant, while the other strives to satisfy a psychical stimulus; proof that dreams are psychical acts with a sense; their two chief characteristics—wish-fulfilment and hallucinatory experience. [*ibid.*, p. 131]

The importance attributed to children's dreams in the understanding of adult dreams is also shown in the extract from *From the History of an Infantile Neurosis* (1918b), below, where, after affirming that child neuroses have a great theoretical interest for the understanding of adult neuroses, Freud added, "They afford us, roughly speaking, as much help towards a proper understanding of the neuroses of adult as do children's dreams in respect to the dreams of adults" (*ibid.*, p. 9).

Also, when Freud exposed his theory of dreams to the difficult audience of a "country which is devoted to practical aims" (the USA) (1910a, p. 33) on the occasion of the lectures at Clark University in 1909, the first subject tabled was exactly the information obtained from observing children's dreams. Similarly, the utility of his study on children's dreams was to be reaffirmed during the years in different circumstances (Freud, 1901a, p. 643, 1916–1917, pp. 213, 363, 1925d, p. 46).

While children's dreams are mainly useful for understanding dreams in general, Freud also pointed at another way of using them, that is, the possibility that childhood dreams reported by adult patients may represent a source of information that would be helpful in understanding the development of their present neurosis.

Dreams which occur in the earliest years of childhood and are retained in the memory for dozens of years, often with complete sensory vividness, are almost always of great importance in enabling us to understand the history of the subject's mental development and of his neurosis. [Freud, 1900a, p. 522, fn. 1]

Freud's invitation to his colleague analysts to collect from adult patients those dreams which occurred in childhood and which are remembered from that period "whose interpretation justifies the conclusion that *the dreamers had been witnesses of sexual intercourse in their early years*" (Freud, 1918b, p. 4), also shows his conviction that those dreams could be clinically useful. In this specific case, one year later, Freud published another note on the matter in which he thanked Dr Mira Gincburg of Breitenau-Schaffhausen for her first contribution, but postponed any related opinion until a greater number of cases were available (Freud, 1913 [quoted in Freud, 1918b, p. 4]).

Dream collection method

Before describing the method used by Freud to collect children's dreams, his concept of "dream" should be specified. Freud defined dreams in general as follows:

> We can help to overcome the defect of the uncertainty in remembering dreams if we decide that whatever the dreamer tells us must count as his dream, without regard to what he may have forgotten or have altered in recalling it. [Freud, 1916–1917, p. 85]

The writings reviewed suggest that Freud apparently did not use a systematic method and a standard interview to collect the dreams of his own children. He rather seemed to have the habit to take note of the dreams that his children spontaneously told him in the morning:

> But next morning he came to me with a radiant face and said: "Last night I dreamt we were at the Simony Hütte". [Freud, 1900a, p. 128]

Freud often brought as examples his children's reports of dreams experienced the night before, and then he sought the explanation of those dreams in what the children had done during the day before. In other words, in these dream reports, the maximum time span between dream experience and dream recall was generally known (Table 2.1).

The dream examples reported by Freud are almost always a verbatim transcription of the child's narration, made in most cases in direct form (in first person), with the words and the slang used by the child. For instance, "Hermann eaten all the chewwies!" (Freud, 1900a, p. 131).

Freud considered as dreams also very short reports consisting of one or two words, even without any action or verb (see Chapter Three, p. 20).

Table 2.1.   Children's dreams reported by Freud.

Child	Age in years/months	No. of dreams	When reported	Source
Anna[1]	1.7	1	Words spoken in sleep	A-B-E-F
A grandson[2]	1.8	1	Words spoken in sleep	A
A grandson[2]	1.10	2**	Morning after/ on morning awakening	A-B-E
Sophie[1]	3.3	1	Morning after	A-B-E
Boy[3]	3.5	1	On morning awakening	A
Little Hans	3.9	1	—	C
Robert[4]	< 4	1	—	A-D
Girl	< 4	1	Morning after	B
Little Hans	4.3	1	On morning awakening	C
Little Hans	4.9	1	On morning awakening	C
Oliver[1]	5.3	1	Morning after	A-B-E
Girl[5]	6*	1	Morning after	A-B
Martin[1]	8	1	—	A-B
Mathilde[1]	8.6	1	Morning after	A
Total		15		

Notes

[1]Child of S. Freud; [2]grandson of S. Freud; [3]an unspecified child; [4]son of W. Fliess; [5]daughter of friends.

*In *The Interpretation of Dreams*, the age of this child is eight years; **one of these dreams appears only in *The Interpretation of Dreams*.

A = *The Interpretation of Dreams* (1900a); B = *On Dreams* (1901a); C = *Analysis of a Phobia in a Five-year-old Boy* (1909b); D = Letters to W. Fliess, 6 and 27 August 1899; E = *Introductory Lectures on Psycho-analysis* (1916–1917); F = Letter to W. Fliess, 31 October.

Apart from spontaneous dream recall, Freud always had information available on the child's life experiences which occurred the day before, which he obtained by asking either the mother or the child. For example, referring to certain details ("bars of chocolate", Freud, 1900a, p. 128) of a dream reported by his daughter Mathilde, he affirmed:

> It had been precisely on that point that I had been in the dark, but the girl's mother now gave me the explanation. On their way home from the station the children had stopped in front of a slot-machine from which they were accustomed to obtain bars of chocolate of that very kind, wrapped in shiny metallic paper. They had wanted to get some. [*ibid.*, p. 128]

In other cases, Freud himself had information on his children's lives that could explain their dreams. This kind of information was considered necessary, as an essential appendix to clarify certain details of dream content and understand it: Freud was never able to explain the dream without any information about the day before the dream. In particular, this kind of information allowed him to understand whether or not a dream was related to a wish.

For example, about the dream had by Fliess's son Robert, Freud said, "His [Robert's] experiences during the dream-day must enlighten us on the subject" (*ibid.*, p. 268).

Again with respect to the methodology used to collect and analyse children's dreams, Freud stated at least twice that in order to understand children's dreams there is no need to apply psychoanalytic techniques or to question children. In his lectures at Clark University, he affirmed:

> Small children always dream of the fulfilment of wishes that were aroused in them the day before but not satisfied. You will need no interpretative art in order to find this simple solution; all you need do is to enquire into child's experiences on the previous day (the "dream-day"). [Freud, 1909b, p. 34]

And, in a similar manner a few years later,

> No analysis, no application of any technique is necessary in order to understand these dreams. There is no need to question a child who tells us his dream. One has, however, to add a piece of information to it from the events of the child's life. There is invariably some experience of the previous day which explains the dream to us. [Freud, 1916–1917, p. 126–127]

About this aspect, Freud went as far as saying that the method used to collect and understand children's dreams could be applied by any psychologist; in other words, no psychoanalytic formation was needed, at least as far as the dreams of young children were concerned, where dream distortion is absent. This is the reason why Freud was surprised by the scarcity of research on child dreams.

> But consider what a large amount of light has been thrown on things by our examination of children's dreams, and with scarcely

any effort . . . Any psychologist, knowing nothing of the postulates of psycho-analysis, might have been able to give this explanation of children's dreams. Why have they not done so? [*ibid.*, p. 131]

Freud used this dream collection method with "normal" children, not with children suffering from a neurosis, like little Hans, for instance; also, when trying to explain childhood dreams, as in the case of the "wolf-man", Freud availed himself of dream interpretation.

Children and dreams used by Freud

In his writings (1900a, 1901a, 1909b, 1916–17) Freud reported various examples of children's dreams. There were the dreams of his own children Oliver, Martin, Sophie, Mathilde, and Anna, and those of one grandson. Other dreams were collected from children of friends, in one case Robert, the son of Wilhelm Fliess. There were also the dreams of little Hans at different ages. As a whole, Freud described fifteen examples of dreams reported by eleven children (six boys and five girls), the youngest aged eighteen months, the oldest eight years and six months (see Table 2.1).

Freud also reported thirteen examples of childhood dreams reported by adults, seven of which belonged to the young "wolf-man" (Table 2.2). I have decided to consider these dreams, too, because, as we will see, Freud used them to obtain indications about child dreams. On the other hand, Freud affirmed that " childhood dreams . . . are so well preserved that after thirty years they remain in the memory like some fresh experience" (Freud, 1916–1917, p. 91). This issue was reaffirmed in a note added in 1919 to *The Interpretation of Dreams*, in which Freud stated that "Dreams which occur in the earliest years of childhood are retained in the memory for dozens of years, often with complete sensory vividness" (Freud, 1900a, p. 522).

While Freud reported in full only these dreams as examples, the extract below would lead one to think that he based his observations on a wider sample, a sort of personal collection of children's dreams obtained primarily from his own children.

Table 2.2.   Childhood dreams reported by adults.

Subjects	Age in years*	No. of dreams	Source
Adult woman (patient)	4	1	(1900a)
Adult woman (patient)	4	1	(1900a)
Adult man	4	1	(1900a)
Adult man	6	1	(1900a)
Adult woman	childhood	1	(1900a)
Adult man	infancy	1	(1900a)
Wolfman	< 4	1	(1918b)
Wolfman	7–8	1	(1918b)
Wolfman	< 10	1	(1918b)
Wolfman	< 10	1	(1918b)
Wolfman	Not stated	1	(1918b)
Wolfman	Not stated	1	(1918b)
Wolfman	Not stated	1	(1918b)
Total		13	

Note
*Supposed age at which dream was had.

I have been able to collect a few instances of such dreams from *material provided* by my own children. [Freud, 1900a, p. 127, my italics]

If I may include words spoken by children in their sleep under the heading of dreams, I can at this point quote one of the most youthful dreams *in my whole collection.* [*ibid.*, p. 129–130, my italics]

CHAPTER THREE

The characteristics of children's dreams described by Freud

Main characteristics

Formal simplicity and brevity

Freud noticed that in children it is possible to find the simplest forms of dreams. Children's dreams are very brief, clear, coherent, and with an elementary structure. In 1909, during the third lecture held at Clark University, he affirmed, "If you inspect the dreams of very young children, from eighteen months upwards, you will find them perfectly simple and easy to explain" (Freud, 1910a, p. 34).

Similarly, in Lecture VIII of *Introductory Lectures on Psycho-Analysis*, Freud stated, "They [children's dreams] are short, clear, coherent, easy to understand and unambiguous; but they are nevertheless undoubtedly dreams" (Freud, 1916–1917, p. 126).

Actually, the children's dreams described by Freud frequently consist of a short sentence made of a subject, a verb, and a complement; discontinuities hardly appear in dream narration.

Two typical examples dealt with here are the dreams of his son Oliver (5.3 years) and of those of his daughter Sophie (3.3 years):

> Last night I dreamt we were at the Simony Hütte. [Freud, 1900a, p. 128]

> Last night I went on the lake. [*ibid.*, p. 129]

Freud also reported the example of a dream (considered as such) told by his grandson that simply consisted of two words,

> He had been in the habit every morning of telling his mother that he had a dream of the "white soldier"– a Guards officer in his white cloak whom he had once gazed at admiringly in the street. [*ibid.*, p. 131]

We can notice that Freud, in his classification of dreams according to the level of distortion (see pp. 34–35), tends to underline that the shortness of the dream is associated to its simplicity, as happens in the dreams of children, while he associates greater length to greater complexity (Freud, 1901a, pp. 642–643).

Absence of distortion

One of the characteristics of children's dreams, underlined by Freud on different occasions, is their absence of distortion.

> For *children's* dreams are of that kind—significant and not puzzling. [Freud, 1901a, p. 643]

> They raise no problems for solution. [Freud, 1900a, p. 127]

The dreams of children can be interpreted and explained easily because they do not show the difficulties of dream distortion:

> Before we made our last attempt at overcoming the difficulty of distortion in dreams by the help of our technique, we were saying [p. 117] that our best plan would be to get round the difficulty by keeping to dreams in which there was no distortion or only a very little . . . The dreams we are in search of occur in children. [Freud, 1916–1917, p. 126]

From the existence of dreams like those of children, Freud drew two important theoretical indications on the nature of dream distortion. First, these dreams suggest that "not all dreams are alien to the dreamer, incomprehensible and confused" (Freud, 1910a, p. 34);

second, the existence of these dreams leads one to deduce that *"dream-distortion is not part of the essential nature of dreams"* (1916–1917, p. 128).

As we will see, Freud made certain points with respect to the general thesis that the dreams of children are exempt from distortion.

Valid, intelligible, and interpretable mental act

The simple form and the absence of distortion of these dreams shows them as comprehensible, valid, and sensible psychic acts.

Freud used these characteristics to criticize the medical theories of dreaming, which affirmed that dreams are the result of a redoubt psychic activity:

> Moreover, an examination of these dreams offers advantages from another standpoint. For *children's* dreams are of that kind—significant and not puzzling. Here, incidentally, we have a further argument against tracing the origin of dreams to dissociated cerebral activity during sleep. For why should a reduction in psychical functioning of this kind be a characteristic of the state of sleep in the case of adults but not in that of children? [1901a, p. 643]

> As we can see, these children's dreams are not senseless, They are intelligible, completely valid mental acts. You will recall what I told you of the medical view of dreams and of the analogy with unmusical fingers wandering over the keys of a piano (p. 87). You cannot fail to observe how sharply these children's dreams contradict this view. It would really be too strange if *children* could perform complete mental functions in their sleep while *adults* were content under the same conditions with reactions which were no more than "twitchings". Moreover, we have every reason to think that children's sleep is sounder and deeper. [Freud, 1916–1917, pp. 127–128]

According to Freud, the easy interpretability of children's dreams would lead one to assume that, although with different levels of difficulty, as a general rule all dreams may be interpreted:

> And if one further takes into consideration the argument from the theory of dreams that the model dream-products of children

invariably have a clear meaning and are easy to interpret, then it will be justifiable to assert that dreams are quite generally mental structures that are capable of interpretation, though the situation may not always allow of an interpretation being reached. [Freud, 1925d, p. 129]

Wish-fulfilment

Direct wish-fulfilment

Children's dreams show contents in which the direct fulfilment of a wish appears, it is not necessary to proceed with an interpretation:

> The dreams of young children are frequently pure wish-fulfilments and are in that case quite uninteresting compared with the dreams of adults. They raise no problems for solution; but on the other hand they are of inestimable importance in proving that, in their essential nature, dreams represent fulfilments of wishes. [Freud, 1900a, p. 127]

> The common element in all these children's dreams is obvious, . . . The dreams were simple and undisguised *wish-fulfilments*. [Freud, 1901a, p. 644]

> Small children always dream of the fulfilment of wishes that were aroused in them the day before but not satisfied. [Freud, 1910a, p. 34]

In a "strong" version of this hypothesis Freud also suggested that the wishes appearing in the dreams are also their "cause". Regarding children's dreams he wrote, "What instigates a dream is a wish, and the fulfilment of that wish is the content of the dream—this is one of the chief characteristics of dreams" (Freud, 1916–1917, p. 129).

The daytime affective state from which the wishful dream originates

Freud suggested that children's dreams are a reaction, in sleep, to a daytime experience that has aroused and left in the child an affective state such as regret, nostalgia, disappointment, sorrow for a denied enjoyment, or for a unresolved wish or a state of impatience (Freud, 1900a, pp. 128–130, 1901a, p. 644, 1916–1917, p. 128).

A typical example is the one reported below:

> She had crossed the lake for the first time, and the crossing had been too short for her: when we reached the landing-stage she had not wanted to leave the boat and had wept bitterly. Next morning she said: "Last night I went on the lake". [Freud, 1900a, p. 129]

In his lecture on children's dreams in *Introductory Lectures On Psycho-Analysis*, where the general characteristics of these dreams are listed in a more systematic way, Freud stated that

> A child's dream is a reaction to an experience of the previous day, which has left behind it a regret, a longing, a wish that has not been dealt with. *The dream produces a direct, undisguised fulfilment of that wish*. [Freud, 1916–1917, p. 128]

Among these daytime experiences, Freud also mentions hunger: "we should not forget what a fruitful source of disappointment and renunciation, and consequently what a stimulus to dreaming, may be provided by the other of the two great vital instincts" (Freud, 1900a, p. 130).

Children's dreams seem to satisfy, in a hallucinatory way, what has remained unresolved during the day: "The dream was a compensation" (*ibid.*, p. 128); "She was thus retaliating in her dream against this unwelcome verdict" (*ibid.*, p. 130); "He made up in his dream for what the previous day had failed to give him" (Freud, 1901a, p. 644).

The dream sometimes may show a clear wish-fulfilment but, at the same time, does not succeed in transforming the daytime affective state; therefore, contents and affection do not match in the dream:

> If I am not greatly mistaken, the first dream that I was able to pick up from my grandson, at the age of one year and eight months, revealed a state of affairs in which the dream-work had succeeded in transforming the *material* of the dream-thoughts into a wish-fulfilment, whereas the *affect* belonging to them persisted unchanged during the state of sleep. On the night before the day on which his father was due to leave for the front, the child cried out, sobbing violently: "Daddy! Daddy!—baby!". This can only have meant that Daddy and baby were remaining together; whereas the tears recognized the approaching farewell. [Freud, 1900a, p. 461, n.1]

At other times, it may happen that the wish refers to something that will occur on the following day or in the future, that is, the dream anticipates the occurrence of the event. For instance, Freud reported a dream recalled by his "wolfman" patient from his child-hood, a while before Christmas Day, which was also the day of the patient's fourth birthday. It was the famous dream of a tree with wolves in it. (As is known, this dream contained other symbolic aspects and a distorted content that required interpretation [see Freud, 1918b, pp. 42–44, fn. 2].)

Regarding this, Freud wrote:

> On another occasion an association which suddenly occurred to him carried us another step forward in our understanding of the dream: "The tree was a Christmas-tree" . . . He had gone to sleep, then, in tense expectation of the day which ought to bring him a double quantity of presents. We know that in such circumstances a child may easily anticipate the fulfilment of his wishes. So it was already Christmas in his dream . . . [ibid., p. 35]

Types of desires

The wishes that are satisfied in children's dreams are only those objectively more important, or that are such, subjectively, for the child. These are intensely felt wishes. Less important experiences of the day do not enter the dream.

> The wishes which are fulfilled in them are carried over from daytime and as a rule from the day before, and in waking life they have been accompanied by intense emotion. Nothing unimportant or indifferent, or nothing which would strike a child as such, finds its way into the content of their dreams. [Freud, 1901a, p. 645]

The types of wishes that instigate dreams in young children can easily be inferred by the examples of dreams brought by Freud. Furthermore, he summarized these wishes as follows:

> I had mentioned the variety of the wishes whose fulfilments are to be found in children's dreams (wishes to take part in an excursion or a sail on a lake, or to make up for a missed meal, and so on). [Freud, 1900a, pp. 160–161, fn. 1]

These wishes originate from a precise range of time during the daytime.

> This small collection throws a direct light on a further characteristic of children's dreams: their connection with daytime life. . . . The wishes which are fulfilled in them are carried over from daytime and as a rule from the day before . . . [Freud, 1901a, p. 645]

Precise statements on the absence of distortion

During the years, Freud introduced certain precise limitations to the general assumption that all the dreams of children are exempt from distortion.

Transformation from optative to simple present

In 1901, Freud noticed that in the dreams of young children there is a minimum of distortion that, however, does not hinder the simplicity and understandability of the dream:

> Every one of these dreams can be replaced by an optative clause: "Oh, if only the trip on the lake had lasted longer!"—"If only I were already washed and dressed!"—"If only I could have kept the cherries instead of giving them to Uncle!" But dreams give us more than such optative clauses. They show us the wish as already fulfilled; they represent its fulfilment as real and present; and the material employed in dream-representation consists principally, though not exclusively, of situations and of sensory images, mostly of a visual character. Thus, even in this infantile group, a species of transformation, which deserves to be described as dream-work, is not completely absent: *a thought expressed in the optative has been replaced by a representation in the present tense.* [Freud, 1901a, p. 647]

Here, Freud asserted that the optative thoughts of the dream are turned into a visual representation of their realization. It is this form of distortion that he referred to in still other extracts from 1916–1917:

> But when we examine these dreams more closely, we shall recognize a small piece of dream-distortion even in them, a certain distinction between the manifest content of the dream and the latent dream-thoughts. [Freud, 1916–1917, p. 128]

The other, equally constant one, is that a dream does not simply give expression to a thought, but represents the wish fulfilled as a hallucinatory experience."*I should like to go on the lake*" is the wish that instigates the dream. The content of the dream itself is: "*I am going on the lake*". Thus even in these simple children's dreams a difference remains between the latent and the manifest dream, there is a distortion of the latent dream-thought: *the transformation of a thought into an experience.* [*ibid.,* p. 129]

Dream distortion and age

Freud also suggested specific limitations to the hypothesis of the lack of distortion in children's dreams that concern the age of the child.

For example, in 1911, Freud changed the sentence that appeared in the first edition of *The Interpretation of Dreams,* "The dreams of young children are [frequently] pure wish-fulfilments . . .", adding the word "frequently" (Freud, 1900a, p. 127, n. 1).

Elsewhere, he described the contents of child dream that had "becomes complicated and subtle" (1901a, p. 645), with reference to a dream recounted by his son Martin, aged eight.

In *Analysis of a Phobia in a Five-year-old Boy* (the case of little Hans), Freud (1909b) described three dreams had by little Hans at three different ages. A first dream report by little Hans at three years and nine months was explained as a fulfilment of a wish (*ibid.,* pp. 11–12). About a second dream reported by Hans at four years and three months, Freud affirmed that it was "the first dream of his that was made unrecognizable by distortion" (*ibid.,* p. 19). Really, the comprehension of this dream will require an interpretative work (*ibid.,* p. 107).

The experience of this analysis shows, therefore, that some dreams of young children can be more complex. The first direct reference to this issue appeared in 1911, in a note added to *The Interpretation of Dreams.* After bringing the example of a very simple dream, Freud added,

The fact should be mentioned that children soon begin to have more complicated and less transparent dreams, and that, on the other hand, adults in certain circumstances often have dreams of a similarly simple, infantile character. The wealth of unexpected material that may occur in the dreams of children of four or five is shown by examples in my "Analysis of a Phobia in a Five-Year-Old Boy" (1909b) and in Jung (1910a). [Freud, 1900a, p. 131, fn. 1]

Another example of child dream (around four years of age) that already shows the beginning of distortion was the "dream of the wolves" reported by the wolf-man patient (Freud, 1918b, p. 29). Then there are other writings in which the issue of relationship between dream distortion and age of child is mentioned.

For instance, in *The Interpretation of Dreams*, if, on one hand, Freud defined the form of a dream had by a patient at the age of four as "only slightly influenced by the censorship" (Freud, 1900a, p. 253), on the other hand, he reported the dream of Fliess's child Robert, aged under four, defined as a dream "which exhibits the beginning of dream-distortion" (Freud, 1900a, p. 268) and, subsequently, in an addendum of 1909, he reported a childhood dream recalled by an adult, defined as "a very peculiar dream, which also deserves to be noticed as having been dreamt by a child" (Freud, 1900a, p. 413). In 1901a, in the writing *On Dreams*, Freud reported a dream of a child aged under four, that "at first sight it is not quite easy to understand" (p. 644).

Although Freud here did not directly assert a relationship between age and dream distortion, he indirectly pointed out that certain distorted dreams could be found also among four-year-olds.

On the occasion of the "Five lectures on psycho-analysis", at Clark University, Freud limited the characteristic of simplicity of children's dreams only to the dreams of "very young children, from eighteen months upwards" (Freud, 1909a, p. 34).

In 1916–1917, in the lecture on children's dreams in *Introductory Lectures on Psycho-Analysis*, the relationship between dream distortion and age was formulated in a more direct way:

> Dream-distortion sets in very early in childhood, and dreams dreamt by children of between five and eight have been reported which bear all the characteristics of later ones. But if you limit yourselves to ages between the beginning of observable mental activity and the fourth or fifth year, you will come upon a number of dreams which possess the characteristic that can be described as "infantile"... [Freud, 1916–1917, p. 126]

Furthermore, in *The Interpretation of Dreams*, the following remark was added in 1925 to the affirmation that "The dreams of the young children are frequently pure wish-fulfilments" (p. 127):

> Experience has shown that distorted dreams, which stand in need of interpretation, are already found in children of four or five; and this is in full agreement with our theoretical views on the determining conditions of distortion in dreams. [Freud, 1900a, p. 127, n. 1]

In conclusion, although Freud was aware of the presence of distorted dreams in four-year-old children, he believed that up to four or five years of age the simplest and undistorted forms of dreams are frequent, while beginning from the age between five and eight there are numerous distorted dreams, more similar to those of adults. The fifth year of age can be regarded as an important moment of "passage", where dreams, from clear and simple, become progressively distorted.

Dream distortion and sexual drives in childish form

The writings above underline that Freud started to review his affirmation that all children's dreams are undistorted wish-fulfilment in around 1911. This revision follows the discoveries made by Freud on child personality and sexuality (Freud, 1905c) and the analysis of little Hans (Freud, 1909b). The existence of child sexuality suggests the possibility that dream materials may derive from this sphere, which would require the intervention of dream censorship (and, therefore, the appearance of dream distortion). Two extracts from *The Interpretation of Dreams* seem to support the foregoing.

> Though we think highly of the happiness of childhood because it is still innocent of sexual desires, we should not forget what a fruitful source of disappointment and renunciation, and consequently what a stimulus to dreaming, may be provided by the other of the two great vital instincts [it follows the dream of Freud's grandson Hermann eating cherries]. [Freud, 1900a, p. 130]

And then, in 1911, he added the following note:

> A closer study of mental life of children has taught us, to be sure, that sexual instinctual forces, in infantile form, play a large enough

part, and one that has been too long overlooked, in the psychical activity of children. [*ibid.*, fn. 2]

Elsewhere he wrote,

> ... dreams of the death of parents apply with preponderant frequency to the parent who is of the same sex as the dreamer: that men, that is, dream mostly of their father's death and women of their mother's. I cannot pretend that this is universally so, but the preponderance in the direction I have indicated is so evident that it requires to be explained by a factor of general importance. It is as though—to put it bluntly—a sexual preference were making itself felt at an early age: as though boys regarded their fathers and girls their mothers as their rivals in love, whose elimination could not fail to be to their advantage. [Freud, 1900a, p. 256]

In conclusion, we also notice that Freud described childish dreams with more evident distortion in the case of children who showed a neurosis, or other forms of psychopathology, rather than among normal children

Symbolism

Freud (1916–1917) considered symbolism as a second factor of dream distortion, together with dream censorship activity; both may serve the same goal of disguising dreams. He observed that children's dreams may present certain symbolic aspects. In a 1919 addition to *The Interpretation of Dreams*, he presented the following example:

> A man who is now thirty-five years old reported a dream which he remembered clearly and claimed to have had at the age of four. *The lawyer who had charge of his father's will*—he had lost his father when he was three—*brought two large pears. He was given one of them to eat; the other lay on the window-sill in the sitting-room.* ... It is most remarkable, of course, that symbolism should already be playing a part in the dream of a four-year-old child. But this is the rule and not the exception. It may safely be asserted that dreamers have symbolism at their disposal from the very first. [1900a, pp. 372–373]

In 1919, in the same work, in the part titled "Dream of castration in children", there were two other examples of dreams had by children aged three years and five months and six years, respectively, that introduced evident symbolic aspects (pp. 366–367). In another part, Freud mentioned the dreams of flying in children, in which one may see a symbolic misrepresentation of the wish "to get big and do what grown-ups do" and "to be able to do it" with reference to adult sexuality (Freud, 1910c, p. 126).

Dream distortion and development of intrapsychic censorship activity

Dream distortion and topographic theory

Freud's dream theory ascribed dream bizarreness to motivational and psychological factors. In *The Interpretation of Dreams*, the explanation of dream bizarreness was elaborated from the standpoint of the topographic theory of the mind, which is formulated in the seventh chapter of the book. The topographic theory divided the psychic apparatus into three systems: Unconscious (*Unc.*), Preconscious (*Pcs.*) and Conscious (*Cs.*). Freud assumed that among the *Unc.* and *Pcs.* systems a sort of intrapsychic selective mechanism is activated. It reviews and excludes (repression) the contents unacceptable under the ethical, aesthetical, or social profile that cannot be admitted to the *Pcs.* (or *Cs.*) system because they would cause the development of unpleasant affects. As we know, Freud, in analogy with the political censorship of his times, considered this mechanism as a sort of "censor" watching over the passage of these contents to the conscious system.

The distortion and bizarre aspect of dreams was attributed to a series of defensive transformations of the latent elements of dreams, activated by the same censorship agent, normally active between *Unc.* and *Pcs.*, and that continues its action during sleep, although in a softer manner. The latent contents of a dream that are potentially sorrowful and painful for the individual are disguised and distorted until they become unrecognizable before being admitted to the conscious system and forming the manifest content of the dream.

When Freud described the differences between children's dreams and adult dreams (absence of distortion in the former), he really attributed them to the differences existing in the respective psychic apparatuses:

> We may expect to find the very simplest forms of dreams in *children*, since there can be no doubt that their psychical productions are less complicated than those of adults" (Freud, 1900a, p. 127); "in the case of children, where there is as yet no division or censorship between the *Pcs.* and the *Ucs.*, or where that division is only gradually being set up. [*ibid.*, p. 553]

> In them the various psychical systems are not yet sharply divided and the repressions have not yet grown deep, so that we often come upon dreams which are nothing more than undisguised fulfilments of wishful impulses left over from waking life. [Freud, 1925d, p. 46]

The wish that arouses child dreams is supposedly not an unconscious (repressed) wish but merely "an unfulfilled, unrepressed wish from waking life" (Freud, 1900a, pp. 553–554), or "a wish which is known to consciousness, which is left over from daytime life" (Freud, 1901a, p. 674) that therefore supposedly does not demand any distortion. Vice-versa, in the distorted dreams, the origin of wishes is unconscious:

> We have learnt, lastly, from numerous analyses that wherever a dream has undergone distortion the wish has arisen from the unconscious and was one which could not be perceived during the day. [Freud, 1900a, p. 552]

On this point he also wrote,

> We cannot help concluding, then, that there is a casual connection between the obscurity of the dream-content and the state of repression (inadmissibility to consciousness) of certain of the dream-thoughts, and that the dream had to be obscure so as not to betray the proscribed dream-thoughts. [Freud, 1901a, p. 672]

Dream distortion and structural theory

In the second model elaborated by Freud, the "structural model", where the psychic apparatus is differentiated into *Id*, *Ego*, and *Superego*, the concept of "intrapsychic censorship" is replaced by the "superego" (Freud, 1923b). The development of superego functions makes it possible—and necessary—to dissimulate those wishes at the base of dreams that, again due to the development of these functions, have been removed and now return in the form of unconscious wishes in the dreams. Where these conditions are not present (i.e., children who have not yet developed the superego functions) dreams are mostly free from distortion. In other words, in Freud's view, the dreams of young children are frequently clear and simple because children lack those intrapsychic conditions that enable and require the disguising of the dreams' latent content.

While the assumption of a relationship between the development of the superegoic functions (censorship functions) and dream distortion is implicitly present in various works by Freud, in at least one of these it is expressed in a direct form. (The effect of superegoic functions on dream distortion is expressed elsewhere with regard to dreams in general [e.g., 1916–1917, p. 143].) See the dream example below:

> A child of under four years old reported having dreamt that *he had seen a big dish with a big joint of roast meat and vegetables on it. All at once the joint had been eaten up—whole and without being cut up. He had not seen the person who ate it.* [Freud, 1900a, pp. 267–268]

Freud attempted to explain the bizarre element of the dream, that is, "*He had not seen the person who ate it*":

> Who can the unknown person have been whose sumptuous banquet of meat was the subject of the little boy's dream? His experiences during the dream-day must enlighten us on the subject. By doctor's orders he had been put on a milk diet for the past few days. On the evening of the dream-day he had been naughty, and as a punishment he had been sent to bed without his supper. [Freud, 1900a, p. 268]

Here, Freud showed the daytime origins of the dream, but did not explain why the eater fails to appear in the dream. Freud later attributed the bizarre element of the dream to the fact that the child had started the development of the interiorization of moral norms, particularly, *to obey the prohibition on dining* by his parents. Therefore, the child supposedly performed a minimum dissimulation, that is, he omits, in the manifest content of the dream, the person who ate the meal. (This dream was reported by Freud with regard to egoism in dreams. Freud wrote that all dreams are egoistic "the beloved ego appears in all of them, even though it may be disguised" [Freud, 1900a, p. 267]. The fact that the dreamer's ego does not appear in this dream is explained as the effect of the beginning of dream distortion.)

> He had been through this hunger-cure once before and had been very brave about it. He knew he would get nothing, but would not allow himself to show by so much as a single word that he was hungry. Education had already begun to have an effect on him: it found expression in this dream, which exhibits the beginning of dream-distortion. There can be no doubt that the person whose wishes were aimed at this lavish meal—a meat meal, too—was himself. But since he knew he was not allowed it, he did not venture to sit down to the meal himself, as hungry children do in dreams. (Cf. my little daughter Anna's dream of strawberries on p. 130.) The person who ate the meal remained anonymous. [Freud, 1900a, p. 268]

Dreams as guardians of sleep

Freud suggested that dreaming preserves the desire to sleep by treating the stimuli that disturb sleep in order to allow sleep to continue (Freud, 1900a, 1916–1917). Therefore *"dreams are not disturbers of sleep,* as they are abusively called, but *guardians of sleep which get rid of disturbances of sleep"* (Freud, 1916–1917, p. 129). This assumption, too, according to Freud, is particularly clear in the case of children's dreams.

> It is commonly said that sleep is disturbed by dreams; strangely enough, we are led to a contrary view and must regard dreams as *the guardians of sleep.* In the case of children's dreams there should be no difficulty in accepting this statement. The state of sleep or the psychical modification involved in sleep, whatever that may be, is brought about by a resolve to sleep which is either imposed upon the child or is reached on the basis of sensations of fatigue; and it is only made possible by the withholding of stimuli which might suggest to the psychical apparatus aims other than that of sleeping . . . It is clear that any wishes or needs that may arise have an inhibiting effect upon falling asleep . . . Since a dream that shows a

wish as fulfilled is *believed* during sleep, it does away with the wish and makes sleep possible. [Freud, 1901a, p. 678]

We learnt from children's dreams that it is the intention of the dream-work to get rid of a mental stimulus, which is disturbing sleep, by means of the fulfilment of a wish. [Freud, 1916–1917, p. 213]

Differences between children's dreams and adults' dreams

Classification of dreams with respect to the relationship between latent and manifest content

According to Freud, dreams can be classified with respect to the relationship between their latent and manifest content. Different quantities of transformation of latent thoughts generate different forms of manifest dream contents. In Freud's view, there are three categories of dreams that are differentiated with respect to their different formal aspect (plausibility in comparison to common experience, strangeness, consistency of the dream in itself, degree of incomprehensibility and bizarreness). In brief, we have: (a) sensible and intelligible dreams, mainly short; (b) consistent dreams, with a clear meaning that nevertheless strike us because unlikely and/or implausible compared to our experience; (c) dreams without meaning and intelligibility, inconsistent, confused, and senseless, mostly long.

> Dreams can be divided into three categories in respect of the relation between their latent and manifest content. In the first place, we may distinguish those dreams which *make sense* and are at the same time *intelligible*, which, that is to say, can be inserted without further difficulty into the context of our mental life. We have numbers of such dreams. They are for the most part short and appear to us in general to deserve little attention, since there is nothing astonishing or strange about them. . . . A second group is formed by those dreams which, though they are connected in themselves and have a clear sense, nevertheless have a *bewildering* effect, because we cannot see how to fit that sense into our mental life. . . . The third group, finally, contains those dreams which are without either sense or intelligibility, which seem *disconnected, confused*

and *meaningless*. . . .The most evident signs of incoherence are seldom absent, especially in dream-compositions of any considerable length and complexity. [Freud, 1901a, 642–643]

Based on his experience in dream interpretation, Freud noted that certain formal qualities always corresponded to a given amount of dream-work; children's dreams, which are placed in the first category, differed in that they do not show any dream-work activity.

The contrast between the manifest and latent content of dreams is clearly of significance only for dreams of the second and more particularly of the third category. It is there that we are faced by riddles which only disappear after we have replaced the manifest dream by the latent thoughts behind it . . . *there is an intimate and regular relation between the unintelligible and confused nature of dreams and the difficulty of reporting the thoughts behind them.* Before enquiring into the nature of this relation, we may with advantage turn our attention to the more easily intelligible dreams of the first category, in which the manifest and latent content coincide, and there appears to be a consequent saving in dream-work . . . For *children's* dreams are of that kind—significant and not puzzling. [Freud, 1901a, p. 643]

This aspect of the classification refers to a quantitative difference: in short, different degrees of dream distortion/bizarreness (three categories) of manifest dream content apparently reflect different quantities of dream-work. Children's dreams differ in the fact that they introduce a lower level of distortion and dream-work activity.

Types of wish-fulfilment and children's dreams

As to the way in which wishes are fulfilled, Freud divided dreams into two groups. Some dreams, like those of children, fulfil wishes in a clear and direct form, others (the majority) achieve wish-fulfilment in a distorted manner, with evident intervention of dream censorship activity:

We have already been led by wish-fulfilment itself to divide dreams into two groups. We have found some dreams which appeared

openly as wish-fulfilments, and others in which the wish-fulfilments was unrecognizable and often disguised by every possible
means. In the latter we have perceived the dream-censorship at
work. We found the undistorted wishful dreams principally in children. [Freud, 1900a, pp. 550–551]

Freud resumed this classification of dreams in 1901, adding a
third type of dreams, that is, anxiety dreams. Elsewhere, Freud
reported anxiety dreams in children (see, for instance, 1909b, p. 23,
1918b, p. 29).

Dreams fall into three classes according to their attitude to wish-
fulfilment. The first class consists of those that represent an unrepressed wish undisguisedly; these are the dreams of an infantile
type which become ever rarer in adults. Secondly there are the
dreams which express a repressed wish disguisedly; these no doubt
form the overwhelming majority of all our dreams, and require
analysis before they can be understood. In the third place there are
the dreams which represent a repressed wish, but do so with insufficient or no disguise. These last dreams are invariably accompanied by anxiety, which interrupts them. In their case anxiety takes
the place of dream-distortion. [Freud, 1901a, p. 674]

*Origin (location in the mind's apparatus) of wishes
and children's dreams*

Freud distinguished three possible origins for the wishes that are
the bases of dreams. Such origin is related to the different location
in the mind's apparatus in terms of the topographic model (*Cs.,
Pcs., Unc.*):

We may next ask where the wishes that come true in dreams originate. What contrasting possibilities or what alternatives have we in
mind in raising this question? It is the contrast, I think, between the
consciously perceived life of daytime and a psychical activity which
has remained unconscious and of which we can only become aware
at night. I can distinguish three possible origins for such a wish.
(1) It may have been aroused during the day and for external
reasons may not have been satisfied; in that case an acknowledged
wish which has not been dealt with is left over for the night. (2) It
may have arisen during the day but been repudiated; in that case

what is left over is a wish which has not been dealt with but has been suppressed. (3) It may have no connection with daytime life and be one of those wishes which only emerge from the supressed part of the mind and become active in us at night. [Freud, 1900a, p. 551).

Child dreams represent an "unfulfilled, unrepressed wish from waking life" (Freud, 1900a, pp. 553–554) or "a wish which is known to consciousness" (Freud, 1901a, p. 674). This type of wish may be located, according to Freud, in the system *Pcs.* (Freud, 1900a, p. 551).

Formation process of dreams and children's dreams

The model of dream formation process in the psychoanalytic theory is formulated especially in "economic" terms (Freud, 1900a, 1905c, 1917d). The dream is apparently formed after a stimulus that threatens to interrupt the sleep that the dream-work would turn into a dream.

> In so far as a dream is a reaction to a psychical stimulus, it must be equivalent to dealing with the stimulus in such a way that it is got rid of and that sleep can continue. [Freud, 1916–1917, p. 129]

This is a stimulus that tries to arouse the interest of the sleeper. While, at the moment of going to sleep, the individual loses interest in the elements of the surrounding world, it may happen that certain diurnal residues maintain an interest to the individual that gives rise to the dream:

> Observation shows that dreams are instigated by residues from the previous day—thought-cathexes which have not submitted to the general withdrawal of cathexes, but have retained in spite of it a certain amount of libidinal or other interest. [Freud, 1917d, p. 224]

These diurnal residues must be considered latent thoughts of the dream and should be regarded as *Pcs.* mental representations. According to Freud, the state of narcissism of sleep implies that the investment of interest that these daytime residues have is not enough to arouse the attention of the conscience, so "these day's residues must receive a reinforcement which has its source in unconscious instinctual impulses" (*ibid.*).

When the diurnal residues get strength from their unconscious "ally", that which Freud defines the "dream wish" is formed. In conclusion, in Freud's view, a wish that may trigger the dream formation process must be "strong" enough, meaning that it must possess an important investment of energy (of interest) by the sleeper. According to this pattern, we may distinguish the dynamics of formation of children's dreams from those of adults.

In the adult, a wish that arose in daytime and remained unsatisfied, in itself, would not attract enough interest to result in a dream without an unconscious ally. Conversely, in children, a wish unsatisfied during daytime is enough to stimulate a dream. However, this is due to the different psychic structure of children, who do not abandon their wishes easily, so they keep an intense interest also during sleep.

> It is true that children's dreams prove beyond a doubt that a wish that has not been dealt with during the day can act as a dream-instigator. But it must not be forgotten that it is a *child's* wish, a wishful impulse of the strength proper to children. [Freud, 1900a, p. 552]

On the other hand, adults do not maintain intense wishes, thanks to the progressive domain of thought over drives.

While, in adults, dreams are supposedly caused by an unconscious wish (of childish origin), in children, wishes originate from the consciousness sphere. On this, Freud confirmed in 1905 the difference in the dynamics of the dream formation process between adults and children:

> Experience derived from analyses—and not the theory of dreams—informs us that in children any wish left over from waking life is sufficient to call up a dream, which emerges as connected and ingenious but usually short, and which is easily recognized as a "wish-fulfilment". In the case of adults it seems to be a generally binding condition that the wish which creates the dream shall be one that is alien to conscious thinking—a repressed wish—or will possibly at least have reinforcements that are unknown to consciousness. [Freud, 1905c, p. 161]

In adults, the only dreams that can be aroused by wishes not removed are the dreams of "childish type":

I have never maintained the assertion which has so often been ascribed to me that dream-interpretation shows that all dreams have a sexual content or are derived from sexual motive forces. It is easy to see that hunger, thirst, or the need to excrete, can produce dreams of satisfaction just as well as any repressed sexual or egoistic impulse. The case of young children affords us a convenient test of the validity of our theory of dreams. In them the various psychical systems are not yet sharply divided and the repressions have not yet grown deep, so that we often come upon dreams which are nothing more than undisguised fulfilments of wishful impulses left over from waking life. Under the influence of imperative needs, adults may also produce dreams of this infantile type [Freud, 1925d, p. 46]

In the same period, Freud re-stated his thesis that adults also may have "dreams of hunger [p. 131 n.], dreams stimulated by thirst [p. 123 f.] or by excretory needs" against the accusations levied against psychoanalysis that "all dreams have a sexual content" (Freud, 1900a, pp. 160–161, fn. 1, added 1925).

"Infantile" adult dreams

The term "infantile" dream, sometimes used by Freud as synonym for dreams of children, is also a term that designates the type of adult dreams which show the same characteristics as children's dreams (Freud, 1916–1917, p. 126). In his Lecture VIII, "The childish dreams", of *Introductory Lectures On Psycho-Analysis*, Freud put together dreams of children and "infantile" dreams of adults. The latter were also defined as dreams "constructed on infantile lines" (*ibid.*, p. 134) or dreams showing the "infantile type of fulfilment" (Freud, 1901a, p. 646). These dreams can appear under conditions of major deprivation of vital needs and/or under unusual living conditions.

Numerous examples of dreams of this infantile type can be found occurring in adults as well . . . Under unusual or extreme conditions dreams of this infantile character are particularly common. Thus the leader of a polar expedition has recorded that the members of his expedition, while they were wintering in the ice-field and living on a monotonous diet and short rations, regularly dreamt like children of large meals, of mountains of tobacco, and of being back at home. [Freud, 1901a, pp. 645–646]

On the other hand, dreams of an infantile type seem to occur in adults with special frequency when they find themselves in unusual external circumstances. [Freud, 1900a, p. 131 n. 1]

Dreams of the infantile type also include the so-called *dreams of convenience* "in which a person who would like to sleep longer dreams that he is really up and is washing, or is already at school, whereas he is really still sleeping" (Freud, 1916–1917, pp. 134–135) and the *dreams of impatience*, i.e., "if someone has made preparations for a journey, for a theatrical performance that is important to him . . . he may dream of a premature fulfilment of his expectation" (p. 134).

Other characteristics

Tendency to exaggeration in dreams

Freud noticed that children's dreams show a tendency to exaggeration. He mentioned this matter for the first time in a letter to Fliess, after reporting the dreams of his daughter Anna and those of Fliess's child, Robert:

> At some point the "bigness" in children's dreams must indeed be considered; it is related to children's yearning to be big; to be able for once to eat a bowlful of salad like Papa: the child never has enough, not even of repetitions. Moderation is the hardest thing for the child, as for the neurotic. [Freud, 1985, letter dated 6 August 1899, p. 365]

The matter is resumed later in *The Interpretation of Dreams*:

> The appearance in dreams of things of great size and in great quantities and amounts, and of exaggeration generally, may be another childish characteristic. Children have no more ardent wish than to be big and grown-up and to get as much of things as grown-up people do. They are hard to satisfy, know no such word as "enough" and insist insatiably on a repetition of things which they have enjoyed or whose taste they liked. It is only the civilizing influence of education that teaches them moderation and how to be content or resigned. [Freud, 1900a, p. 268, fn. 1]

From this writing, we can notice that also this characteristic of childish dreams, like dream distortion, is put in connection with the incomplete educational development of the child. Freud returned to this topic in *Jokes and Their Relation to the Unconscious* (1905c, pp. 226–227).

Fairy tale materials in dream contents

In *The Occurrence in Dreams of Material From Fairy Tales* Freud (1913d) noticed that materials from fairy tales may appear in the contents of both child and adult dreams. Freud showed that in the famous dream of the "wolf-man" (Freud 1918b) had by the patient at the age of four, in which the wolf—the element of anxiety—was taken from a book of tales (the tales of *Little Red Riding Hood* and *The Wolf and the Seven Little Kids*).

> The effect produced by these stories was shown in the little dreamer by a regular animal phobia. This phobia was only distinguished from other similar cases by the fact that the anxiety-animal was not an object easily accessible to observation (such as a horse or a dog), but was known to him only from stories and picturebooks (Freud, 1913d, p. 286).

The influence of reading a history on the dream is also evident in the case of Martin, Freud's son, who, at the age of eight, reported a dream in which he was Achilles:

> An eight-year-old boy had a dream that he was driving in a chariot with Achilles and that Diomedes was the charioteer. It was shown that the day before he had been deep in a book of legends about the Greek heroes; and it was easy to see that he had taken the heroes as his models and was sorry not to be living in their days. [Freud, 1901a, p. 645]

This dream was reported by Freud also to show that "There are some dreams which consist merely in the repetition of a day-time phantasy which may perhaps have remained unconscious" (Freud, 1900a, p. 492).

Table 3.1. Synthesis of Freud's principal observations on children's dreams.

- The dreams of children are valid and meaningful psychic acts, since they are a finalized (and not random act [i.e., the fulfilment of wish]).
- These dreams have a simple form, that is, essential and elementary.
- Children's dream are short, they may also consist of a few words.
- The content of children's dreams is clear, consistent, and directly connected with daytime life, particularly of the day before the dream.
- They are easily comprehensible and it is easy to understand that they are a direct fulfilment of wish.
- Children's dreams are frequently a direct (undisguised) fulfilment of conscious wishes experienced in the previous day but not satisfied.
- These dreams are a psychological reaction, a reward, to a daytime unsatisfied wish.
- The daylife experience which originates the dream has left behind an affective state of regret, nostalgia, sorrow, and similar.
- Children's dreams may represent a fulfilment of wish with respect to something that will occur in the future("dreams of impatience").
- The wishes that appear in children's dreams are accompanied by intense emotions (objective or subjective) in day-life time.
- Scarcely important emotional elements hardly ever appear in children's dreams.
- The dreams show a wish fulfilled in present time.
- Children's dreams are frequently free from distortion up to about five years of age.
- Children's dreams may be similar to those of adults (distortion, length, formal aspect), beginning from five to eight years of age.
- Sexual drives in infantile forms may give rise to dreams.
- Children's dreams can present symbolic aspects.
- Children's dreams begin to show bizarre elements when censorship functions are developed.
- Compared to adult dreams, they show little difference between latent and manifest content and a small amount of dream-work.
- Unlike adult dreams, children's dreams show the fulfilment of wishes in an undisguised way.
- Unlike the majority of adult dreams, children's dreams may be instigated by a simple conscious wish that was unsatisfied.
- From an "economic" point of view children's dreams and "infantile dreams" in adults show that the dream may be instigated by a conscious wish.
- Dreams of infantile type can appear under conditions of major deprivation of vital needs and/or under unusual living conditions also in adults.
- In children's dreams there is a tendency to exaggeration.
- Children's dreams clearly show how material from tales may appear in dreams.

Table 3.2.   General deductions from the study of children's dreams.

- Dream is a valid, sensible and finalized psychic act.
- All dreams in principle can be interpreted.
- Dream distortion is not intrinsic to the nature of dream processes.
- Not all dreams are bizarre.
- Dream is instigated by wishes.
- Dream is a hallucinatory wish-fulfilment.
- Not all dreams are fulfilment of repressed sexual wishes.
- Dream is a formation of compromise.
- Dream is the guardian of sleep.

CHAPTER FOUR

Are Freud's hypotheses on children's dreams empirically testable?

In the following pages, I try to show that Freud's statements on children's dreams have been formulated in such a way that they may be subject to empirical control.

Before doing this, two matters preliminary to this discussion should be analysed, at least briefly. These are, first, the question of the empirical testability of psychoanalysis in the recent epistemological debate and, second, the issue, viewed particularly within the scientific community on dream research, of the alleged empirical untestability of Freud's dream theory.

The question of the empirical testability of the psychoanalytic theory in the modern epistemological debate: A. Grünbaum vs. Karl R. Popper

Karl R. Popper: psychoanalysis as a pseudo-scientific theory

Popper's criticism (1959, 1963) of psychoanalysis moves from his attempt to analyse the scientific method in order to identify a specific criterion to dividing empirical sciences on one side and pseudo-sciences on the other (i.e., the problem of demarcation).

Popper believed that the *inductivist method criterion* used until then to distinguish scientific theories from metaphysical ones had to be abandoned for being too permissive. In fact, according to Popper, the inference based on a certain number of observations as the foundation for building a theory, apart from being unreasonable, cannot or should not be considered a scientific procedure. Psychoanalysis represented, for Popper, the paradigmatic example of a theory that, even if lacking scientific standards, would be recognized due to the excessively broad range of the inductive demarcation criterion.

According to Popper, the inductive demarcation criterion was to be replaced by the *falsifiability criterion*, according to which any theory may be regarded as scientific when it can exclude the occurrence of a certain number of events (i.e., basic statement). A scientific theory must have the inherent logical ability to distinguish, in an unambiguous way, the events it denies from those it allows (theory predictions). The events clearly denied by a theory are referred to as *potential falsifiers* of that theory.

> I propose the following definition. A theory is to be called "empirical" or "falsifiable" if it divides the class of all possible basic statements unambiguously into the following two non-empty subclasses. First, the class of all those basic statements with which it is inconsistent (or which it rules out, or prohibits): we call this the class of the *potential falsifiers* of the theory; and secondly, the class of those basic statements which it does not contradict (or which it "permits"). [Popper, 1959, p. 86]

When a theory does not have a class of potential falsifiers, it will never be contradicted by experience data and cannot be falsified or challenged. "Every 'good' scientific theory is a prohibition: it forbids certain things to happen. The more a theory forbids, the better it is" (Popper, 1963, p. 48).

Therefore, in Popper's epistemology, the control of a scientific theory should not proceed by demonstrations of its verifiability, that is, the finding of supporting data, but, rather, by attempts to falsify it.

> In other words: I shall not require of a scientific system that it shall be capable of being singled out, once and for all, in a positive sense;

but I shall require that its logical form shall be such that it can be singled out, by means of empirical tests, in a negative sense: *it must be possible for an empirical scientific system to be refuted by experience.* [Popper, 1959, pp. 40–41]

When a theory withstands the attempts to falsify it by means of experimental observations, we will say that the theory in question is "corroborated" because it has passed this test.

According to the *falsifiability criterion*, psychoanalysis (as well as the Marxist theory of history and Adler's individual psychology) cannot be regarded as scientific. In fact, according to Popper, as psychoanalysis does not exclude any possible human behaviour, it is supposedly impossible to challenge it empirically. In other words, the structure of the psychoanalytic theory does not have any potential falsifiers, or classes of events capable of denying it.

> . . . every conceivable case could be interpreted in the light of Adler's theory, or equally of Freud's. I may illustrate this by two very different examples of human behaviour: that of man who pushes a child into the water with the intention of drowning it; and that of a man who sacrifices his life in an attempt to save the child. Each of these two cases can be explained with equal ease in Freudian and in Adlerian terms. According to Freud the first man suffered from repression (say, of some component of his Oedipus complex), while the second man had achieved sublimation. According to Adler the first man suffered from feelings of inferiority (producing perhaps the need to prove to himself that he dared to commit some crime), and so did the second man (whose need was to prove to himself that he dared to rescue the child). I could not think of any human behaviour which could not be interpreted in terms of either theory. [Popper, 1963, p. 46]

Adolf Grünbaum: a criticism of the thesis of the empirical untestability of psychoanalysis

Grünbaum (1984) has strongly criticized psychoanalysis, particularly the theory of repression and the role it was said to have in the causes of neuroses and in the explanation of dreams, forgetfulness, and lapsus.

I am not going to deal with his criticism, because what I am particularly interested in are its premises: Grünbaum's assumption that, to the contrary of what Popper affirmed, psychoanalysis is a theory that can potentially and logically be subject to empirical control. Grünbaum wanted to demonstrate that the clinical psychoanalytic method and the aetiologic hypotheses based on it are defective from an epistemologic standpoint, but for other reasons than the non-falsifiability asserted by Popper (Grünbaum, 1984). According to Grünbaum, psychoanalysis is based solely on clinical evidence, and clinical data are unavoidably epistemologically contaminated by the suggestion. Furthermore, for this author, the psychoanalytic clinical method is not able to validate the aetiologic causal hypothesis of neuroses, since it is invalidated from the fallacy of *post hoc ergo propter hoc*. In Grünbaum's view, the empirical control of psychoanalysis should be mostly of non-clinical experimental nature.

Grünbaum showed the groundlessness of Popper's assumption by reporting and studying in depth various examples of empirical falsifiability in psychoanalysis and, in particular, he analysed Freud's writing on *A Case of Paranoia Running Counter to the Psychoanalytic Theory of the Disease* (Freud, 1915f). He suggested that the psychoanalytic theory introduces different aetiologic hypotheses where a specific factor is "causally necessary" (but non-causally sufficient), and that have "a high degree of empirical falsifiability" (Grünbaum, 1984, p. 110). In other words, Freud's aetiologic hypotheses allow the making of predictions about the increase of the incidence of a psychopathological syndrome whenever a given causal factor is present, and these are similar to hypotheses commonly present in medicine. The fact that these hypotheses have a limitation to predictability, in the sense that they deny that a necessary causal factor may also be considered sufficient, does not justify the accusation of non-disconfirmability brought by Popper.

> An apologist for Popper was thereby led to conclude that the limitation on predictability in psychoanalysis thus avowed by Freud is tantamount to generic nonpredictability and hence to nondisconfirmability. But oddly enough this apologist is not inclined to regard the causal relevance of heavy smoking to cardiovascular disease as wholly nonpredictive or nondisconfirmable, although chain smoking is not even held to be a specific pathogen for this disease, let alone a universal predictor of it. [*ibid.*, p. 112]

According to Grünbaum, the fact that no example of testable consequences could be found in the review of Freud's theory was not to be held as proof of their untestability, nor could it allow the presumption of the intrinsic impossibility to submit psychoanalysis to empirical control. On the contrary, if these examples of falsifiability do exist (as Grünbaum showed), some philosophers of science (the Popperians), far from having given proof of any scientific want in psychoanalysis, have shown a lack of knowledge of it. (Other authors suggested that it is not so automatic to think that the general theory of psychoanalysis [of which dreams are part] is widely known and understood (Erdelyi, 1985; Rapaport, 1960). With regard to this, Grünbaum stated,

> It is as if those with only a rather cursory exposure to physics concluded by inspection that its high level hypotheses are not falsifiable, just because *they* cannot think of a way to test them. [1984, p. 113]

Besides, Grünbaum, in the case of "drowning child" (see above), affirmed that this was a "grossly contrived" example and he suggested that Popper "gives no indication whatever whether he drew this example from any actual case history or publication of Freud's (or Adler's)" (*ibid.*, p. 114). This example brought by Popper, together with the accusation that any behaviour is explicable in Freudian terms, fails to do justice to the fact that

> Freud scorned the attribution of such universal explanatory power to his theory as a vulgar misunderstanding, when he referred to psychoanalysis and wrote : "It has never dreamt of trying to explain 'everything'" (*S.E.* 1923, *18*: 252). [*ibid.*]

According to Grünbaum, not only psychoanalysis can develop falsifiable predictions, but Freud himself as *methodologist* showed, at least in certain circumstances, a certain "intellectual hospitality" to accepting the objections expressed by others and to highlighting those events that he discovered and that questioned his own prior hypotheses.

> In his instructive 1895 "Reply to Criticisms of My Paper on Anxiety Neurosis" (*S.E.* 1895, 3; 123–139), Freud stated explicitly what sort of finding he would acknowledge to be a *refuting* instance for his hypothesized etiology of anxiety neurosis. Indeed, this reply, as well as the original paper defended in it, throw a great deal of light

on Freud's understanding of the standards that need to be met when validating causal hypotheses. [*ibid.*, p. 118]

J. Allan Hobson and the presumed empirical untestability of Freud's dream theory

Hobson has developed the "activation-synthesis" theory of dreaming processes (Hobson & McCarley, 1977), which proposes alternative hypotheses to the psychoanalytic model, in particular with regard to dream activation, considered as "motivationally neutral" (McCarley & Hobson, 1977, p. 1219) and identified with the activation of REM sleep, and to the explanation of dream bizarreness, directly attributed to the neurophysiological events of REM sleep (random ponto-geniculo-occipital activation and aminergic demodulation). The former hypothesis wants to reject the Freudian thesis of dream as wish-fulfilment, the latter intends to replace the disguise–censorship model of dream bizarreness. Here, I will not go into detail about the theory of dream processes developed by Hobson, or about its unconvincing aspects (elsewhere, I have suggested that there are several data in literature that are not consistent with the "activation-synthesis" hypothesis and, in particular, with the hypothesis on dream bizarreness [Colace, 1997b, 2003]), but about Hobson's criticism of Freud's dream theory.

Hobson is, among dream researchers, the one who, more than any other, has pointed at the question of the scientific untestability of psychoanalysis within the framework of the psychoanalytic dream theory (Hobson, 2006). He attributed three vital defects to the psychoanalytic theory of dream.

First, this theory "is not scientific because it is not empirically based" (Hobson, 1988, p. 53). The theory is seen as more like a "proto-scientific" and "essentially religious" approach (Hobson, 2002, pp. 17, 19).

Second, "psychoanalytic theory is not logically constructed in such a way as to make it amenable to direct experimental test" (Hobson, 1988, p. 53) and it does not allow either quantitative observations or exact predictions (*ibid.*, p. 55).

Third, "psychoanalysts have never even defined the sort of evidence that could refute the theory" (*ibid.*, pp. 53–54) and there is no evidence to support the Freudian dream theory (Hobson, 1986). Here, Hobson seems to return to Popper's empirical non-falsifiability thesis.

Finally, Hobson criticized Freud as a methodologist and, accusing him of having unfairly criticized the medical theories of his times on dream (Hobson's book "is firmly dedicated to a scientific resuscitation of the 'medical theory of dream life', which Freud disdained" [Hobson, 1988, p. 51]), he wrote,

> Regardless of its nature, the literature that Freud reviewed confirmed his theory: he simply explained away any puzzling or contradictory data. By 1936, his thinking was characterized by arbitrariness, authoritarianism, and a failure to specify rules or imagine data that could contradict his theory. [*ibid.*, pp. 58–59]

Are Freud's observations on children's dream empirically testable?

Freud has used a scarcely systematic method to collect child dreams, and his results are mainly based on the spontaneous dreams reported by children on early morning awakening. Having said this, we need to establish whether the characteristics of the dreams described by Freud are verifiable against a sample of dreams collected in a more systematic way. Based on the premise of this intrinsic limit to Freud's observations, we will examine how Freud formulated his hypotheses.

1. *Methodological conditions.* Notwithstanding the scarce systematicity, Freud clarified certain basic conditions of his method. In the first place, he gave a clear definition of what he meant for "dream"; in the second place, he pointed out, as a necessary condition for understanding dreams, the availability of detailed information on the dreamer's daytime experiences.
2. *Hypothesis on frequencies.* Freud gave two clear indications about the frequency of specific types of dreams in young children. Particularly, clear wish-fulfilment dreams are very frequent and bizarre dreams are very scarce. These predictions can be easily checked with a congruous sample of dreams of young children.

3. *Correlational hypothesis.* Freud formulated various explicit correlational hypotheses according to which it is possible to make certain predictions that can be empirically valued by using statistic validity indices. For example, the hypothesis of the relationship between dream bizarreness and age, or the hypothesis of the relationship between dream bizarreness and development of superego functions.

4. *Measurability.* The measurement of the variables considered by Freud shows the same difficulties as other positions of the psychological research. For instance, dream bizarreness or other aspects of dream content can be measured by means of "content scales", as usually happens in dream research (Winget & Kramer, 1979). The aspects of personality that are grouped by Freud under the concept of "superego functions" (moral conscience, prohibitions, self-observations, etc.) can be measured, like other aspects of personality, through indirect indices by means of psychological research tools such as questionnaires, tests, etc. As to the wish-fulfilment variable in dreams, it must be kept in mind that, unlike in adult dreams, in child dreams there are various conditions offering greater control opportunities: in particular, Freud specified that (a) with these dreams there is no interpretation problem and wish-fulfilment is clearly present in dream contents (provided that information on the child's diurnal experiences are available), (b) the wish portrayed in these dreams is known to the child, and often also to the person(s) present in the child's daytime experience, and is therefore easily detectable, (c) the daytime experience from which the dream originates lies within a precise time range (e.g., the day before the dream), (d) these dreams concern only important wishes, "intensely felt" by the child.

5. *Classifications.* Freud also introduced criteria to measure those aspects of dream that formed the subject of his hypotheses, and developed at least three explicit classifications of dreams (dream bizarreness, origin of wishes, ways of satisfying wishes) that allow one to make a systematic distinction between child dreams and adult dreams: these classifications can be used to assess "objectively" the changes that intervene in dream contents and in the process of dream formation in developmental age.

Other clear predictions that can be controlled are, for instance, those related to the relationship between length and bizarreness of dreams, to the narrative simplicity of dreams, to the type of experiences and daytime affective states that are supposedly the basis of children's dreams, to the types of wishes appearing in children's dreams, all aspects on which Freud made unambiguous statements.

From the standpoint of Popper's epistemological criterion (*falsifiability criterion*), we may see that these hypotheses of Freud's do have clear potential falsifiers, that is, facts that, if found to be true, would clearly deny the theory (see Table 4.1). Freud himself, after all, while developing his theories showed that some of his starting assumptions could be falsified, and that therefore there were events that could prove his theory wrong or at least suggest a change to its original hypothesis: it is the case of Freud's revision of his 1900 thesis according to which all children's dreams are mere fulfilment of wishes, which he changed after his investigations on personality and sexuality in children and on cases of neurosis in children. This is evident in the notes he added in 1911 to *The Interpretation of Dreams*, which limit the scope of absence of dream distortion to children up to four or five years of age.

In conclusion, I believe that the system of observations and statements about children's dreams delineated by Freud has enough credentials of systematicity and is built in such as way that it may actually be subject to empirical control. The systematic features of Freud's hypotheses on children's dreams are summarized in Table 4.1.

Has the empirical testing of Freud's observations on child dreams any evidence value for the general theory of dreams?

The control of the hypotheses on children's dreams, apart from being able to establish an empirical base for Freud's observations on this type of dream, introduces a certain value of evidence for the purposes of a judgement on certain more general hypotheses of Freud's dream theory.

1.   *The dream as a valid and meaningful psychic act.* If the observations on children's dreams showed that these indeed have an

Table 4.1. Systematic features of Freud's observations about children's dreams.

Method	• Operational definition of "dream"; • Conditions for repetition of the observations: availability of information on the child's daytime experience.
Hypotheses on frequencies (examples)	• Low frequency of distorted dreams up to age 4–5; • High frequency of clear wish-fulfilment dreams up to age 4 5.
Correlational hypotheses	• (positive) Dream distortion and age; • (positive) Dream distortion and super-ego functions development.
Measurability	• In children's dreams the fulfilment of wishes is evident; • The wishes that appear in the dream can be easily traced in the daytime experience; • The wishes that find place in the dream are only the important ones.
Classifications	• Dream distortion: definition of three levels (quantitative and qualitative); • Origin of the wishes; • Ways to satisfy the wishes in dreams.
Potential falsifiers (examples)	• Observation of a high frequency of long dreams in children (hypothesis: children's dreams are often brief); • Observation that young children's dreams are frequently bizarre (hypothesis: young children's dreams are often not bizarre; • Observation that in young children many dreams do not show a clear fulfilment of wish (hypothesis: the dreams of children are frequently direct fulfilment of wishes).

easily understandable content related to the dreamer's diurnal experience, they would contribute to clarifying whether dreams can be regarded, in principle, as psychic acts with a sense and an individual meaning, rather than as random processes.

2. *The dream as wish-fulfilment.* The empirical control of the assumption that the dreams of children often represent the direct *Pcs.* wish-fulfilment may also have a certain probative importance for the general assumption that "a dream is a (disguised) fulfilment of a (suppressed or repressed) wish" (Freud, 1900a, p. 160) for the following reason: if it were proved, through systematic observations, that, even in children, where observation conditions are privileged (according to Freud himself), dreams do not often represent the fulfilment of a wish, this would be a piece of evidence against the general adoption of this assumption, as it would be shown that *there are at least some dreams that do not present the fulfiment of a wish.*

3. *The nature of dream bizarreness.* If the observations on young children's dreams showed that these are more often simple than bizarre, this would be in agreement with Freud's general assumption that: (a) *"dream-distortion is not part of the essential nature of dreams"* (Freud, 1916–1917, p. 128), and (b) dream-distortion is not a characteristic of all dreams (*ibid.*, p. 143).

4. *The disguise–censorship theory of dream bizarreness.* The Freudian model of disguise–censorship is not alien to the results of a control of the statistic validity of the relationships between dream bizarreness and the development of the superego functions in children. If it were shown that the levels of dream bizarreness have no relation to the indices of the development of the superego functions and, particularly, that children who have not completely developed these functions report bizarre dreams, this would be a piece of evidence against the general disguise–censorship model of dream, that assumes a central role of the censorship functions, later superego functions (in the ego), in the possibility/necessity to disguise the dream's latent contents (Freud, 1916–1917, pp. 142–143).

5. *The function of dream as guardian of sleep and as "safety valve".* Freud suggested that dreams preserve the individual's desire to sleep, treating sleep-disturbing stimuli in order to favour its continuation (see Freud, 1900a, 1916–1917, p. 129). Another function of dreams that Freud resumes from Robert (1886) is that of discharging the psyche as a sort of "safety valve" (Freud, 1900a). Information for an investigation of these possible

functions of dreams may be obtained from an observation of those children's dreams, if any, that are a clear fulfilment of wish, where there is a known connection with diurnal experiences.

5.   *The existence of dreams that satisfy unrepressed wishes.* The verification of the existence of dreams that appear as the fulfilment of *Pcs.* wishes from the daytime experience is consistent with Freud's assumption that certain dreams may also be aroused by simple non-repressed wishes (Freud, 1900a, pp. 160–161, n. 1, 1925d, p. 46).

PART II

EMPIRICAL EVALUATION OF FREUD'S OBSERVATIONS ON CHILDREN'S DREAMS

CHAPTER FIVE

Dream research in children: general and methodological aspects

When do children start dreaming?

D ifferent authors have attempted to establish at what stage of development children start dreaming. However, it is very difficult to discover this until children develop their language abilities, since their dream experience is accessible only when it can be verbally reported.

Some authors have assumed, based on behavioural signs shown by children during sleep (e.g., movements, smiles, cries, vocalizations), that there is a certain "rudimentary" dreaming activity already at around one year of age (Hug-Helmuth, 1919; Fraiberg, 1959; Diatkine, 1975). Niederland (1957), for example, noticed the presence of "nightmares" (not yet reported in words) in children between seventeen and twenty months, and vocalizations during sleep have been observed at around 13–14 months of age (Mack, 1965; Fraiberg, 1950).

However, Piaget (1945) suggested that these behavioural signs probably do not evoke any mental images. In this sense, the presence in young children of dreams like those dreamed by older children and adults should be excluded. As we have seen, Freud reported examples of dreams in children aged eighteen months; Piaget, likewise, affirmed that the first dreams appear in children aged 1.9–2 years, who spoke in their sleep and reported the dream upon awakening (*ibid.*).

Some authors have confirmed the presence of these first dream reports around 24–30 months of age (Grotjahn, 1938; Niederland, 1957).

Kohler, Coddington, and Agnew (1968), in their sleep laboratory studies, also found early dream reports at this age. These authors, after selecting a sample of children with good verbal ability, observed that some of these were able to report dreams on awakening from REM sleep at around two years of age.

Foulkes (1982, 1999), in his classical studies in sleep laboratories, clearly distinguished the presence of REM sleep (that is present, for instance, also in several kinds of animals) from the possibility of having a complex mental activity such as dreaming. On the neurophysiological side, REM sleep is certainly present from the moment of birth. In fact, in the early months of life, the REM stage accounts for around 40% of the sleep, and for 25–30% at around the second year of life (Bosinelli & Cicogna, 1991). The problem lies in establishing whether this corresponds to the presence of a dreaming activity. Foulkes (1982) found that pre-school children recall dreams only in 27% of REM awakenings. He suggested that children may not generate dreams until they have developed visual-spatial abilities (e.g., the ability to think of images or to imagine visually). Indeed, Foulkes found that the percentage of dream recalls following REM awakenings is positively correlated with the tests that measure these abilities (i.e., Block design score, Wechesler Test) (Foulkes, 1982; Foulkes, Hollifield, Sullivan, Bradley, & Terry, 1990). Foulkes concluded that children can report their first dreams at around 3–4 years of age (Foulkes, 1982, 1999).

The first dream collected in my studies is that of a girl aged two years and eleven months: "The dog 'Baruba' was running with me towards the road and then he encouraged her to climb up and run faster, but there was an officer."

Methods for collecting dream reports

Three main methods have been employed in the investigations on child dreaming.

1. *Dream reports collected by means of standard interviews at school.* This method consists of interviewing children one by one at school at a given time in the morning, in a room arranged for the purpose. The interviewer usually asks the child to tell the dream, generally "the last dream had" by means of a standard interview. Dream reports are recorded and then transcribed verbatim. The transcripts of dream reports may be classified in different forms by content scales used to measure and score objectively the frequency of certain given dream contents (e.g., Colace & Violani, 1993; Levi & Pompili, 1991).

    This methodology allows researchers to collect dream reports in a systematic and homogeneous way. A variation of this method is the one represented by the Most Recent Dream Method, which consists of asking the children to write the most recent dream they can remember (regardless of whether it was had the night, the week, or the month before) and note the date on which the dream was had. This method has been used with children aged eight years and upwards (Avila-White, Schneider, & Domhoff, 1999; Saline, 1999).

2. *Dream reports collected at home setting upon morning awakening.* Children are interviewed in their homes when they wake up in the morning, for a given period of time, for example, a week or a month (e.g., Colace, 1997a; Colace, Tuci, & Ferendeles, 1997; Foulkes, 1979; Resnick, Stickgold, Rittenhouse, & Hobson, 1994). The interviewer is usually a parent (often the mother) instructed on how to conduct the standard interview in order to minimize the risk of errors, straining, and interpretation. The latter methodology, compared to the one mentioned previously, gives greater guarantees that children report a recent dream experience (i.e., from the period of sleep that precedes their awakening) and there is less risk of dream alteration than in reports made at a certain distance in time.

Both these methods, and particularly the former, are subject to the limitation that the dreams collected after a certain amount of time has elapsed from when they were experienced can only represent a partial (and biased) sample of the whole of child dreams. In my opinion, one merit of these methods lies in the fact that they allow us to collect dream reports in a familiar and comfortable environment for the child.

3. *Dream reports collected in sleep laboratories.* This method consists of interviewing children in "sleep laboratories" on awakenings pre-arranged at specific stages of the sleep (e.g., REM sleep) defined by physiological indexes (i.e., through the use of the EEG electroencephalogram, EOG electro-oculogram, EMG electromyogram). This method reduces considerably the risks of an alteration of the dream content due to recall at distance, and the dream reports collected provide a more representative sample of children's dreaming (Foulkes, 1982). Some authors have noticed that this method may introduce a greater risk from the possibly inhibiting and artificial effect of the laboratory on the child, especially for younger children (i.e., foreign and unusual environment) (Resnick, Stickgold, Rittenhouse, & Hobson, 1994; Schwartz, Weinstein, & Arkin, 1978; Van de Castle, 1994). Differences in contents were actually observed between laboratory dreams and home dreams (Foulkes, 1979). However, Foulkes (1979, 1999) suggested that these differences are not due to the effect of the laboratory in itself, and may be explained by the above-mentioned principle of partial dream sampling in home studies. Foulkes's assumptions are actually supported by empirical data. This author showed that when children are woken up always at the same time (six o'clock in the morning), in both settings (laboratory and home), in order to have an identical sampling of dreams, the differences in dream recall percentages was not significant. This apparently suggests that there is no inhibiting effect of the laboratory in dream recall. Nevertheless, given the small number of studies, particularly on the dreams of children aged between three and seven, I believe any conclusion on the possible effects of the method (school/home *vs.* laboratory) on the general contents and other aspects of children's dreams would be premature.

I believe that the criticism brought against the sleep laboratory method (Resnigk, Stickgold, Rittenhouse, & Hobson, 1994) is excessive and, in any case, the validity of this method in scientific dream studies is certain, while there is too much concern about the fallacy of the home collection method (Foulkes, 1999). Foulkes (1999) has recently developed a more radical position, distinguishing "Dreams A", collected in sleep laboratories, as the only credible sources of empirical study on children's dreaming, from "Dreams B", "told to an obviously interested parental audience around the breakfast table", which might have value only for "personalistic and social disciplines" Foulkes (1999, pp. 39, 37). A thorough investigation on dreams would require all of the methodologies described above. If, on the one hand, the dream reports collected in sleep laboratories are more reliable and representative of children's dreaming, on the other hand, it is useful to compare these laboratory dreams with the dreams collected in more familiar settings, such as home and school, and with methodologies that allow one to observe the relationships between dream contents and the child's recent daytime experiences, also with the help of parents.

Dream reports' collection, at home and in sleep laboratories, is the most reliable dream study methodology; it is worth noting, however, that it implies major costs (e.g., skilled personnel, organizational arrangements) and implementation problems, such as, for instance, difficulties in bringing the children and their parents to the sleep laboratories, or in finding parents willing to interview their children at home on morning awakening. These may be serious obstacles to the research on children's dreams. In fact, very few studies have been made so far, and therefore there is a risk of excessive generalization of data based on small groups of subjects.

An attempt was made recently to collect data on children's dreams through a Questionnaire on Dream in Evolutionary Age (QDEA) filled out by parents. This methodology has allowed researchers to collect data in an easier and more cost-effective way and from wider groups of children. Even though this method cannot be used as a substitute for conventional ones, the results of the employment of the QDEA show that parents may provide, through their answers, reliable indications on various characteristics of young children's dreams that, besides, prove consistent with what is known in literature (e.g., brevity of dreams, presence of animal characters, etc.). From this point of view, this methodology may be useful to supplement and confirm the existing knowledge base on children's dreams (Colace, 2004b,c, 2006a; Colace et al., 1999; Colace et al., 2000; Colace, Ferendeles, Tuci, & Celani, 2000).

The issue of credibility of children's dreams

Authors who have been dealing with children's dreams have long stressed how this research is useful to understand dreams in general and the psychological development of children. However, they have also pointed at the various methodological difficulties of this research, and particularly those concerning the evaluation of dream report credibility, usually a problem for the researcher (Ablon & Mack, 1980; Becker, 1978; Cicogna, 1991; De Martino, 1955; Despert, 1949; Foulkes, 1982, 1993b, 1999; Kimmins, 1937; Piaget, 1945) (Table 5.1).

Young children may have *problems in understanding the term "dream"*: the experimenter should evaluate the extent to which the child can understand what it means when he is asked to relate a dream. If, on the one hand, Piaget's studies (1926) suggest that young children have a different concept of dreams than adults, on the other hand, it is unclear whether, and to what extent, certain types of child beliefs may imply less credibility of the dream reported. As we will see later in this chapter, the literature on this suggests that children are already able at 3–4 years of age, for instance, to understand that dream is a private mental state and not a real event (Woolley & Wellman, 1992).

Table 5.1. Main difficulties in the evaluation of the credibility of children's dreams

- Problems with the understanding of the term "dream";
- Problems with the evaluation of the accuracy of dream reports as well as of the effects of a possible distorted recall;
- Problems with the detection of what is really of dream origin out of the stories reported by the child.

All dream research is based on verbally reporting dreams after a certain time from experiencing them. If this is difficult for adults, it can be a serious obstacle when it comes to children. With children, we have the problem of evaluating the *accuracy of the dream report* as well as the *effects of a possible distortion due to its recall*. Foulkes (1982), with regard to the accuracy with which children describe their dreams, used tests where children had to describe some pictures (number of details noticed) and, after a short time, remember those details without the pictures (number of details remembered): this latter condition was for the purpose of reproducing a situation similar to that of dream recall after laboratory awakening. For Foulkes, however, the fact that children have not yet developed self-reflective ability would reduce the risk that the dream is altered at a later time.

Finally, how is it possible to establish what is *really of dream origin* out of what the children report? There is, especially in young children, the possibility that they may report a dream that is not real, but, rather, something made up on the spur of the moment to gratify the interviewer. About this, Cicogna (1991) suggested that Foulkes's experimental data point out that young children show a modest percentage of dream recall following REM awakening, and report only few dreams following NREM awakening: now, if young children were inclined to "invent" their dreams, these percentages should be greater. In any case, the issue of the possible mix of elements of imagination and dream material remains an inherent open risk in every research of this type with young children.

A study on the identification of the indices of child dream credibility

At present, in the research on child dreams, the inherent problems of their credibility remain open for the most part: the evaluation of the credibility of these dreams is often based on the ability and the experience of the interviewer and, in any case, on subjective criteria (Colace, 1997a; Colace & Violani, 1993; Foulkes, 1982, 1993b). From this point of view, Foulkes' statement that "it must be stressed that there's no absolute way to verify dream reports, whether those of children or of adults" (Foulkes, 1999, p. 24) remains acceptable.

In my studies on children's dreams, which will be the subject of following chapters, I have developed some observations on dream reporting in order to identify those characteristics that may represent more "objective" indices of their credibility (Colace, 1998a). To this end, seventy-eight dream reports by seventy-eight children aged between three years four months and seven years two months were reviewed (see Study II, p. 91). Repeated listening to the recordings and a detailed analysis of written dream reports showed some individual differences in the narration (time/speech) and in dream contents. Some dream reports, unlike others, show characteristics that suggest they may be more credible than others. Eight characteristics were found, listed in Table 5.2. The first two concern the way (time/speech) in which the dream is told, and may be identified only by listening to the tape recordings of dream reports. The other characteristics can be traced in dream transcriptions. A description of these characteristics is given below.

1. *Short interval before start of dream report.* The child starts to report the dream immediately after the interviewer has put the question. He/she answers without hesitation.
2. *Rapidity of reporting.* The dream is reported quickly, in one go, without interruptions and hesitations.

These two characteristics seem to appear together frequently: one has the impression that the child is referring to something already lived through and ready to hand that he/she quickly remembers, rather than inventing a story on the spot, which is, on the other hand, something that would presumably require more time and it involve more hesitation during the narration.

Table 5.2.   Characteristics of credibility of dream reports.

1. Short interval before start of dream report
2. Rapidity of reporting
3. Self-definition of the mental experience as dream
4. Context-placement of the mental experience in the period of sleep
5. Intrinsic coherence
6. Good comprehension
7. Consistency between dream report and general concept of dream
8. Consistency between the dream and its recall through a drawing

3. *Self-definition of the mental experience as dream.* The child self-defines his/her verbal report as a "dream" (not all children do so). The report begins with such expressions as "I dreamed that . . ." and/or finishes with such expressions as "And then the dream ended".

4. *Placement in context of the mental experience in the period of sleep.* The child clearly points out that his/her story occurred during his/her rest or sleep. The child makes such statements as "I have made this dream while I was sleeping", or "then the dream ended because mother woke me up".

Below are a few examples of indices 3 and 4 (the interviews on dreams [Studies I, II, III] that appear here and in other parts of the book are not reported entirely for reasons of space. Nevertheless, the part I am reporting is the verbatim transcription of tape-recorded interviews. The child's answers are between quotation marks. The interviewer's questions, when not necessary to understanding the child's answers, are omitted. Where the interviewer's questions or comments are included, they are within square parentheses).

Dream 48: child aged five years and eleven months (Study II)
A girl was amazed, on awakening, seeing that dolls she had dreamed of were not there!

> "*I dreamed that* I was in a toy shop, there were plenty of dolls, all Barbies, all bicycles, all toys and then, and then and I went back home, and there were no more toys and that's it".

About the dream, she added: "I played with the dolls, I discarded them and then when I went back home there were no more. I tried to play, there were those big dolls that speak and then that's it, it ended that, *it was a dream*. I was sad, because *it happened that it was a dream*. Later, *when I woke up*, I told mother: give me the dolls! [here mother answered] But I don't have any! [the girl]. *Then it was a dream!*"

Dream 76: child aged six years and five months (Study II)
A boy spontaneously affirmed that his dream ended because his mother woke him up.

"*I dreamed that* I, my mother and my brother . . . they wanted me to get into this room, and there were plenty of dinosaurs, but they were remote-controlled, they were not real. One of them wanted to eat me and I got into the elevator, and then I escaped, we all escaped. One of the dinosaurs would not let us go, because . . . then mother, *I was sleeping, she woke me up and I could not go on*" [with the dream].

Dream 90: child aged three years and ten months (Study II)

"I dreamed the tree near where the garage is. There was a rose." [Were you doing something?] "*I turned off the light . . . I fell asleep.*"

Dream 72: child aged six years and ten months (Study II)

"The one when my aunt, myself, dad and mum and uncle and aunt, my aunt had arrived from the hospital and we jumped to her, because we were happy, *then, I woke up!*" [the girl laughs].

5.   *Intrinsic coherence.* The contents of the free dream report are consistent with the answers given to more specific questions about the dream and with the answers about the daytime experience the dream refers to.

Dream 21: child aged four years and four months (Study II)

"When I was going to grandpa M's place and then mother said go play a while with Ma! Then L arrived and said, 'Shall we go and play with the slide?' and *we went to the slide.*"

[What were you doing?] "I was going there with a small motorcycle." [A small motorcycle. Were you riding it? Or was it a toy motorcycle?] "A real one." [Who was riding, you?] "I was riding alone." [Do you have this motorcycle for real?] "Yes". [And you also dreamed it?] "Yes". [But where were you in the dream?] "In the vineyard." [Have you ever really been to the vineyard, or only in the dream?] "Always." [Do you always go there?] "Yes." [So who was there in this dream, is L a friend of yours?] "No, she is my little sister." [Was another friend also there, then?] "Yes, Ma." [Were there any animals in the dream?] "Yes, but they were most on the road. I was sad." [Why?] "Because L. said "You stay by the slide so when I fall down badly you catch me.'" [And you didn't want to catch her?] "No." [Why?] "Because I wanted to slide down too!"

Dream 13: child aged six years and three months (Study II)

"I was the princess, and then, then *I did like Cinderella*, I lost my shoe, I lost my shoe, and then, then . . . then Prince Charming came!" [she laughs].

[Listen, in this dream you were the princess, but in what place were you?] "I was in the castle." [But was it a castle you really know or not?] "Yes." [And where is this castle?] "It is in Rome. I saw it and then I dreamed it, because dad once took us to see it, and then I dreamed it." [And who was the Prince Charming, someone you know?] "He was a boy who was at the kindergarten with me, that I liked." [Were there any animals too in this dream?] "There was two horses . . ."

6.   *Good comprehension.* The child gives meaningful and/or original explanations of his/her dream experience, that suggest a "good understanding" of it.

Dream 77: child aged six years and four months (Study II)

About the dream reported. [While you were having this dream, did you know that it was only a dream or did you think it was happening really?] "No, I thought that it was happening for real, only when I woke up there wasn't anything, so I realised." *About the general concept of dream.* [What do you think a dream is?] "A dream is when you dream something that however is not true." [Where do you think dreams come from?] "I think they come from thought." [But where is the dream, while you are dreaming?] "Well, I think the dream is in the mind."

Dream 47: child aged five years and nine months (Study II)

About the concept of dream. [Do you dream at night?] "A little, but then mother wakes me up . . . and then this morning I was sleepy I could not even walk." [How do dreams come up?] "They come up that you see something during the day and then at night you remember it and dream it." [What do you dream with?] "With the mind."

Dream 12: child aged six years and five months (Study II)

About the concept of dream. [Can you tell me what a dream is?] "Yes, it's that at night when you sleep if you sleep really deeply, but I never really sleep at night, however, when I sleep tight I do dream something." [Where do you think dreams come from?] "From the brain, you imagine them . . ." [What do you think we dream with?] "With the brain." [But are dreams inside or outside us?] "Inside." [Do dreams come when one sleeps or when one is awake?] "Well! When one is awake you say he is thinking, and when one sleeps you say he is dreaming."

7.   *Consistency between dream report and general concept of dream.* The child, in the attempt to give an explanation of dreams in general, refers to his/her dream report and gives elements consistent with it; besides, the explanation of his/her dream experience falls within the known forms of understanding of young children (Piaget, 1926).

In the examples below, the dream is seen as an event of external origin "the dream originates from the place of the dream" (the second level established by Piaget).

Dream 96: child aged three years and eleven months (Study II)

"I had a dream, I dreamed a cow, it went eating and drinking and that's it."

Later:

Concept of dream. [Where do you think dreams come from?] "From the farm." [How do dreams come up?]] "From the animals." [But where is the dream, while you are dreaming?] "The dream is at the farm." [But if mum and dad are next to you while you are dreaming, can they see your dream?] "No." [But can you touch a dream?] "No." [What are dreams made up of?] "Of animals." [What do we dream with?] "Animals." [But are dreams inside or outside us?] "Outside us."

In other words, when this boy was asked to explain dreams, being convinced, like other children of his age, that dreams come from the place of the dream, he referred to his dream and logically affirmed that it came from the farm. The same applies to the example below.

Dream 55: child aged five years and two months (Study II)

"The Befana brought me the bicycle and my father took me to ride the bicycle (I was riding it) in the park of C." [Initial of the town where the child lives.]

Later:

Concept of dream. [Where do dreams come from?] "From C." [Initial of the town where the child lives.] [But are dreams inside or outside us?] "They are outside."

8. *Consistency between dream and its recall through a drawing.* The child, after a considerably long period of time (one month), can remember the reported dream and draw a picture that appears consistent with the verbal dream report. This was noticed in a group of twenty-four children (aged 5–7 years) (see Chapter Six, p. 100). Eight children (33%) remembered the dream reported previously and drew it. Some of these even portrayed details of the dream content as they had reported them in words. In order to evaluate the credibility of the dreams reported, another aspect to be observed in their drawings is *the way dreams are presented.* In fact, a sign of good credibility of the dream origin of the story might be the fact that the child presents the dream in the ways known in literature: the content of the dream set in a "balloon" floating above the bed, in which the dream scene is portrayed. (See Lucart, 1977, who observed that, in a sample of thirty children aged between 5.6 and 6.3 years, 23% graphically represented the dream setting in a balloon; other children drew the content of their dream to their side or above their head. Based on this finding, the author assumes that when children aged five and upwards locate their dreams above their heads, this means that they have taken cognizance of the existence of a mental space, separate from objective space. In the drawings collected here, we found the same methods of graphic representation of dream contents, with a greater frequency of representations of dreams inside balloons.) Examples are shown below.

Dream 71: child aged six years and eight months (Study II)

"There were mum and dad who bought me a toy, no, a toy car, then it broke up with my brother, then when I woke up I looked for the car but there was none, neither broken nor new."

The drawing made by this boy (the arrows are mine) shows the toy car, new and broken (see Figure 5.1).

Dream 76: child aged six years and five months (Study II)

"I dreamed that I was brave, and C [girl schoolmate] she was like that, with her head down, and I jumped at her, without hurting her [and then?], and then that's all." [Was C lying down on the floor?] "No, she was on the chair. She was sitting on the chair with the head back." [And

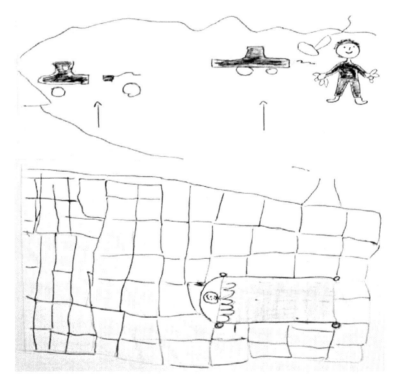

Figure 5.1.   Pictures of dream report (the toy car),

you jumped at her, how?] "I did . . . without hurting her, I jumped in the air."

In Figure 5.2, the drawing shows the girl (C) appearing in the dream, sitting on the chair with her head stretched back, this detail may be seen very well in enlarged detail (Figure 5.3). I remember in particular that this child, while recounting the dream, mimicked the way he was playing with his friend, in a manner that was very similar to the scene later drawn by him.

Dream 01: child aged six years and eight months (Study II)

"I dreamed Santa Claus coming here (to school) and reading my letter, then he went away with his sleigh, there were fawns, and that's it."

Figure 5.4 shows the drawing of this dream, in which the girl put even the smallest details, with Santa Claus's eyes looking at the letter because he is reading it and the fawns on the bed (see details in Figure 5.5).

Figure 5.2.   Drawing of dream 76.

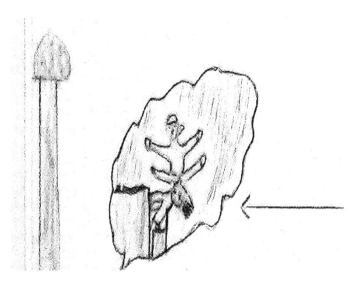

Figure 5.3. Detail of drawing of dream 76.

Figure 5.4. Picture of the Santa Claus dream (01).

Figure 5.5.   Details of the drawing of the Santa Claus dream (01).

Dream 78: child aged six years and four months (Study II)

"My grandmother was telling me, 'Mark come inside!' because I was
playing ball out in the garden, and as grandmother was feeling cold,
she told me 'Mark come inside', and I said, 'No! I am playing here',
because I was playing with my friends. My grandmother said, 'Come
inside,' and I replied, 'No' and she told me, 'Watch out, I am going to
call your mother!' Then I stopped playing." (see Figure 5.6).

Another example of convergence of details between the verbal
report of dream and its drawing is that of a child who, after having
dreamed of embracing his aunt leaving the hospital, was also able
to represent the smiles on the faces of the dream characters in the
drawing of the dream (see Chapter Nine, pp. 171–172).

Figure 5.6.   The drawing of this dream shows the boy playing football. In the balloon the boy wrote: "I am playing football" (i.e., *Io gioco a pallone*, in Italian).

In my view, the characteristics described above may help researchers to direct their evaluation of the credibility of the dreams reported by children.

Probably, those children who use the term "dream" to denominate what they are telling (characteristic 3, above) and those who provide a meaningful explanation of their dream experience (characteristic 6, above) will have fewer difficulties in understanding the term "dream" and will have greater capability of understanding what the researcher means when he or she asks them to tell their dream (task).

The systematic use of drawing the dreams after a given amount of time since they were reported verbally might offer useful information about their credibility. The ability to draw a dream with a correspondence of details between verbal report and visual presentation (characteristic 8, above) may suggest that the child is really making reference to an "important" mental experience, that is, the dream; on the other hand, it is improbable that a child could remember and reproduce, after some time, details that were invented during the interview about dreams. Also, the graphic pattern (e.g., use of the "balloon" to present the contents of the dream, the dreamer drawn with the eyes closed, etc.) used by children to represent their dreams may suggest that their verbal reports really have a dream origin, rather than being the description of an invented story.

For an evaluation of dream accuracy (which is difficult even with adults), it can be useful to observe how the various aspects of the free report of the dream are true, and not the product of momentary confabulation, verifying the consistency between these and the answers given by the child later, during the systematic detailed interview on dream contents and on the daytime experience the dream refers to (characteristic 5, above).

A positive indicator of the actual dream origin of a child's verbal report may be the hints given by the child, through direct expressions, that the mental experience being reported is set in the time space of rest or sleep (characteristic 4, above).

As for the first two indices, "short interval before start of dream report" and "rapidity of reporting", we may assume that children would take more time to begin to answer (interval) and tell (slower reporting) a false dream or an invented story (confabulation), rather than a real dream. From this point of view, these two indices should be associated to other indices of credibility in the dream report.

Equally useful in the research on dreams in different developmental ages would be to investigate the general concept of dream, as the interviewed child, instead of "explaining" dreams in general, might refer to his/her particular dream reported, returning to it, giving useful elements of agreement/disagreement (characteristic 7, above). On the other hand, I feel it is less important to establish how the level of comprehension of the dream is close to that of adults; in fact, a different concept of dreaming does not necessarily reflect automatically less credibility of dream reports recounted by children and/or their incapability of understanding the task.

The other two aspects that may give a positive indication of the reliability of children in this type of study are their *interest in dreams in general* and *their ability to self-evaluate their dream recall*.

The data from my QDEA study (see Chapter Six, Study IV) suggest that, in the parents' opinion, already at the age of five children begin to show a certain interest in dreams by asking questions about them (Colace, 2006a).

In the school (Study II) and home studies (see below), we asked the young participants (3–7-year-olds) to tell us if they remembered any dreams in the morning, when they wake up (1. "never or almost never"; 2. "seldom"; 3. "sometimes"; 4. "often"). Quite unexpectedly, we observed that the children's self-evaluation is "reliable", or at least consistent with the actual frequency of their dream recall. Particularly, in the school study (Study II), the group of children who reported their dreams after the standard request valued their recall of dreams by placing themselves in categories 2,"seldom", or 3, "sometimes" (mean: 2.71), while those who did not report any dream after our standard request self-placed themselves in categories 1, "never or almost never", and 2, "seldom" (mean: 1.82). The differences are statistically significant (Mann–Whitney U-test, $p = 0.02$). This indication has emerged even more clearly in the home study. Here, the children's self-evaluation of dream recall frequency appears to be positively correlated with the actual percentage of dream reports on morning awakening (number of recalled dreams/number of requests) (Table 5.3). I believe that these two indications suggest that children may be "interested" and "competent" subjects in this type of study.

Table 5.3. At-home study: self-evaluation of dream recall and actual frequency of dream recall of each child.

Dream recall self-evaluation	Dream recall percentage	
Seldom	12.50%	
Never or almost never	14.20%	
Never or almost never	28.50%	
Often	71.40%	
Seldom	28.50%	$Rho = 0.71, p = 0.01$
Sometimes	66.66%	
Often	57.10%	
Sometimes	62.50%	
Seldom	42.80%	
Often	57.10%	
Sometimes	100.00%	

The literature, on the other hand, suggests other positive indicators to the fact that small children can produce reliable dream reports. For example, those authors who have dealt directly with child dreams have attributed to these a degree of credibility that would encourage future investigations. Piaget (1945), referring to the need to compare dreams with play, suggested that although children, in telling their dreams, may partly make them up, there always remains a sufficient amount of spontaneous dream content, so that the attempt to collect children's dream is legitimate. Foulkes (1993, 1999), who conducted extensive research on child dreams, identifying different methodological risks, also suggested that, in general, in children aged five and upwards, dream reports may be regarded as believable attempts to describe the dream experience. He also pointed out that the ability to recognize a believable dream develops with experience in the collection of children's dreams.

Other data may be derived from the studies on how children understand the phenomenon of dreaming. Woolley and Wellman (1992), for instance, have found that 3–4-year-old children give proof of understanding the fantastic (unreal), non-physical, and mental/private nature of dreams. Accordingly, Kinoshita (1994) suggested that children of pre-school age are able to distinguish dream entities from real ones. Woolley and Boerger (2002) found that children up to five years of age have an idea of dreams similar to that of older children and adults. Nevertheless, the concept of dreams in these young children is marked by the fact that they believe dreams can be controlled. Meyer and Shore (2001) have shown that five-year-old children, despite their scarce ability to recall dreams, begin to understand that dreams are an unreal, private, and psychological event. Other studies found that children, as early as the age of four, use mental categories to define dreams (Cassi, Pinto, & Salzarulo, 1999) and seem to be able to recognize the boundary between imagination and reality better than we would commonly suppose (Sharon & Wolley, 2004). These data are consistent with Lucart's observations (1977) on dream drawings (see p. 71).

In conclusion, I believe that the issue of the credibility of children's dream reports should be studied by means of specific research focused on this aspect. More can be done to identify and collect many of these indicators of dream report credibility and to observe their convergence. At present, I believe more caution is required when comparing to studies on adult dreams before the knowledge derived from studies of children's dreams may be taken for granted.

Main lines of research

There are very few studies on children's dreams, especially compared to the amount of research conducted on adult dreams. This gap may be due, on the one hand, to the methodological difficulties explained above; on the other hand, given the opportunities to understand the dreaming processes offered by these studies, the gap is not justified. Before presenting my studies, I provide a brief summary, with no claim to exhaustiveness, of the main lines of research with children up to 7–8 years of age that have been developed after Freud's observations, in order to provide an overview of these studies. (Readers interested in more detailed reviews on the research on children's dreams may refer to the following more specific papers: Despert [1949], De Martino [1955], Ablon and Mack [1980]. For reasons of space, I have not considered the studies on "nightmares" here [e.g., Schredl & Heuser, 1999].) Then I return in greater detail to some of these studies in order to compare the results that emerged from my research. At least the following trends may be singled out in the progress of studies on children's dreams: (a) the early pioneering studies conducted between the 1930s and 1950s; (b) the studies of Piaget; (c) the early systematic research on the general contents of children's dreams by Hall, Van de Castle, and Domhoff; (d) the early experimental studies in sleep laboratories conducted by Foulkes and colleagues; (e) the studies on dream bizarreness in children's dreams; (f) the insights of the studies on self-representation in children's dreams.

The pioneering studies

In the period that followed Freud's observations, there were some early attempts to study the dreams of children in a more systematic way. However, according to the judgement of the authors who have revisited this literature, these attempts gave few results (De Martino, 1955; Despert, 1949). Some of these pioneering investigations deserve to be mentioned because they used for the first time a more systematic method of collecting dreams and/or because they were based on wider samples of children. These studies compared themselves with the psychoanalytic tradition, trying to give an early evaluation of it. Coriat (1920) observed that the dreams of children under ten years of age appear to be mere fulfilment of wishes. These dreams show a simple structure and are supposedly very useful in the study of dream mechanisms. This author also found that the dreams of primitive tribes are very similar to those of children and often show the fulfilment of a wish. Hill (1926), based on the observation of 240 dreams of children between two and sixteen years of age, suggested that these present various forms of wish-fulfilment. Kimmins (1937) made one of the first attempts at systematic study on dreams according to developmental age based on a wide sample. He collected stories of dreams in various schools over a period of two years, interviewing 5,600 children aged five to sixteen years (150 children were 5–7 years old). This author found that the dreams of younger children are very realistic, lack fantastic and unreal elements, and often contain references to the preceding day. Kimmins also observed that the greater part of the dreams had by young children are of the "simple wish-fulfilment" type, although there are other dreams that cannot be included in this category. Jersild, Markey, and Jersild (1933) conducted a study of 400 children aged between five and thirteen years, based on interviews and administration of questionnaires. These authors noticed that the content of children's dreams frequently concerns their daily life. The theme of wish-fulfilment is not frequent; conversely, the presence of frightening dreams is frequently observed. Despert (1949), apart from conducting an accurate review of the available literature, developed a study of thirty-nine children aged between two and five years. This author collected 190 dream reports using three different methods: (a) dreams collected during individual situations of play activities, (b) dreams collected through daily diaries on the behaviour of the child, and (c) dreams collected at home from notes taken by the parents. Despert noticed that an important characteristic of these dreams is their simplicity and their essential structure; he also observed a characteristic that will be confirmed by different subsequent studies, that is, the frequent presence of animal characters. In this period, De Martino (1959) accurately reviewed the literature on children's dreams before the discovery of REM sleep, with particular reference to age, gender, and personality differences. This author also reviewed the studies on the dreams of sight-impaired and hearing-impaired children.

The observations of Piaget

Piaget (1945), in his study on the development of symbolic activity, observed the dream reports of children using a methodology similar to the one used by Freud (spontaneous dream recall and information about the daily life of the children). According to Piaget (1945), as happens in symbolic play, dreams become more complicated as thought develops, and contain first conscious (primary) symbols, that have a transparent meaning to the child, and later unconscious (secondary) symbols that include more than the conscious meaning. Piaget, based on observations of a group of spontaneous dreams, identified six categories of dreams: (1) dreams that fulfil wishes through the direct evocation of the wish result; (2) dreams that introduce primary conscious symbols; in these dreams Piaget noticed that the primary symbols represented things loved by the child; (3) dreams of painful events with a positive ending; (4) nightmares; (5) dreams of punishment and self-punishment; (6) dreams with (secondary) symbols of actual organic drives, such as, for instance, the dream of eating a stone as the expression of a heavy stomach. Piaget concluded that some of his observations were consistent with Freud's theses. The dreams belonging to the second category may be considered to be wish-fulfilment type, provided that "wish" is given a broader meaning; that is, assimilation of reality to the self as it happens while playing. Piaget noticed that when the content of children's dreams refers to the introduction of unpleasant external stimuli and/or when it symbolically translates an unpleasant internal stimulus, the dream can be seen as a "guardian of sleep."

The systematic analyses of the contents of children's dreams: Hall,
Van de Castle, Domhoff, and Domhoff

These authors were the first to apply a dream content classification
system (Hall & Van de Castle, 1966) to children's dreams, establishing certain frequency rules by age and gender. Hall and Domhoff (1963a, 1963b, 1964) studied children between two and twelve
years of age, collecting a broad sample of dreams with different
methodologies (e.g., dreams collected by teachers at school, kindergarten, and at home). These authors found that the dreams of
children are shorter than those of teenagers and of young adults.
Furthermore, in these dreams, children are often the victims of
aggressive actions (by animals) and have negative endings. These
information were later reorganized by Domhoff (1996). These
authors found that young children's dreams (2–6 years) frequently
present animal characters. This result was also replicated in a later
study based on 741 dream reports, where it was also observed that
the frequency of these characters decreases as age increases (Van de
Castle, 1970, 1983).

The studies in a sleep laboratory by Foulkes

The discovery of REM sleep (Aserinsky & Kleitman, 1953) made it
possible to investigate dreams in a more complete and systematic
way, waking the subjects at given stages of their sleep. Foulkes's
research group conducted the early studies on children's dreams
using this methodology (Foulkes, 1982, 1999; Foulkes, Pivik,
Steadman, Spear, & Symonds, 1967; Foulkes, Larson, Swanson, &
Rardin, 1969). Their longitudinal study started in 1968 and was
completed in 1973. Foulkes studied two groups of children who, at
the beginning of the study, were 3–5 years old (fourteen children),
and 9–10 years old (sixteen children): both groups were followed
and examined for five years. Then six children (aged eleven and
twelve) and seven children (aged seven and eight) were added.
These children spent nine nights (in one year) at a sleep laboratory
and were woken up three times per night, primarily (but not
always) during the REM stage. This allowed the monitoring of the
evolution of dream contents with respect to different variables tied
to age. Foulkes and his colleagues were interested in the first place
in the relationship between the dream processes and the cognitive

development of the children. I feel it is important also to provide a brief description of the characteristics of these dreams, because they are the only ones currently available. Although other studies exist of children's REM dreams, they concern older children and teenagers (e.g., Strauch & Meier, 1996). Foulkes observed that young children (3–5 years old) have a low percentage of dream recall. Their dream contents are characterized mainly by the presence of static images related mostly to bodily aspects such as hunger, fatigue, etc. In these dreams, social relationships are absent, there is no active self-representation in the dream setting, and there are often animal characters. At 5–7 years old, dreams change and show more movement and a more accurate definition of the scene and setting. Animal characters continue to be present, and active self-representation is still missing. As to formal aspects, Foulkes (1982) found that children's dreams present a direct and realistic connection with the daytime experience, show an ordinary and essential content, and are extraordinarily concise. The dreams of 3–5-year-old children are not bizarre at all, nor do they present distortions from everyday reality, or alterations of the common laws of physics. The dreams of 5–7-year-old children show a greater presence of bizarreness (i.e., "characters' distortion") compared to those of 3–5-year-old children. Foulkes also observed that, from 5–7 years of age, distortion tends to become a general characteristic of children's dreams; furthermore, the dream reports of 5–7-year-old children are longer. Many observations arising from this first study were later confirmed by the same authors. Particularly, Foulkes, Hollifield, Sullivan, Bradley, and Terry (1990), investigating 193 REM dream protocols in eighty children aged between five and eight years, confirmed that dreams up to the age of 7–8 show a static imaginative, an extremely simple narrative structure, and the dreamers are self-represented only passively, from the viewpoint of an observer. These authors also found confirmation that the development of visual-spatial abilities, rather than of verbal–descriptive ones, is a necessary condition for the appearance of dreams.

Bizarreness in children's dreams

In the 1990s, the first studies on bizarreness in children's dreams were conducted, based on specific content scales (Colace & Tuci,

1996a,b; Colace & Violani, 1993; Colace, Doricchi, Di Loreto, & Violani, 1993; Colace, Tuci, & Frendeles, 1997; Colace, Violani, & Solano, 1993; Resnick, Stickgold, Rittenhouse, & Hobson, 1994). These studies were based on dreams collected at school and at home. With regard to my studies, the first partial results were published in those years and will be the subject of the following chapters. Resnick, Stickgold, Rittenhouse, and Hobson (1994) conducted a study on children of 4–5 and 8–10 years of age, interviewed about their dreams upon awakening in the morning. They criticize the assumptions of Piaget and Foulkes, according to which young children lack the cognitive abilities for dreaming. Resnick and colleagues suggested that the dreams of children show characteristics similar to those of adults as far as bizarreness and self-representation are concerned. They considered their results consistent with the "activation–synthesis hypothesis" according to which the formal characteristics of dreams are constant in so far as they are due to the neurophysiological substrate of REM dream (e.g., Hobson, 1988). I address this study in further detail in the following chapters, in comparing the results of my studies with those of the literature. Another study conducted in this period found conflicting results with the one referred to above. Levi and Pompili (1991), based on a study of 369 children aged between three and five years interviewed at school, found that the dreams of the younger children (3–4 years) show less "conflicting and fantastic themes" and a greater prevalence of "ordinary and realistic themes" compared to those of older children.

Self-representation in children's dreams

Some authors have studied self-representation in the dreams of children and found that children even as young as three years of age can represent themselves in their dreams in an active role (Colace, 2006a; Colace, Tuci & Ferendeles, 2000; Colace, Violani, & Tuci, 1995; Resnick, Stickgold, Rittenhouse, & Hobson, 1994). These results clash with Foulkes's observations on REM dreams, according to which children up to 7–8 years seem to appear in their dreams in a passive way, as mere observers (Foulkes, 1982; Foulkes, Hollifield, Sullivan, Bradley, & Terry, 1990). According to Foulkes, certain differences between home-collected dreams and REM dreams do not depend on the setting (i.e., the possibly inhibitory effect of the laboratory) but, rather, on the effects of recall selectivity (i.e., partial and biased sampling, see above p. 62). However, it remains to be seen whether this explanation may also apply to the differences observed in self-representation in dreams. At present, based on the dreams reported outside sleep laboratories (at home, at school, in questionnaires), the assumption that young children lack the cognitive ability to actively represent themselves in their dreams remains improbable.

CHAPTER SIX

Four studies on children's dreams

I n the decade 1989–1999, I conducted four studies on children's dreams, with the purpose of submitting Freud's main observations on children's dreams to an empirical control. Particularly, those related to dream bizarreness with respect to age and development of the superego functions and, subsequently, those related to undisguised wish-fulfilment.

Two of these studies were based on interviews with the children at their schools. The first study (Colace & Violani, 1993) (Study I, school study) represented an attempt to define a methodology for the research on the dreams of very young children; in fact, at least in Italy, there were very few examples of research on this subject (e.g., Levi & Pompili, 1991). The principal purpose of this study was to measure the level of bizarreness of children's dreams by a specific contents scale and to test in a systematic way Freud's assumptions concerning: (1) the scarce presence of bizarreness in the dreams of young children, (2) the increase of bizarreness in the dreams of older children, and (3) the relationship between dream bizarreness and development of the superego functions. The encouraging results (Colace & Violani, 1993) led me to try to replicate them in a more articulated manner with a second study (Colace, 1997a) (Study II, school study) that included other measures of dream bizarreness and a greater number of indices of the superego functions.

The third study (Colace, 1997a) (Study III, home study) was certainly the most ambitious one, in as much as it tried to replicate with further detail the results found in the research conducted in schools through a more methodologically reliable collection of dream reports. In fact, in this research, dream reports were collected upon morning awakening at home. This study also led to some preliminary systematic observations on the frequency of wish-fulfilment dreams.

The fourth study (Study IV, questionnaire study) I conducted with children was considerably different from the previous ones in both method and purposes (Colace, 2006a, Colace et al., 2000). This study represented an attempt to try out a methodology, simpler and more cost-effective than the classical methods, of collecting information on dreams in developmental age on the basis of a wider sample of children. This was done by developing a questionnaire that was completed by the parents, who investigated their children's dreams and also their television-watching habits and the characteristics of their sleep (Colace, Dichiacchio, & Violani, 2006a,b).

In the end, these studies have allowed us to contact 748 children aged between two years, nine months old and nine years, four months old, and to collect 537 dream reports. Many variables regarding the various aspects of dreaming (i.e., dream recall, understanding of dream concept, etc.), the development of the superego functions, and cognitive abilities were also considered.

In the following pages, I present the general methodology of these studies, so as to give readers an idea of how these were conducted. With regard to Study I, below is a short description of the method, already described elsewhere in detail (Colace & Violani, 1993; Colace, Violani, & Solano, 1993), and the same applies to study IV (Colace, 2006a; Colace et al., 2000). With regard to Studies II and III, I give a more exhaustive description of the method, as the detailed presentation of these studies has only appeared in my PhD dissertation. However, while treating specific matters, I will return to the methodology of these studies, and provide a detailed description of individual tests and measures of variables.

The first study conducted in the school setting

This study was conducted in the period 1989–1990 in two schools, a kindergarten and a primary school in Rome. Every child was interviewed individually between 9.00 and 11.00 a.m. in a classroom arranged for the purpose. The interviews generally did not take more than fifteen minutes. Each child was scrutinized twice at an interval of fifteen days. Standard interviews were entirely tape-recorded, so that they could be listened to later and transcribed verbatim. In the first session, we tried to make the child feel at ease and started to ask some questions aimed at understanding the child's conceptions of dreams. These questions are similar to those formulated by Piaget in his studies (Piaget, 1926) and by Foulkes (1982). In order to collect dream reports, we asked, *Will you please tell me the last dream you have had?* and, at the end of each free verbal report, we asked, *Why do you think you had this dream?* With this last question, we tried to obtain information about the possible relationship between dream content and daytime experience of the dreamer. The answers to this difficult question have often provided precious details and allowed us to detect unsuspected abilities in the children of this age. Apart from requesting the dream reports, we also administered some tests, distributed in both sessions, concerning certain cognitive abilities and certain indices of the development of the superego functions (see Chapter Eight). I have to say that almost all the children were enthusiastic about this experience and very few were non-co-operative. The general impression was that the children took very seriously the task of trying to remember their dreams.

This study involved seventy-five children aged between three years, four months and seven years, four months (mean group: five years, seven months). In the first session, we asked each one of them to report his or her dream. In the second session, we repeated the attempt to collect the dreams with sixty-six of these children. In total, 101 dream reports were collected, of which fifty-seven came from the first session and forty-four from the second (Tables 6.1 and 6.2).

Table 6.1. Study I: children by age and gender.

Age in years	Boys	Girls	Total
3	4	1	5
4	11	10	21
5	8	12	20
6	12	13	25
7	2	2	4
Total	37	38	75

Table 6.2. Study I: dream reports frequencies by age group and gender.

Age	Gender	No. of children interviewed		Dream reports		No recall	False dream reports (i.e., not credible)*	Frequency percentage of dream reporting	
		Sessions		Sessions				By	By age
		I	Returned in session II	I	II			gender	group†
3–5	Girls	17	12	12	9	5	3	21/29 (72%)	48/68 (70.5%)
	Boys	21	18	16	11	8	4	27/39 (69%)	
5–7	Girls	21	21	17	15	9	1	32/42 (76%)	53/73 (72.6%)
	Boys	16	15	12	9	8	2	21/31 (67%)	
		75	66	Total 101	30	10			

*These dream reports were discarded as hardly credible (agreement between two judges). These were, essentially, stories that seemed to have been conjured up at the moment, or reports of something that had happened during the day.

†Dream recall age group difference was not statistically significant: Session I = $\chi^2 = 0.226$, df = 1, $p = 0.634$; Session II = $\chi^2 = 0.000$, df = 1, $p = 1.00$

Frequency percentage of dream reports

About 72% of the children interviewed reported a dream (for all ages). No difference was observed in the percentage of dream reports between different age groups (see Table 6.2).

The second study conducted in the school setting

This study was conducted in the period 1993–1994 and was intended to replicate and expand the results of the first research. This study, however, presents two variations compared to the first one. First, the interview about the dreams was more articulated, with more detailed questions. Second, there were a greater number of cognitive variables and various indices of the development of the superego functions (see Chapter Eight). The study was conducted in two kindergartens and two primary schools in a small town of about 20,000 inhabitants in central Italy. Two sessions were held with each child, between 8.30 and 11.30 a.m., lasting about thirty-five minutes each.

The first session started with the first two questions from the standard interview about the understanding of the concept of dream, followed by the request to tell the dream. After the initial question, *Will you please tell me the last dream you had?*, the child was left free to answer without any further form of encouraging. The free dream report was then followed by the standard interview aimed at investigating the followings aspects: pleasant/unpleasant theme, self-representation, setting, degree of proximity (plausibility) between dream contents (setting, people, objects, actions) and common daily-life experiences, presence of animals, test of reality and emotions (Table 6.3). During this session, the first part of the tests on superegoic functions and cognitive abilities was also administered. Both these types of tests were completed in the second session. Both sessions were tape-recorded.

The number of children contacted in this study was 105; however, thirteen of these wanted to return to their teachers just after starting the interview, while the other ninety-two participated quietly in the study (12% abandonment rate). Of these ninety-two children, the youngest was three years, four months old, and the

Table 6.3.   The dream interview of the second study. This interview followed the free report of the dream. Its purpose was to obtain more detailed information on the various aspects of dream contents.

Was this dream a good or a bad one?

(Where required) Were you there in the dream?

(If Yes) Were you doing something in this dream or were you just watching?

In what place were you in the dream?

For every person/fantastic character/setting mentioned in the dream content, it was asked:

This person (name) who was in the dream, do you know him/her?

This place (name) that was in the dream, do you know it?

Have you ever been there?

For every thing and main action appearing in the dream content, it was asked:

This thing (name) that was in the dream, do you know it?

This action (name) that you were doing in the dream, do you actually do it also during the day, sometimes? When was the last time you did this action (name)?

Were there any animals in this dream?

While you were dreaming, did you know that what was happening to you was only a dream, or did you think it was for real?

Were you happy during this dream?

Were you sad?

(The use of synonyms was allowed for particularly difficult questions, especially with the younger children)

---

eldest was seven years, two months old. The mean age of the sample was five years, four months. Sixty-four dream reports were collected from this group of children (Table 6.4).

Frequency percentage of dream reporting

Seventy per cent of the children interviewed reported a dream (for all ages). There is no statistically significant difference in the percentage of dream reports between the younger and the older age groups (Table 6.5).

Table 6.4. Study II: children by age and gender.

Age in years	Boys	Girls	Total
3	7	4	11
4	15	11	26
5	8	11	19
6	21	12	33
7	2	1	3
Total	53	39	92

Table 6.5. Study II: frequency of dream reports by age group and gender.

Age	Gender	N	Dream reports	Non recallers	False dream reports*	Frequency percentage of dream reporting[†]
3–5	Girls	20	16 (80%)	3 (11%)	1	30/46 (65%)
	Boys	26	14 (54%)	3 (11%)	9	
5–7	Girls	19	14 (73%)	3 (16%)	2	34/46 (74%)
	Boys	27	20 (74%)	5 (19%)	2	

*These "dreams" were, essentially, stories that seemed to have been conjured up at the moment, or reports of something that had happened during the day. In dream reporting frequency these "dreams" were considered as non-report.

[†]Age group difference: χ^2 (df 1) = 0.821, p = 0.365.

The study conducted in the home setting

This study was conducted in the period 1994–1996, partly in Rome and partly in the same small town of school study II. The purpose of this research was to replicate the results of the two previous studies through a different and more reliable methodology, that is, to collect the dream reports through a systematic interview performed by the parents upon morning awakening at home. To the best of my knowledge, an attempt of this type with young children had never been made in Italy. The most difficult part was finding parents willing to co-operate, and this was the reason why the study lasted much longer than we expected (consider that, in this study as in the others, as we had no funds available for our research, and the participants (children and parents) did not receive any form of compensation). As a first attempt, we published an article about dreaming in a local paper of the place in which the research was to be performed; the article ended with the notice that a scientific study on children's dreams was about to begin and any parents interested and wishing to participate would be welcome. Unfortunately, this attempt did not produce any results. Therefore, we decided to proceed in this way: we handed out leaflets to the parents at the schools, saying that a scientific study on children's dreams was about to be started. With this method we succeeded in contacting a few (daring!) parents, later followed by others.

The dreams were collected with the same interview used in the second school study, adequately adjusted so that it could be administered by the mothers (Table 6.6). Nevertheless, as in this case we also had the opportunity to interview mothers, too, the research protocol also included the mothers' remarks on the dreams with reference to the children's daytime experiences. This allowed us to

Table 6.6.   Study III: dream interview form.

Instructions:

Children should be asked to tell their dreams as soon as they wake up in the morning. Requests should be considered as mere attempts, as the children will not necessarily recall their dream, so please consider also the possibility that your child may simply answer, "I can't remember any dream!" The request should be "determined but not insistent", otherwise you may risk that your child conjures up a dream only to please you.

Were you dreaming while you were sleeping?

(If the answer is no: that's OK, you don't always remember dreams, sometimes I can't remember them, either.)

(If the answer is yes)

Will you tell me your dream?

When the child begins to tell the dream he/she should not be interrupted, but allowed to continue the story until he/she stops and appears to have finished. You should then wait a little and then ask:

And then?

If child does not add anything else, you may proceed with the specific interview on the dream (identical to the one used in Study II (see Table 6.3).

perceive possible connections. The research was structured in different stages: a *preliminary meeting*, in which the study programme was described, a *dream collection week*, during which the dream reports and the mothers' comments were collected, and the *tests session*, in which we administered cognitive development and superego functions development tests.

Preliminary meeting

We generally explained the tasks for the children and the mothers that the research programme implied. The mothers were reassured about the simplicity of the interview on dreams, as they had merely to follow a pre-written form. Furthermore, in order to make sure that the mothers had understood, we simulated a dream collection interview. Even at this stage we made it clear that the request to tell a dream was a mere attempt, as the child would not necessarily recall one. The request was supposed to be "determined but not insistent". Then we explained that there are certain ordinary differences in each individual's ability to remember dreams.

The dream collection week

For seven consecutive days, the mothers asked their children to tell a dream after waking up in the morning, using the standard interview form (see Table 6.6). One parent continued to request dream reports for two days more, once per day, while another parent made one attempt less. Every interview was tape-recorded. At the end of interview, the mothers noted down their impressions about the child's behaviour and whether the child had woken up spontaneously or not (e.g., to go to school). The next morning they would continue with a second attempt, and then again until the end of the week. During this week, the presence of the researcher was limited to one or two afternoon meetings, in which mothers were asked to comment on the dreams collected. The first afternoon meeting was usually held on the third day of the test week, to comment on the first three dreams reported, if any; the second meeting was held in the afternoon of the last day of the test week, to comment on any dreams reported during the last four days. During these afternoon meetings, the interviews were played back and listened to together with the mothers, and the researchers asked for comments on the dream. In particular, we asked, *How would you comment on your child's dream?*; *Do you recognize the characters, events, places as familiar, ordinary for your child?*; *Do you think the dream can be related to any specific circumstance or situation that happened to your child during the day?*

Test sessions with children

After the *dream collection week,* two test sessions were developed in which the researcher proceeded with the administration of the cognitive tests (Wechsler Preschool and Primary Scale of Intelligence [WPPSI] or Wechsler Intelligence Scale for Children Revised [WISC-R] and tests on the indices of superego functions (see Chapter Eight). Each session lasted around thirty minutes and was held at home, generally in the afternoon.

This research programme involved sixteen children (five boys, eleven girls) but three of them could not complete the sessions (two boys aged six and seven, respectively, and one seven-year-old girl). The youngest child was three years and four months old; the eldest was seven years and eleven months old (Table 6.7) (mean group: five years of age). One of these children was interviewed at two different ages, one week at four years and six months, and another one at five years and six months. The child is Lisa, whose dreams are the subject of Chapter Ten. In the analyses by age groups, the dreams of this child appear in both groups, 3–5 years and 5–7 years.

Table 6.7. Study III: children by age and gender.

Age in years	Boys	Girls	Total
3	1	1	2
4	1	4	5
5	1	2	3
6	-	2	2
7	-	1	1
Total	3	10	13

Dream recall frequency

One hundred and one attempts were performed in as many morning awakenings. We obtained forty-seven dream reports (46% of the attempts) (for all ages). The older group showed a tendency to report a greater number of dreams (Table 6.8).

The study conducted with the QDEA

The main purpose of this study was to develop a simpler methodology to collect children's dreams from a wider sample. In particular, we tried to evaluate whether a simpler and less expensive methodology could allow us to collect data on dreaming that appeared consistent with the data obtained from the researches carried out with the classical methods.

This research was performed in twenty kindergartens and primary schools in a number of small towns near Viterbo, Frosinone, and Bologna, and in the town of Udine, with the help of various psychologists. The data on children's dreams were collected through a questionnaire developed for the purpose (QDEA). The QDEA mainly considers three content areas: the first one concerns the parent's compliance in comparison to the dream (seven items), the second is about children's dreaming and particularly about the different aspects of the last dream related by the child (twenty-one items), the last is about the child's sleep habits (eighteen items) (Colace, 2006a) (Table 6.9). Other items were on television-watching habits (Colace, Dichiacchio, & Violani, 2006a,b). All questionnaires

Table 6.8. Study III: frequency percentage of dream recall by age and gender.

Age	Gender	Ss.	No. of attempts	No. of dream reports	% of dream recall by gender	% of dream recall by age group[*]
3–5	Girls	5	38	12	31.5%	36% (21/58)
	Boys	3	20	9	45%	
5–7	Girls	6	43	26	60%	60% (26/43)
	Boys	—	—	—	—	

[*]Dream recall by age group: t-test $= -0.1986$ (df $= 12$) $p = 0.070$.

Table 6.9. QDEA: selection of items about children's dreaming, particularly on their latest dream.

Does your child ask you questions about dreams?

☐ Often   ☐ Sometimes   ☐ Rarely   ☐ Never

Is your child interested in his/her dreams?

☐ Very highly   ☐ Highly   ☐ Enough   ☐ Little   ☐ Very little
☐ Not at all

How many dreams has your child reported in the previous month? ____

Can you remember the last dream your child has reported?

☐ Yes, well   ☐ Yes, well enough   ☐ No

When did he/she report this dream?

☐ Waking up in the morning   ☐ During the same day
☐ At another time

Was the dream reported

☐ Spontaneously   ☐ On demand   ☐ Uncertain

While the child was reporting his/her dream, did you feel he/she was

☐ Anxious   ☐ Quiet   ☐ Happy   ☐ Gloomy

About this last dream reported:

Your child reported this dream using

☐ Brief sentences   ☐ Brief and elaborate sentences   ☐ A short story
☐ A long story   ☐ A long and elaborate story

Which was the main setting of the dream?

☐ Home   ☐ School   ☐ Recreational environment   ☐ Other _____
☐ Vague

Were there animal characters in the dream?

☐ Yes   ☐ No   ☐ Uncertain

Were there TV characters (cartoons, famous characters, etc.) in the dream?

☐ Yes   ☐ No   ☐ Uncertain

Were there family members in the dream (e.g., parents, brothers, sisters, grandparents, etc.)?

☐ Yes   ☐ No   ☐ Uncertain

Were there other children known to your child in the dream?

☐ Yes   ☐ No   ☐ Uncertain

In the dream your child was:

☐ The protagonist   ☐ A secondary character   ☐ Not present
☐ Uncertain

(continued)

Table 6.9 (continued)

Did your child interact with other people in the dream (e.g. speaking, playing, etc.)?

☐ Yes   ☐ No   ☐ Uncertain

Were there violent and aggressive actions in the dream?

☐ Yes ☐ No   ☐ Uncertain

The content of the dream (e.g., characters, settings) was:

☐ Ordinary and realistic   ☐ Realistic, but with some strange elements
☐ Strange and improbable

Please describe the dream the answers you have provided above refer to:

Did the dream content show evident connections with recent real-life events that happened to the child?

☐ Yes   ☐   No   ☐ Uncertain

(*If answer is Yes*) These events were mostly

☐ Pleasant   ☐   Neutral   ☐ Unpleasant

Please describe these events and their connection with the dream

---

were given in an envelope by teachers to parents, together with a cover letter containing a brief presentation of the research and guarantees on the anonymity and privacy of the personal information. The parents were asked to return the questionnaires in a sealed envelope after one week. About three days after distributing the questionnaires, the teachers reminded the parents to return them, and, if they were not returned, they prompted the parents again twice. The questionnaires were distributed to 1,148 parents. Of these, 652 returned them (return rate: 57%); of these in turn 565 were useable (usability rate: 49%) and related to children aged between two years, nine months and nine years, four months. In 325 questionnaires, the parents were able to write down their child's most recent dream report (Table 6.10).

Dream recall

We asked the parents to note down how many dreams their children had reported in the last month. The results show that 60.7% of the younger children had remembered at least one dream, while 39.3% had not reported any dream. The situation was similar for

Table 6.10.   QDEA Study: number of children by age, gender and number of dream reports.

Age in years	Girls	Boys	Total	Children whose dreams were noted down by parents
3[a]	28	37	65	30
4	29	56	85	44
5	46	60	106	71
6	58	56	114	70
7	61	64	125	68
8[b]	33	37	70	42
Total	255	310	565	325

a. This group includes two children under the age of three.

b. This group includes four children under the age of nine.

older children: 72.7% had reported at least one dream, 27.3% did not report any dream (Table 6.11).

A preliminary study on the drawings of dreams with 5–7-year-old children

We conducted a brief pilot experiment on the drawing of dreams with a small subgroup of children who had participated in Study II. The main purpose was to observe the possible convergence between the contents of the dream as they appeared in the verbal reports and their drawing made after some time. We asked a group of thirty-five children, aged 5–7, to make a drawing about one month after the dream they had reported previously. The question was: "*Make a drawing of yourself dreaming. You are sleeping and having a dream. If you can remember the dream you told me (interviewer), please draw that one.*"

Among these children, twenty-four had previously told a dream; eleven had not remembered any dream. Overall, we collected thirty-five dream drawings. Of the twenty-four children who had previously given a verbal dream report, eight drew that same dream (33%). As we have seen in the preceding chapter, dream drawings have proved to be quite useful for the evaluation of dream credibility. Furthermore, these dreams have started also to

Table 6.11. QDEA Study: frequencies of dream recall by age group and gender.

Age	Gender	No. of dreams reported in the last month						
		None	1	2	3	4–5	6–9	10–20
3–5	Girls 131	56 (41%)	20 (14.5%)	18 (13%)	13 (9%)	16 (12%)	3 (2%)	5 (4%)
	Boys 93	32 (34%)	16 (17%)	16 (17%)	13 (14%)	6 (6%)	7 (7.5%)	3 (3%)
	Total	88 (39.3%)	36 (16.1%)	34 (15.2%)	26 (11.6%)	22 (9.8%)	10 (4.5%)	8 (3.6%)
6–8	Girls 136	38 (28%)	23 (17%)	23 (17%)	29 (21%)	9 (6.6%)	10 (7%)	4 (3%)
	Boys 146	39 (27%)	34 (23%)	32 (22%)	13 (22%)	19 (13%)	4 (2.7%)	5 (3.4%)
	Total	77 (27.3%)	57 (20.2%)	55 (19.5%)	42 (14.9%)	28 (9.9%)	14 (5.0%)	9 (3.2%)
	All ages	165 (32.6%)	93 (18.4%)	89 (17.6%)	68 (13.4%)	50 (9.9%)	24 (4.7%)	17 (3.4%)

Age group differences: $\chi^2 = 9.112$, df = 6, p = 0.167.

prove useful for the study of the phenomenology of the dream (see Chapter Nine).

Statistical analyses

Statistical analyses were developed using the Statistical Package for Social Science (SPSS) 11.0 software.

CHAPTER SEVEN

Formal characteristics of children's dreams

I n this chapter, I describe the formal characteristics of children's dreams with respect to three indicators: the *length of dream reports,* the *narrative complexity,* and the *measure of dream bizarreness.*

Length

Children aged 3–5

We assessed dream length by measuring the number of words contained in the verbatim transcription of dream reports. That is, the number of words employed by the child to describe his/her dream that provide actual information on it, removing repetitions and comments. This assessment was made through the "word count" feature of a common word processing package.

The dreams of children of preschool age (3–5 years) are really short. Most of them are composed of a story of two sentences. The analysis of the dream reports collected in Study I shows that in children aged 3–5 (mean age group: four years, eight months) the median measure of dream length is twenty-three words. This find-ing was repeated in Study II: here, too, in the group of 3–5 year-old children (mean age group: four years, six months), the median measure of dream length is twenty-three words.

The results obtained from Study III (home study) are close enough to the findings above. In the 3–5 years age group (mean age group: four years, two months) typical dream reports do not exceed thirty-five words.

It is noteworthy that, although the three studies mentioned above were based on different types of dream collection methods, the results are similar (Table 7.1). In the at-home study, the inter-views on dreams were conducted by parents and the children were presumably more at their ease in telling the dreams recalled than they were when they reported their dreams to a stranger (i.e., the interviewer), which might have encouraged them to extend their verbal report. Notwithstanding this, the reports collected at home and at school appear very similar in terms of length. Besides, in the group of children involved in the home study, the median length of dreams was greater because of one dream that clearly distinguishes itself from the others due to its exceptional length (277 words).

Below are a few typical examples of dreams.

Table 7.1.   Length of dream reports by age groups.

Length (word count)	Age groups					
	3–5 year-old			5–7 year-old		
	Studies			Studies		
	I	II	III	I[1]	II[2]	III[3]
Median	23	23	35	41	46	46
Min–max	2–134	2–85	2–277	8–539	9–194	10–150

[1]Mann–Whitney U-test , $p = 0.00$;

[2]Mann–Whitney U-test , $p = 0.00$;

[3]Mann–Whitney U-test , $p = 0.01$

Dream 01: child aged three years and six months (Study III)

"I dreamed that I woke you [the mother] up and caressed you, gave you a little kiss and hugged you, and then gave a kiss to dad."

Dream 20: child aged four years and two months (Study II)

"I slipped on the snow. Along a road with the mountains, going to Rieti [a town in Italy], I was with mum and dad and there were the farm animals."

Dream 90: child aged three years and ten months (Study II)

"I have dreamed the tree near the house, where the garage is. There was a rose."

Dream 18: child aged four years and five months (Study II)

"I dreamed of Dylan, the one from Beverly Hills, he was with Brenda."

[Beverly Hills was a popular TV series in 1993–1994, the period in which the dream was collected.]

Dream 13: child aged four years and eight months (Study I)

"I dreamed that I was at school and I was drawing."

Dream 67: child aged five years and six months (Study II)

"I, mum and sister, on Sunday, we had gone to the beach and . . . I tried to build a sand castle."

Dream 96: child aged three years and eleven months (Study II)

"I have had a dream, I dreamed a cow, it went eating and drinking and that's it." [This child lives in the countryside.]

There are also a few very short dreams of one or two words:

Dream 51: child aged four years and two months (Study II)

"I dreamed the police."

Dream 06: child aged four years (Study III)

"I dreamed lizards."

These very short dreams of two or three words were also noticed during the first study; however, I discarded these stories as anomalies and/or non-credible reports for mere lack of experience (Colace & Violani, 1993). Actually, I hold these dreams as reports of a dream experience that, even though elementary, is real.

This brevity of the early childish dreams is also confirmed by the parents' evaluations collected in the questionnaire study (Study IV). We asked the parents to measure the length of their child's most recent dream report according to a five-level scale: "Brief sentence", "Long and articulate sentence", "Short story", "Long story", "Long and elaborate story". Fifty-eight per cent of the parents of children of this age answered that the dream report consisted of a "Short story" and a good percentage (33%) even found that the dream report consisted of one sentence only (brief, 21%; long, 11%) (3–5 year-old children) (Colace, 2006a) (Table 7.2).

I believe that these results show that the brevity of early dreams of children can be considered the most peculiar and well verified characteristic of these dreams. It is the characteristic that best defines them and that makes them special compared to the common idea we have of dreams as long and complex stories (i.e., adult dreams).

Children aged 5–7

In older children, dreams are longer. In Study I, the median score of the dreams had by 5–7-year-old children (mean age of group: six

Table 7.2.   Parents' evaluation of dream length (Study IV).

Age in years	Subjects/ dreams	Brief sentence	Long and elaborate sentence	Short story	Long story	Long and elaborate story
3–5	$n = 144$	31 (21.5%)	16 (11.1%)	83 (57.6%)	7 (4.9%)	7 (4.9%)
6–8	$n = 178$	21 (11.8%)	22 (12.4%)	110 (61.8%)	17 (9.6%)	8 (4.5%)
All	$n = 322$	52 (16.1%)	38 (11.8%)	193 (59.9%)	24 (7.5%)	15 (4.7%)

($\chi^2 = 7.373$, df = 4, $p = 0.117$)

years, six months) is forty-one words. In Study II, in the 5–7 years age group (mean age of group: six years, four months), the median score is forty-six words.

In the dreams collected at home, the typical length in the 5–7 years age group (mean age of group: six years, two months) is also forty-six words.

The greater length compared to younger children's dreams is statistically significant (see Table 7.1)

Below are a few typical examples for this age group.

Dream 62: child aged six years and three months (Study I).

> "My mother told me, 'A, go buy the bread'—I went to buy the bread, when I got in I saw there was nobody in the bakery, there was nobody not even that lady, then I got in and saw a witch, then I went to mother and said, 'Mum, there's a witch inside!'—and that's all."

Dream 10: child aged seven years and ten months (Study III)

> "I dreamed that we were due to go on a trip with some friends and so— and then I didn't know what to wear, and I was upset because I didn't know what to wear. It was supposed to be a trip in the woods. I had to put on a skirt but could not find it. I found a pair of trousers that were too small for me. The friends were making lunch. We were at home. There were seven cats playing around."

Dream 12: child aged six years and five months (Study II)

> "The last dream I had is very very short. I, dad, mother and grand- mother were in the woods, I told daddy 'Dad I have seen a mole!' I picked the mole up then threw it to the ground at once because it was biting me! Then dad saw another one, picked it up, laid it down on the ground, and then the dream ended."

Dream 13: child aged six years; and four months (Study III)

> "There was a witch that made us turn old, and afterwards she leaned out from the window and I saw grandmother L., but she was not grandmother L., she was an angel that looked like grandmother, then grandmother, the true one, was already there at the market, but she really was the true one and the other one was false, and then . . . there was me, crying and crying."

One can see clearly that these dreams, although short, are decidedly longer than those of younger children. Besides, the increase in dream length in older children may not be statistically significant if we used a less sensitive measure than word count. For instance, by counting the number of verbs, in a subgroup of the sample from Study I, no statistical significant increase in length was found among older children (Colace & Violani, 1993). Also, the five-level scale used by parents did not prove sensitive enough to find a statistically significant difference in 6–8-year-old children, although these seem to have fewer dreams of one "brief sentence" (see Table 7.2).

Narrative complexity

Children aged 3–5

The dream reports of small children, apart from being short, show a simple narrative. There are also dreams that lack a real narrative sequence, that is, they are static in terms of space–time. The systematic evaluation of this aspect of dreams was made in Study II, using the measurement developed by Foulkes and colleagues (1990) that classifies the narrative complexity according to four levels: 0, non-narrative; 1, narrative with single temporal unit; 2, more than one temporal unit, (discontinuous); 3, more than one temporal unit (continuous). The measurement was applied independently by two judges (agreement rate = 82%).

The dream reports of 3–5-year-old children show a very basic narrative: 20% of these dreams have a "non-narrative" aspect, 50% have a "narrative with single temporal unit", 3% have a "narrative sequence within multiple, discontinuous temporal unit", and 27% have "a narrative sequence within multiple, continuous temporal units" (generally two). The median score in this age group is "1" (Figure 7.1).

The dream reports of older children (5–7 years) show a less elementary narrative (median score 1.5); 3% of dreams have "non-narrative sequence", 47% have a "narrative sequence within one temporal unit", 3% a "narrative sequence within more than one temporal units, discontinuous", 47% a "narrative sequence within

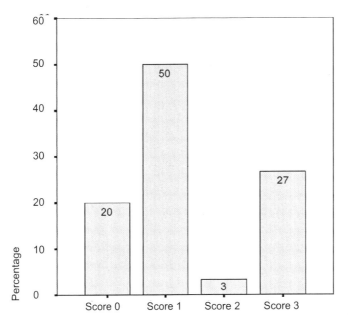

Figure 7.1.   Narrative sequence in the dreams of 3–5-year-old children.

more than one temporal units, continuous" (usually two) (Figure 7.2). The differences between the two age groups are statistically significant (Mann–Whitney U-test, $p = 0.03$).

It should be pointed out that these dreams (for all the ages) rarely show a discontinuous narration (only around 3%). As will be seen in more detail later, discontinuity is considered a characteristic that contributes to dream bizarreness.

Dream bizarreness

Defining and measuring dream bizarreness

Dreams frequently show impossible and/or improbable aspects compared with everyday life experiences, which have been referred as to "dream bizarreness". For example, we may dream of meeting people we have not seen in years, or find ourselves in unknown situations or environments; sometimes the whole plot of the dream is entirely surreal. Several terms have been used in literature to describe bizarreness, for example: "distortion from reality", "meta-

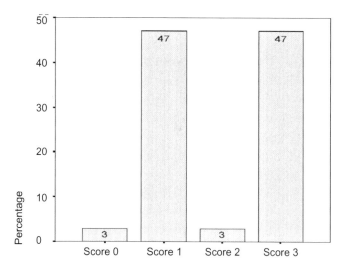

Figure 7.2. Narrative sequence in the dreams of 5–7 year old children.

morphosis", "implausibility", but many authors agree that the concept of bizarreness includes both (a) impossibility, and (b) improbability and/or oddness compared to "common daily experiences". The first dimension includes those situations that are impossible from a physical and/or logical point of view; the second dimension implies statistical improbability (Colace, 2003). This is one of the most enigmatic aspects of dreaming, which all the most important theories on dreams have tried to explain since ancient times (Colace, 1997b, 2003, 2006c) (Table 7.3).

Until the 1980s, the study of dream bizarreness was based primarily on research on adult dreams. The few studies on children's dreams considered measuring this aspect only marginally.

For example, Foulkes's study measured this aspect of dream by two categories only, that is, "characters' distortion" (all the unfamiliar characters appearing in the dream) and "setting distortion" (unfamiliar setting with respect to the child's ordinary everyday experience).

In order to measure this factor, I started applying those specific dream bizarreness content measures that had been used until then only in the studies on adults' dreams, such as, for example, the "Distortion scale" developed by Zepelin (1979), or the "Bizarre

Table 7.3. Synthesis of the principal modern theories on dream bizarreness.*

Freud's theory of dream bizarreness

According to the disguise–censorship theory, dream bizarreness is an expression of a motivated effort to disguise unconscious wishes that are unacceptable to the conscience. The dream-censorship agency and, later, the superego functions (in the ego) are responsible of the effort to disguise latent dream contents. In Freud's view, dream bizarreness is not an invariant property of dreams, as there are dreams that are typically non-bizarre (e.g., young children's dreams, and adult dreams directly engendered by the frustration of vital needs) (Freud, 1905c, 1916–1917). Bizarre elements are psychologically meaningful, and dreams do have a meaning. Motivations play an important role in this model, while other models reviewed give little relevance to them.

Activation–synthesis hypothesis

This model (Hobson, 1988; Hobson & McCarley, 1977) ascribes dream bizarreness exclusively to the unique neurobiological conditions of the brain during the REM phase of sleep ("dreaming is the cognitive by-product of a physiological state, REM sleep" [Mamelak & Hobson, 1989, p. 202]). The original theory stated that bizarreness is the result of a temporally random and non-cognitive input from the brainstem (ponto-geniculo-occipital spikes) and that dreams are merely the product of "the best of a poor job" that the forebrain makes to give sense to this random bombardment (*forebrain synthesis*). Later on, it was suggested that the aminergic demodulation found in REM sleep (or the lack of the inhibiting influence of norepinephrine and serotonin) causes defects in cognitive functioning (e.g., attention, memory, etc.) during forebrain synthesis, which contributes to dream bizarreness (Hobson, 1988; Hobson, Stickgold, & Pace-Schott, 1998; Kahn, Pace-Schott, & Hobson, 1997; Mamelak & Hobson, 1989). In Hobson's view, dream bizarreness is a constant formal property of all dreams and it has no particular psychological significance.

"Reverse learning" theory

According to the "reverse learning" theory (Crick & Mitchison, 1983), dreaming and bizarreness are merely the result of the effort to erase from memory redundant associations or "parasitic" thoughts (i.e., information causing an overload in the memory system) during REM sleep. As in Hobson and McCarley's theory, in this model, too, random subcortical PGO activity plays an important role for bizarreness. Dream is inherently meaningless (Crick & Mitchson, 1983, 1986).

(*continued*)

Table 7.3 (continued)

Seligman and Yellen's theory

According to Seligman and Yellen (1987), the bizarreness and discontinuity found in REM dreams are due to the "visual burst" (discharges of eye movements) that supposedly cause intrusions of inconsistent and discontinuous images in the dream plot. As in Hobson and McCarley's model, Seligman and Yellen attributed bizarreness to random PGO activity (PGO spikes are commonly associated with visual bursts) and, therefore, to the difficulty in finding sense in visual bursts.

Foulkes's cognitive model

Foulkes (1982, 1985) indicates three components in dream production: the input, that is, the activation of memory units, their processing, known as "planner", and the output, that is, conscious organization. The dream is an attempt to give a plausible sense to input information. In Foulkes's view, this attempt is generally successful. However, this dream production mechanism may be disturbed by the presence of memory units with a higher and more impinging level of activation, which the planner cannot exclude from processing. This event translates into the presence of thematic changes (i.e., discontinuity) and bizarre elements. Therefore, bizarreness is considered an exception rather than the rule.

Antrobus's General Cortical Activation/Thresholds (GCAT) model

According to Antrobus and colleagues, bizarre mentation is the product of two factors: cortical–cognitive activation and the level of environmental stimulation (or auditory thresholds) (Antrobus, 1983, 1986, 1991; Reinsel, Antrobus, & Wollman, 1992; Reinsel, Wollman, & Antrobus, 1986; Wollman & Antrobus, 1986). Reinsel and colleagues (1992) found that bizarreness is maximal in conditions of high to moderate cortical–cognitive activation when external stimulation is minimal (i.e., REM sleep and relaxed waking).

Phenomenological perspective

Hunt (1982, 1989) elaborated a "phenomenological classification-ratings system for formal anomalies in the dreaming experience" and analysed different samples of dream reports. In Hunt's view, "normative dreams" (i.e., laboratory and home dreams), albeit largely realistic in content and plot (in the sense that they reproduce typical waking situations and capacities), may show aspects of bizarreness that can be assimilated to a mild clinical delirium. Conversely, dreams of Freud's and Jung's collections were characteristically bizarre. This approach does not consider bizarreness an invariant property of dreaming. Bizarreness is of great importance as evidence of creative symbolic imagination (visual–spatial processes) and has a metaphorical significance.

---

*See Colace (2003).

elements" scale developed by Domhoff and Kamiya (1964) (see Colace, 1997a; Colace & Violani, 1993) (for insight on dream bizarreness scales, see Winget and Kramer [1979] and Colace [1997b; 2003]) and, later on, I also decided to apply measurements obtained from the Freudian classification of dreams (see Chapter Three) based on their level of distortion–bizarreness (Colace, Violani, & Solano, 1993).

The application of different measurements of dream bizarreness, some of which certainly did not develop from a psychoanalytic background, such as, for instance, the "Dream bizarreness" scale of Hobson, Hoffman, Helfand, and Kostner (1987), apart from leading to more objective and standardizable results on children's dreams, also allowed me to prove the validity of construction of the Freudian classification. Furthermore, one bizarreness scale may catch certain aspects better than others.

All bizarreness measurements were always taken by two independent judges who did not know the age of the children or the scores obtained from the other tests (see Table 7.4).

The application of bizarreness scales to children's dreams is not particularly problematic; however, our observations led to the identification of certain evaluation criteria that should be followed in the presence of certain peculiar contents of children's dreams.

These criteria that I am describing in these pages came up from the very first applications of bizarreness scales and may be fine-tuned in further research.

Table 7.4. Dream bizarreness scales used in the studies.

Dream bizarreness scales	Interjudges agreement	Study
1. "Distortion/bizarreness scale" (Colace, Violani, & Solano, 1993)[a]	84%–90%	I, II, III
2. "Bizarre elements" (Domhoff & Kamiya, 1964)	84%	II
3. "Distortion from reality " (Zepelin, 1979)	$r = 0.84$ (p 0.00)	I
4. "Dream bizarreness" (Hobson, Hoffman, Helfand, & Kostner, 1987)	67%	I

[a] The scores of this scale are correlated with Domhoff and Kamiya's (1964) scale , $r = 0.71$ ($p = 0.00$).

Television and imaginary characters

There are dreams that present characters belonging to a child's common imaginary world. For example, Santa Claus or the Befana (the "Epiphany witch", who is believed to bring presents on 6 January). Besides, during the holiday season the children may happen to meet people disguised as these characters in the streets. The appearance of these characters in child dreams has always been judged as "plausible" and not as a bizarre dream content, except in those cases in which they have unusual roles and/or commit unusual actions in the dream.

Examples of "plausible" dreams follow.

Dream 32: child aged four years and seven months (Study II)

"I dreamed that Santa Claus brought me the present, the bulldozer, and then came to my bed."

Dream 55: child aged five years and two months (Study II)

"I dreamed of the toy motorbike. The Befana brought me the toy motorbike and dad took me to the gardens (I was riding the toy motorbike), there, there at the gardens, and I rode fast and then jammed on the brakes to make the tyres squeal."

Likewise, other dreams contain more or less known television characters. For instance, characters from cartoons, television series, or famous films, for which there are plenty of toy gadgets available. I am referring to dreams that present such characters as the "Ninja Turtles", the "Power Rangers", or those dinosaurs with weird names from Jurassic Park. In the dreams these characters may appear alone, or they may interact with the child. Even if they are not real characters, they belong to the child's fantastic world. They have been considered as plausible and ordinary. Sometimes the dreamer him/herself confirms that the dream is about a television character he/she watches everyday. I believe that these television characters can be treated in the same manner as those that, in Freud's times, came from illustrated fairytale books. In other words, today we would more often watch a television programme than read a story book.

A few examples are given below.

Dream 81: child aged four years and ten months (Study II)

"I dreamed of 'Captain Flan', he was fighting with a villain, 'Radiragno', and five young men with rings evoked Captain Flan and fought the villain. 'Radiragno' wanted to crash the trees and make the elephants become evil, and there were also kangaroos."

[This is a cartoon the child watches on television every day.]

Dream 18: child aged four years and five months (Study II)

"I dreamed of Dylan, he was with Brenda (TV characters)."

[These are the protagonists of a famous television series of the 1990s.]

Soft and toy animals

Other dreams present soft and/or toy animals that one must take care not to mistake for real animals. While in our evaluation of dream bizarreness soft and toy animals were considered "plausible contents" in the experience of many children, the presence of real animals other than pets can be considered an element of bizarreness. It is also important to consider the role and the actions performed by these animals.

Daytime fantasies

Last but not least, another aspect concerns the evaluation of dream contents that seem to refer to ordinary fantasy in the life of the child. We saw already, in the first study, that in the case of some dreams, truly a very small number, we found it hard to apply the dream bizarreness scale. These were dreams that contained what actually were ordinary fantasies of the child. In our evaluation of dream bizarreness, in the presence of dream contents that probably referred to a waking fantasy, we considered the plausibility of the fantasies with respect to the child's possible common experience. It is important to try to identify which reality elements are likely to be the origin of the fantasy that is re-visited in the dream. For instance, if the child says he/she has dreamed of being in the jungle with

Tarzan, it will be very helpful to know that the evening before the child had watched a Tarzan film, or had read a book on this character. In this case, we are facing a dream with a plain and understandable content. Often, the fantasies that appear in these dreams are mere repetitions or reproductions of fantasies based on real and known diurnal elements. More rarely, dreams show fantasies that cannot be traced in the diurnal elements that are likely to have engendered them.

Information on daytime experiences

A discriminating point in the evaluation of dream bizarreness may be the quantity of information on the dreamer's personal experiences during the state of wakefulness. When we have this information, dreams may be understood more easily and certain contents that at first seemed bizarre may be explained. For instance, in some cases we found difficulty in understanding dreams when we were not sufficiently informed about the newest cartoons broadcast on television, or about the latest fantastic character or attraction for children. This is a methodological aspect that should not be underestimated. Those who collect these kinds of dreams should be aware of these aspects, or at least be supported by someone who is. This is something we understood especially in Studies II and III. In Study II, we obtained information to help us evaluate the plausibility of certain dream contents with respect to the dreamer's specific diurnal experience by asking questions of the child after his/her spontaneous dream report. We asked, referring to the characters, settings, objects, actions that appeared in the dream, if these were also known during the day (i.e., for real) or not, and when was the last time the child had seen them or performed a given action: for instance, if, in the dream, the child was riding a bicycle, we asked when was the last time he had used a bicycle, or if he/she uses it often. In Study III, this and other information was provided by the children's mothers. Actually, the aspect mentioned here is not specific to the evaluation of bizarreness in childish dreams. In adults, when dreamers themselves are asked to evaluate the bizarreness of their dreams by comparing dream contents with their personal experience, the dreams are rated less bizarre than they would be by an independent evaluator (Zepelin, 1989). In any case, in adults there is a positive correlation between self-evaluation of dream bizarreness and evaluation made by evaluators (Foulkes & Rechtschaffen, 1964).

Frequency of bizarre dreams in children

Children aged 3–5

I am primarily reporting here the results based on the application of the bizarreness content scale derived from the Freudian classification (Table 7.5), since it is the measure employed in all studies. Later, I will also report the results based on the application of other bizarreness scales in a single study and/or sub-group of children's dreams.

Dream reports of young children are frequently simple and without bizarre elements. 68% of dreams were valued as sensible, comprehensible, and plausible with common daytime experiences, without strange elements (score I) (altogether Studies I, II, III), 17% as dreams clear, consistent and sensible but strange, since their

Table 7.5. Scale of dream bizarreness developed on the basis of the Freudian classification (Colace, Violani, & Solano, 1993).

The authors attempt to formalize Freud's original classification of dream bizarreness. Dreams are classified as follows.

1. The dream is *sensible, plausible, and without strange elements*. This dream is comprehensible and plausible with respect to common daytime experiences. Example: "I dreamed that I was playing with a teddy bear and I wanted to take it."

2. The dream is *sensible, consistent in itself, but strange compared to everyday life*. The content of the dream is clear and consistent in itself, makes sense, but has a strange effect for its meaning is hardly compatible with common everyday experiences. Example: "I dreamed that they were kidnapping me, then they kidnapped me, but . . . and then they ate me."

3. The dream is *senseless, inconsistent, and bizarre*. The content of the dream is non-understandable, inconsistent, strange, and senseless. Example: "I dreamed that my mother was shut inside a box. I wanted to pull her out but could not because the box was huge, then I took a ladder and opened the lid."

meaning is scarcely compatible with common daytime experiences (score II), 15% of dreams were valued as senseless, not comprehensible, bizarre, and without a meaning (score III) (Table 7.6).

In brief, these dreams are often quite clear and comprehensible, and their content may be easily related, with no need for interpretation, to common daytime situations of the child.

Here are a few examples.

Dream 11: child aged four years and one month (Study II)

"I dreamed that I was skiing with my dad, my mother and L [sister]."

Dream 01: child aged three years and six months (Study III)

"I dreamed that I woke you [the mother] up and caressed you, gave you a little kiss and hugged you, and then gave a kiss to dad."

Dream 23: child aged four years and seven months (Study I)

"I met a girl who was going to the beach and I said hello to her."

Dream 13: child aged four years and eight months (Study I)

"I was at school and I was drawing."

Table 7.6.   Frequency percentage of dreams by bizarreness score by age group.

Age group in years	N dream reports	Score I	Score II	Score III
Study I				
3–5	48	56% (27)	23% (11)	21% (10)
5–7	53	32% (17)	32% (17)	36% (19)
Study II				
3–5	30	77% (23)	17% (5)	6% (2)
5–7	34	59% (20)	18% (6)	23% (8)
Study III				
3–5	21	81% (17)	5% (1)	14% (3)
5–7	26	38% (10)	16% (4)	46% (12)
All studies				
3–5	99	68% (67)	17% (17)	15% (15)
5–7	113	42% (47)	24% (27)	34% (39)

Dream 32: child aged four years and eight months (Study II)

"I dreamed that Santa brought me the present and then came to my bed."

Dream 49: child aged five years and two months (Study II)

"Mother had bought me the Barbie and then I could not find it (when I woke up)."

As we may see from Table 7.6, the percentages of the various categories of dreams found in the three studies are really very similar.

In Study I, the percentage of "sensible and comprehensible dreams" (score 1) is lower compared to those found in Studies II and III, which confirms the fact that, in the presence of further information on the child's daytime experiences (present in Studies II and III), it is possible to explain certain aspects of the dream that otherwise would be considered implausible or improbable.

Children aged 5–7

In older children, dreams start to show more bizarre aspects. Sensible and comprehensible dreams (score 1) decrease to 42%, those sensible but hardly compatible with daytime experiences (score 2) are 24% and those strange and bizarre (score 3) increase to 34% (altogether Studies I, II, III) (see Table 7.6).

By comparing these dreams with those of younger children, we observed a significant increase in the mean score of dream bizarreness in each of the three studies (Table 7.7).

Here are a few examples.

Table 7.7.   Bizarreness mean score by age group.

	Mean bizarreness score		Mann–Whitney U-test
	3–5 years	5–7 years	
Study I	1.65	2.04	$p = 0.01$
Study II	1.30	1.65	$p = 0.08$
Study III	1.33	2.08	$p = 0.00$

Dream 11: child aged five years and eleven months (Study III)

"I remember only one thing, M and I we were in a shop . . . so M and I were in a shop and we had met many children who wanted to take the doll . . . but they were too many, they could not take it, then a policeman came and said, 'What are you doing?' 'We all want that doll but we are too many', and the policeman said, 'Give it to those two girls! They are just two!'"

Dream 9: child aged six years and four months (Study II)

"Well, they cut my head off and I went to the hospital."

Dream 19: child aged six years and six months (Study II)

"I dreamed that mummy was giving two thousand lire to me and then dad put the chair into place and then I dreamed that dad was growing old and died. He was old, he had got many many years old, and he had died."

Dream 59: child aged five years and ten months (Study II)

"There was a horse, it was all green with red eyes, so this horse took mum, made her stand up and made her with red eyes, she was the horse's wife, so she left daddy and myself sleeping but she had transf . . . my eyes had become red because I was the daughter of these two people . . . of this horse and of this and of . . . mother."

Dream 70: child aged six years and five months (Study II)

"A dragon, I was watching it, so I said now I'm going to get myself a knife and attack it. I closed his mouth but didn't kill it. Then uncle too came into the dream, a mess . . . mother, dad, uncle and aunt . . . I was still climbing and then I went behind the dragon's head, I caught it, turned it, slammed it to the ground . . . oh dear! I was fighting with a dragon (he thought it was a Carnival dragon while it was a true dragon). I returned home, took a knife long like this and cut him here [the throat], I caught it, turned it, slammed it to the ground, there were mummy, daddy and G (my sister). I killed it and everybody went away."

The indications above are substantially confirmed by the application of other measures of dream bizarreness.

The "Bizarre elements" scale developed by Domhoff and Kamiya (1964), which identifies three general classes of bizarre elements (metamorphoses, four categories; unusual acts, two categories; magical occurrences, four categories) was applied to sixty-four dream reports (3–7-year-old children, Study II). We observe that thirty-six dream reports do not show any element of bizarreness, while twenty-eight show sixty-two elements of bizarreness. Only sixteen out of the sixty-two bizarre elements originated from the dreams of the 3–5 age group ($X = 0.5$ elements of bizarreness per dream); in the group of older children, there are forty-six elements of bizarreness ($X = 1.3$ elements of bizarreness per dream). The increase of bizarreness is statistically significant ($t = -2.38$, $p < 0.03$).

Hobson and colleagues' "Bizarreness scale" (Hobson, Hoffman, Helfand, & Kostner, 1987), which identifies bizarre items (i.e., impossible or improbable) as exhibiting discontinuity, incongruity, or uncertainty was applied to a sub-group of dreams (Study I, session 1). The results show that 47% of dream reports by 3–4 year-old children do not show any items of bizarreness and another 20% show only one item of bizarreness. In addition, we observed that six-year-old children, compared to four-year-old ones, show a statistically significant increase in dream bizarreness in terms of the number of "inconsistent elements" (Colace, Doricchi, Di Loreto, & Violani, 1993).

Zepelin's "Dream distortion" scale (1979) (see Winget & Kramer, 1979 for detail) that measures the strangeness in dream content (i.e., unknown chararacters and settings, illogical relationships, etc.) in comparison to waking experience (six levels of dream distortion) shows that, in the 3–4 age group (Study I, session I), the mean score of dreams (mean score = 2.40) corresponds to a dream "quite realistic, but in some aspect inconsistent or unusual with subject's everyday experience or with common experience". While this scale gives higher scores of bizarreness to the dreams of older children (mean score: 3.55) the increase is not statistically significant (Colace & Violani, 1993).

Finally, it must be noted that, in the dreams of children (of all ages), as in the dreams of adults (for review see Colace, 2003), we have found positive and statistically significant correlations between bizarreness and length of the dream: $r = 0.32$ ($p = 0.02$)

(Colace & Violani, 1993; Colace, Violani, & Solano, 1993), $r = 0.28$ ($p = 0.01$) and $r = 0.41$ ($p = 0.00$) (Colace, 1997a).

The results of Studies I, II, and III were also confirmed in the QDEA questionnaire study. The parents were required to classify the latest dream report of their child according to three levels of bizarreness: "1, ordinary and realistic dream"; "2, realistic dream but with some strange elements"; "3, strange and improbable dream". The parents, while unfamiliar with "dream bizarreness" classification and notwithstanding their difficulties in evaluating dreams some time after they were reported, clearly classified the dreams (children aged 3–5 years) as "strange and improbable" (score 3) in only 16% of cases. They identified in the majority of cases "ordinary and realistic dreams" (46%) and a larger group, compared to Studies I, II, and III, of "realistic dreams but with some strange elements" (38%), in which we noticed a fair percentage of parents uncertain about the assessment (Table 7.8). The parents of older children (6–8 years) considered their children's dreams more bizarre than the parents of younger children, which suggests an increase, quite close to statistic significance, in "strange and improbable" dreams, and in "realistic dreams with some strange elements", and a decrease in "ordinary and realistic" dreams (Table 7.8).

Briefly, the majority of the dreams of preschool age children show a scarce presence of bizarreness even if this aspect of dreams is measured by different scales. The increase of dream bizarreness in the older age group suggests that there may be a stage in development, around the fifth year of age, in which dreams begin to

Table 7.8. Dream bizarreness in parental evaluation by child's age group.

Age in years	Subjects/ dreams	"ordinary and realistic"	"realistic but with some strange elements"	"strange and improbable"
3–5	$n = 136$	62 (45.6%)	52 (38.2%)	22 (16.2%)
6–8	$n = 167$	64 (38.3%)	57 (34.1%)	46 (27.6%)
All	$n = 303$	126 (41.6%)	109 (36.0%)	68 (22.4%)

χ^2 (df 2) = 5.619, $p = 0.06$

become more frequently bizarre. In this sense, useful information for understanding dream bizarreness may come from the study of those development factors (e.g., cognitive and personality) that usually change during that stage and that may affect the formal characteristics of dreams.

As we have said, the psychoanalytic model is one of the few that involves evolutionary factors, and/or factors related to individual personality differences to explain the presence of dream bizarreness. From this point of view, it is the only model that excludes the possibility that dreams are invariably bizarre due to an inherent peculiarity of the dreaming process in itself. The next chapter will deal with this aspect. Table 7.9 summarizes the formal characteristics of children's dreams.

A comparison with previous studies

Length

The dreams analysed here are close enough to Foulkes's definition of childish REM dreams (at ages 3–5) as ". . . only a sentence or two long" (Foulkes, 1982, pp. 47–48). In the dreams of preschool children, the numerical values found by Foulkes are lower than those observed here (typically 23–35 words in these studies *vs.* fourteen

Table 7.9.   Summary of the formal aspects of children's dreams.

Dreams at age 3–5	• They are brief, typically of 23–35 words • They have a simple narration, generally with one temporal unit • They frequently have a sensible and plausible content with respect to common experience, without bizarre elements
Dreams at age 5–7	• They are significantly longer (41–46 words) (statistically significant increase) • They have a more articulated narration along two temporal units (statistically significant increase) • They are significantly more strange and bizarre (statistically significant increase)

words in Foulkes's study); conversely, in older children the values are very consistent (41–46 words in these studies *vs.* forty-one words in Foulkes's study). I cannot say whether the word count method used here equals the one used by Foulkes. In our studies, dream length was valued with the "word count" feature of a widely available word processing package, including all words, conjunctions, articles, etc. Foulkes, in his study, counted only the number of words of substantive dream content. As the difference in length is related more to the dreams of younger children, we cannot exclude that the latter may be somewhat inhibited by the laboratory environment. Nor can we exclude the hypotheses of partial (and biased) sampling (see Chapter Five). There may also be a third hypothesis: that is, younger children—compared to older children—are more inclined, within a family environment, to embellish their dream report with (invented) details, and therefore the report is longer. This hypothesis may be proved right or wrong by future studies (both in laboratory and home settings). In any case, the brevity of very young children's dreams remains confirmed. Consistently with Foulkes's data on REM dreams, we have found in our studies a statistically significant increase in length (word count) in the dreams of older children.

Narrative sequence

Foulkes affirmed that the REM dreams of young children are static, with no narrative (Foulkes, 1982, p. 48). Here, we have frequently observed instead the presence of a story in these dreams, although very basic and occurring within one temporal unit. In subsequent studies, Foulkes, Hollifield, Sullivan, Bradley, and Terry (1990) observed from 193 REM dream reports of eighty children aged 5–8 that the dreams of children aged up to seven showed an extremely simple narrative sequence or with one temporal unit, without narration discontinuity. The data found here show that the dreams with one temporal unit are 47% (5–7 years), but there are also 47% of dreams with multiple temporal units (frequently two). Therefore, also in this age group, the dreams collected here (Study II) appear more complex when compared to Foulkes's findings (median score: 1.5 in this study *vs.* 1 in Foulkes's study).

Dream bizarreness

In the first place, I would like to point out that the data reported here on bizarreness are in line with the anecdotal and qualitative observations on children's dreams developed by other authors who, even without using any objective content scale, succeeded in capturing the extraordinary simplicity of children's dreams (e.g., Coriat, 1920; Despert, 1949; Kimmins, 1937; see Chapter Five).

These data are in line with two previous studies conducted with methods very similar to those employed here ((Levi & Pompili, 1991; Resnick, Stickgold, Rittenhhouse, & Hobson, 1994). Levi and Pompili (1991), based on a sample of 369 children aged 3–5, interviewed at school ("Do you dream? Will you tell me a dream you had?"), observed that the dreams of younger children (3–4 years) present a "non conflictive and realistic" content, while as age increases (at about five), there are more dream reports with a "conflictive and fantastic" content. Resnick, Stickgold, Rittenhouse, and Hobson (1994) developed research on eighty-eight dream reports (fourteen children aged 4–5 and 8–10) collected at home upon awakening. These authors found that the dreams of younger children, in 66% (27/41) of cases, lacked any element of bizarreness (implausible/impossible elements: "inconsistency", "uncertainty", "discontinuity"), while 34% (14/41) of them showed at least an element of bizarreness. Conversely, in the older children, 51% of dreams (24/47) did not present any element of bizarreness, while 49% had at least one element of bizarreness (23/47). These authors suggested that the increase of bizarreness in the dreams of older children could be explained by their greater length. (Several authors assume that the length of a dream determines a greater presence of bizarreness. Against this trend, Hunt, Ruzycki-Hunt, Pariak, and Beliki [1993] suggested that it is more reasonable to believe that it is bizarreness that makes dreams longer, and not vice-versa. In support of this, Hunt and colleagues [*ibid.*] show that we need more words to describe bizarre images than ordinary images.) Besides, these authors emphasized that the distribution of the various types of bizarreness in children's dreams is similar to that found in the dreams of adults.

The direct comparison with Foulkes's studies on REM dreams is more complex, since it must be kept in mind that this author used a substantially more elementary bizarreness measure than those used here. Foulkes (1982) observed that children's dreams (3–5 years) are not "terribly bizarre" and do not show "deviations from the physical laws characteristic of everyday reality", but refer to family situations of the children's everyday world (*ibid.*, p. 67). Using the categories of "characters' distortion " and "setting distortion" (i.e., the ratio of unfamiliar/familiar characters and settings in dreams), Foulkes found that the dreams of younger children do not show any unfamilar characters or settings. Conversely, the dreams of 5–7 year-old children present a greater "distortion" in dreams in terms of the presence of unfamiliar characters and settings. According to Foulkes, from 5–7 years and upwards, the "distortion" "seemed to be a general property" of children's dreams (*ibid.*, p. 91; see also Foulkes, 1999, pp. 82–83).

It must be said, and I will return to this in the next chapter, that, in Foulkes's view, the presence of distortion in dreams depends on the cognitive ability, which only older children have, to imagine unfamiliar people and settings (*ibid.*). Foulkes also suggested that these dreams seemed plausible and realistic, but really

> the dream contrives to bring together in a plausible, if not always likely, situation images of physical things or events that ordinarily (that is, in waking life) would not be seen or thought of or imagined simultaneously. [Foulkes, 1999, p. 72]

The data found in my studies are in line with Foulkes's observations based on the two categories of bizarreness used; nevertheless, I will add that the dreams classified here as "comprehensible and plausible in comparison with everyday life" (i.e., score 1) did not reproduce reality in an unusual way; quite the opposite, they portrayed scenes of ordinary life, and the individual elements of the dreams were put together exactly as they would occur in the children's daytime experience. Therefore, in this aspect, the dreams collected here differ from REM dreams.

Conclusions

The results of the studies presented here, together with the findings of previous studies, suggest that child dreams are frequently short, simple in their narration, and without bizarre elements up to about five years of age. The dreams of older children progressively lose these characteristics and appear longer and more complex in narration, with contents that start to show more elements of bizarreness. I must point out that more bizarreness was found in the dreams of young children that present with a psychological disease (Freud, 1909b; Foulkes, Larson, Swanson, & Rardin, 1969). Foulkes, Pivik, Steadman, Spear, and Symonds (1967) notice that this is consistent with the correlations between dream bizarreness and personality disease found in adults (e.g., Foulkes & Rechtschaffen, 1964) (for a review see Colace, 1997b, 2003).

This picture of the formal characteristics of children's dreams is consistent with Freud's observations as reported in the first part of this volume. Particularly, first, the data found here are in agreement with Freud's observation of a scarce presence of bizarreness up to about 4–5 years of age and of its increase in the dreams of older children; second, Freud's classification of dreams by degree of bizarreness has proved to be valid and useful, as the results found by applying it to our dream samples are consistent with those obtained from the application of other bizarreness content measures known in literature; third, our data on dream length are consistent with Freud's observation on the brevity of these dreams; furthermore, as Freud had noticed, here we have found a statistically significant positive correlation between the length and the bizarreness of dream; fourth, with respect to narrative sequence, we observed that the examples of young children dreams brought by Freud actually present a story that develops in one temporal unit (as found here). Finally, we also noticed that our data on dream bizarreness are not contrary to two more general Freudian central statements, i.e., (a) bizarreness cannot be considered as intrinsic to the nature of the dreaming process, and (b) bizarreness cannot be considered a property of all dreams (Freud, 1910a, p. 34; 1916–1917, p. 128). In the final chapter, I will return to this point, underlining its implications for the modern theories on dream bizarreness.

Briefly, as far as the formal characteristics of children's dreams are concerned, on the basis of our observations and also by virtue of their material convergence with those from other systematic studies, I feel I can affirm that Freud, in his description of children's dreams, came quite close to how childish dreams appear when they are collected systematically and analysed according to objective measurements of their contents.

CHAPTER EIGHT

Bizarreness in children's dreams and the development of superego functions

Dream bizarreness and superego functions in the psychoanalytic model

In Freud's dream theory, inadmissible latent dream contents (i.e., under the ethical, aesthetical, or social profile threatening for the dreamer) are unconsciously disguised and distorted to become unrecognizable and innocuous to the conscious system. This mechanism, which is responsible for the final bizarre aspect of dream, is described as an intrapsychic selective mechanism that operates as a "censor" in analogy with the known Russian political censorship of the time. While, in the topographic theory of mind, this mechanism is attributed to the normal intrapsychic censor (see Chapter Three), in the "structural model" the concept of "censors" and "censorship" is replaced by the "superego", a sort of special agency existing within the ego, vested with certain important functions such as moral conscience, self-observation, self-evaluation, and formation of ideals. This follows the internalization of parental influence, as well as of the influence of social and cultural impositions (Freud 1914c, 1917e, 1923b, 1924d, 1930a, 1933a).

The progressive appearance of bizarreness in the early form of dreaming is parallel with the completion of the development of the superego functions of personality. These are thought to be responsible for the possibility and the need to disguise the latent material of dreams, and for the peculiar bizarreness of the dream; conversely, where these functions have not reached full development, dreams are more often free from bizarreness (see Chapter Three, pp. 32–33).

I believe that, in Freud's dream theory, dream censorship mechanism remains the most important hypothesis in the explanation of dream bizarreness. However, in Freud's view, other factors also contribute to dream distortion (e.g., symbolism, the considerations of representability, and secondary revision). I believe that it will be useful to proceed with all the various Freudian hypotheses on dream bizarreness, and the data from further studies will tell which of them still has a heuristic and empirical value.

Measuring the development of superego functions

A way to test Freud's hypothesis on the role of the superego in dream bizarreness is to check whether there is a statistically significant correlation between the measures of this aspect of dreams and the indices of development of the superego functions in the dreamer.

Dream bizarreness, as we have seen in the previous chapter, may be evaluated through a specific contents scale. The procedure may imply the measurement of the percentage of bizarre dreams and/or the measurement of the mean level of bizarreness present in the child dreams.

Arranging measures for the dimensions that may be taken as indices of the development of the superego is more complicated. The authors who have attempted to measure this aspect of personality for different research-related reasons have evaluated the following aspects: moral conscience, degree of adaptation to the rules, development of the ability to experience a sense of guilt, resistance to transgression, willingness to help those in difficulty, empathic sorrow (e.g., Amerio, Bosotti, & Amione, 1978; Berkowitz, 1964; Blasi, 1980; Burton, Allinsmith, & Maccoby, 1966; Yarrow & Waxler, 1976).

From a theoretical standpoint, one of the most prominent manifestations of the development of the superego functions is the possibility for a child to experience guilt following "transgressions" of a moral nature. In this regard, Freud stated that

> An interpretation of the normal, conscious sense of guilt (conscience) presents no difficulties; it is based on the tension between the ego and the ego ideal and is the expression of a condemnation of the ego by its critical agency. [Freud, 1923b, pp. 50–51]

> . . . the superego manifests itself essentially as a sense of guilt (or rather, as criticism—for the sense of guilt is the perception in the ego answering to this criticism) . . . [*ibid.*, p. 53]

Anna Freud (1965), on this subject, always affirmed that the appearance of the sense of guilt is a sign of the superego at work.

Some authors have suggested the existence of precursors of the superego (Ferenczi, 1925; Klein, 1932; Spitz, 1958) that are evident in the earlier manifestations of guilt and shame (see, for review, Frank, 1999; Laplanche & Pontalis, 1967).

When I had cope for the first time with the problem measuring those dimensions that might provide information on the development of the superego, my choice fell on measuring the *development of the ability to experience a sense of guilt* (Study I, Colace & Violani, 1993; Colace, Violani, & Solano, 1993). We proposed to the children the following test situation. A stimulus story was told in which the protagonist, a boy or a girl, according to whether the child interviewed was male or female, commits a transgression (story A). The story was interrupted after the protagonist committed the transgressive action. Then the child was invited to continue the story and also, with the aid of standard questions, encouraged to identify with the protagonist of the story, and his/her reactions were observed.

Furthermore, through certain direct questions, we asked the child how he/she would have reacted in the place of the protagonist of the story (role playing). This story was built also taking into account the indications arising from previous studies (Hoffman, 1970; Hoffman & Saltzstein, 1967; Thompson & Hoffman, 1980).

Always with the purpose of measuring the development of the ability to experience a sense of guilt, Study II (Colace, 1997a) continued in this direction, developing a second story (story B), based on the same logic as the first one.

While both these stories measured the sense of guilt in children, they related to different transgressions. This allowed us a greater probability of catching the development of this aspect of personality. Story A shows a *transgression consisting of an aggressive action* that, to a certain extent, might well be considered unintentional. Story B shows a *transgression consisting of the voluntary disrespect of a parental "order"* (see the stories below).

Story A

A boy/girl called Angelo/Anna is playing on a lawn. There are also other younger boys/girls with Angelo/Anna and Angelo/Anna knows that younger children are not so steady and that one needs to watch out so that they do not fall. However, Angelo/Anna starts running very fast and pushing the others, so a young child falls, gets bruised, and starts to cry . . .

Story B

A boy/girl called Stefano (Paola) goes to play with his/her friends. Then his/her friends decide to buy ice cream, but Stefano (Paola) is not supposed to have one, because his/her mum and dad have prohibited him/her to eat sweets and ice creams. However, Stefano (Paola) decides to have the ice cream on the sly, together with his/her friends . . .

Both stories allowed us to identify three levels of development of the ability to experience a sense of guilt.

At the first level, there are those children who, in their answers, did not show any uneasiness or any fear of their parents for what the protagonist did, or "for themselves" in the place of the protagonist.

Example 23: child aged three years and eleven months (Study II), Story A (child's responses are given in italics).

> What is going to happen now? *Angelo runs.* What does Angelo think after he sees that the young child has fallen? *He goes back to the classroom and writes.*

Example 19: child aged six years and six months (Study II), Story B

> What is going to happen now? *He eats the ice cream. He takes the ice cream and eats it.* And what does Stefano think? *He thinks about sleeping.* But how does he feel after he has eaten the ice cream secretly? *He feels OK . . . and goes to school.* Now let's pretend that you are Stefano, how would you feel after eating the ice cream secretly from dad and mum? *Fine . . . I'd go and buy another.* And how would you feel? *Fine.*

Example 85: child aged four years and seven months (Study II), Story B

> What does Stefano think? *That he is going around with the friends.* But how does he feel? *He buys another ice cream.* And what does Stefano do then? *He goes back to play with his friends.* Let's pretend that you are Stefano, how would you feel? *Fine.* Why? *Because I would.* What would you think? *That I'm going to play with my friends.*

At a second level, there are those children who at first did show a certain uneasiness, and fear or worry for the possible consequences of their action, such as, for instance, a punishment by the parents, but who in any case did not show a clear sense of guilt. In these children, uneasiness was due more to the fear of real parental punishment, therefore the source of the possible punishment was rather exterior than interior.

Example 06: child aged four years (Study III), Story A

> What is going to happen now? *They start to cry.* Why? *Because Anna hurt him.* And then? *The teacher says "this is not good".* What do you believe Anna thinks? *She thinks she has hurt him.*

Example 70: child aged six years and five months (Study II), Story A

> What is going to happen now? *It happens that he recovers and puts a bandaid on because he is bleeding.* And then? *The teacher scolds him and sends him indoors in punishment . . .*

Example 71: child aged six years and eight months (Study II), Story B

> What is going to happen now? *His mother scolds him.* Why? *Because he has eaten the ice cream.* What does Stefano think? *He thinks that he shouldn't have taken the ice cream.* How does Stefano feel? *He feels sad.* And how come? *Because his mother has scolded him.* Let's pretend you are Stefano, how would you feel after having eaten the ice cream? *Bad.* How bad would you feel? Very bad, a little bad, or so-so? *Very bad . . .* And what would you think? *That I shouldn't have eaten the ice cream, or mummy would scold me.* And how would you feel? *Bad.* How come? *I'd feel bad because mother would hit me and scold me.*

At a third level, there are those children who said the protagonist would repent for what he has done, feels mean and/or guilty, and tries to help the victim. Uneasiness in these children is due to the awareness that the action committed is wrong in itself. Therefore, it is not so much—or not only—the fear of punishment. Thus, these children seem to have interiorized moral norms and show full development of their superego functions.

Example 73: child aged six years and eleven months (Story A)

> What is going to happen now? *She gets hurt and puts a bandaid on, and Anna won't do it any more.* How does Anna feel? *Anna feels that she won't do it any more, and is sorry because the other child was hurt.*

Example 77: child aged six years and four months (Study II), (Story B)

> What is going to happen now? *Paola eats the ice cream, and her mother and father do not realize . . .* And what happens then? *Paola thinks she is going to tell her mother and father..., then if her mother and father get angry they won't allow her to buy ice cream any more. But if they don't get angry, then they will let her buy ice cream again.* How do you think Paola feels after eating the ice cream? *A bit offended and a bit happy, because if her mother and father scold her she feels offended, but if they don't she feels fine.* If you were Paola, for pretence, how would you feel after eating the ice cream? *A little guilty . . .*

The children's answers were rated by two judges, unaware of both the score of dream bizarreness and the exact age of the children (percentage agreement between the judges was > 85%).

The levels of development established with these stories grow as age increases. The older children show more complete levels of superego functions, highlighted by the possibility and the ability to experience a sense of guilt. For instance, in Study I, the score for sense of guilt (Story A) was correlated with age (range: $r = 0.33$, $p = 0.02$–$r = 0.55$, $p = 0.00$) (Colace & Violani, 1993). The capacity of these stories to discriminate between children of different ages was also confirmed in Study II. Both the scores of stories A and B on guilt correlated positively with the age of the children (rho = 0.42 , $p = 0.00$; rho = 0.52 , $p = 0.00$).

In Studies II and III, over the use of these test stories, we considered other possible indicators in order to access a broader range of dimensions implicated in the superego functions (see Table 8.1). We administered to the children the Wechsler test (WPPSI, Wechsler Preschool and Primary Scale of Intelligence, or WISC-R, Wechsler Intelligence Scale for Children Revised). The Wechsler test include the *comprehension subtest*, which furnishes information about "level of adaptation to reality and social environment" and of the "capacity of judgment and conventionality". The items of this subtest concern, in fact, the ability to understand social and conventional rules and the degree of adaptation to reality. Furthermore, certain items of this subtest may be considered as "moral items" (i.e., items no. 6 and 14, WPPSI, items no. 2, 5, and 6, WISC-R), in as much as they concern more directly the "level of acquisition of moral rules". From this point of view, the score of the *comprehension subtest* may provide information about the level of development of the superego functions. This assumption was tested through a comparison between the raw score from this subtest and the scores from other

Table 8.1.   Superego functions development indices.

Superego functions/indices	Studies
• Ability to experience sense of guilt (story A)	I, II, III
• Ability to experience sense of guilt (story B)	II, III
• Resistance to transgression	II
• Adaptation to reality and the social environment (*Comprehension*, WPPSI-WISC-R)	II, III
• Acquisition of moral rules (*Comprehension*, select items, WPPSI-WISC-R)	II, III
• Helping	II

tests on the superego functions (see above). In addition, the use of this subtest allowed us to try to replicate a result found by Foulkes (1982) on the correlations between "dream distortion" and *comprehension raw score* in children in the 3–7 age group (see above). Thus, from the *comprehension subtest* we obtained two indices: the total raw score of the subtest as a *measure of adaptation to reality and social environment* and the *sum* of the scores of only the "moral items" of this subtest as an index of *acquisition of moral rules* (Table 8.1).

Another index was that of the willingness to help those in difficulty (*helping*). On the basis of previous literature (e.g., Yarrow & Waxler, 1976), to evaluate this aspect we prepared the following situation. During the session with the child, the interviewer, while leaving the room, "inadvertently" caused some sheets of paper to fall and observed whether the child was ready to help to pick them up. During the observation, the interviewer took note of the child's behaviour using a seven-level scale: 1, "active indifference"; 2, "no attention"; 3, "merely notices what happens"; 4, "interest and partial attempt to help"; 5, "help and support"; 6, "help"; 7, "help and support with clear emotional sharing".

Finally, we considered an index based on the evaluation of a real behaviour regarding the *resistance to transgression* ("forbidden toys") (e.g., see Burton, Allinsmith, & Maccoby, 1966; Grinder, 1961). In this test, the experimenter showed a group of toys to a child and asked him/her what was the toy he/she liked best. Then he left the room, asking the child not to touch the chosen toy, with the motivation that "the toy was someone else's". Then the experimenter observed, unseen by the child, whether the latter touched the "forbidden toy" using a four-level scale: "1, touches it"; "2, touches it after a little time"; "3, touches it after a long time"; "4, does not touch it". This test allowed for observations of the child's actual behaviour in terms of obedience to rules.

Altogether, these indicators cover two general aspects of the superego functions: the typical functions of the superego, that is, moral prohibition and self-criticism (all tests except "the willingness to help those in difficulty"), and the positive (so to speak) functions of the superego, that is, those inherent to the ideal of the ego and the moral aspirations of the person (the "helping" test). (Some authors consider these aspects as inherent to two different structures: the superego and the ego ideal [see Frank, 1999].) Using this wide range of indicators for the dimensions implicated in the development of the superego functions, we had greater possibilities than in our first study (where only Story A was used) to identify the possible relationships between these and dream bizarreness and, at the same time, to see if there was any specific function of the superego more involved in the mechanism of dream censorship (see Table 8.1).

Dream bizarreness as a correlate of superego functions' development

In the first study, the hypothesis that dream bizarreness was correlated with the level of development of the superego functions received confirmation. Dream bizarreness measurements were correlated with the level of development of the ability to experience a sense of guilt, measured with Story A (Colace & Violani, 1993; Colace, Violani, & Solano, 1993) (Table 8.2).

Table 8.2.   Study I: Pearson correlations between measures of dream bizarreness and ability to experience sense of guilt (Story A).

Dream bizarreness	Guilt[a] (projected)	Guilt (direct)	Guilt intensity
Dreams: Session I Measure 1 of bizarreness*	$r = 0.17$ (n.s)	$r = 0.28$ ($p = 0.05$)	$r = 0.43$ ($p = 0.01$)
Dreams: Session I Measure 2 of bizarreness[†]	r 0.12 (n.s.)	$r = 0.31$ ($p = 0.02$)	$r = 0.27$ ($p = 0.05$)
Dreams session II Measure 1 of bizarreness*	$r = 0.20$ (0.08)	$r = 0.24$ ($p = 0.06$)	$r = 0.32$ ($p = 0.02$)

[a] In this first study, the answers to Story A were divided into those related to what the protagonist of the story does (projection) and those related to what the interviewee would have done in the protagonist's shoes (direct).

*Distortion/bizarreness scale derived from the Freudian classification of dreams (Colace, Violani, & Solano, 1993).

[†] "Bizarreness scale" (Zepelin, 1979).

These preliminary indications were reapplied and examined more thoroughly in Study II. In fact, a statistically significant positive correlation was observed between the score for Story A and a measure of dream bizarreness. Also, the numerical value of this correlation is quite close to the one found in Study I. In addition, another and more detailed measure of dream bizarreness showed a trend very close to statistic significance, with the scores for Story A (Table 8.3). This result was also replicated with Story B on guilt: in particular, the score of this story was correlated with the dream bizarreness measured with one of the two scales (Table 8.3).

The use of a second story on guilt, based on a different rule-breaking case, could show whether the ability to experience a sense of guilt in general was actually related to dream bizarreness. In other words, we needed to exclude the possibility that it was not only the particular type of guilt portrayed in Story A that was related to dream bizarreness. The second story allowed us to measure the ability to experience sense of guilt in respect of different situations and, therefore, to verify that what we were measuring was a background (general) ability to experience a sense of guilt. An important indication is represented by the fact that the scores of guilt appraised through the two different stories are correlated with each other, which suggests the construct validity of the stories (Table 8.4).

In conclusion, two different studies show that there is a statistical significant relationship between the measure of dream bizarreness (measured with three different scales) and the level of development of the ability to experience sense of guilt.

This relationship appears even more significant if we consider that the results from the tests on other dimensions of the superego functions point at the same direction. As seen in Table 8.3, dream bizarreness is correlated with the indices of "adaptation to reality and social environment" and of "acquisition of moral rules" (comprehension subtest, WPPSI/WISC-R).

The other two measures used for the evaluation of the superego functions (i.e., "resistance to transgression" and "helping") did not show any correlation with dream bizarreness.

The measure of "resistance to transgression" shows a correlation with some other measures of superego functions, and particularly with the "ability to experience sense of guilt" (Table 8.4). From this

Table 8.3. Study II: Spearman's *rho* correlation between measures of dream bizarreness and measures of superego function development.

Dream bizarreness scales	Ability to experience sense of guilt		Comprehension subtest (adaptation to reality and the social environment)		Comprehension subtest, *select moral items* (acquisition of moral rules)		Helping	Resistance to transgression
	Story A	Story B	WPPSI	WISC-R	WPPSI	WISC-R		
Bizarreness I*	0.25 (p <0.03)	0.09 (n.s.)	0.26 (p = 0.04)	0.01 (p = 0.48)	0.39 (p = 0.00)	0.20 (p = 0.21)	0.09 (p = −0.24)	−0.07 (p = 0.59)
Bizarreness II†	0.19 (p < 0.07)	0.26 (p 0.02)	0.37 (p =0.00)	0.25 (p = 0.169)	0.309 (p = 0.01)	0.52 (p = 0.01)	0.09 (p = 0.24)	0.12 (p = 0.38)

*Distortion/bizarreness scale derived from the Freudian classification of dreams (Colace, Violani, & Solano, 1993).
† "Bizarre elements" (Domhoff & Kamiya, 1964).

Table 8.4. Study II: Spearman's *rho* correlation between measures of superego functions.

	Resistance to transgression	Guilt		Comprehension subtest (adaptation to reality and the social environment)		Comprehension subtest, *select moral items* (acquisition of moral rules)	
		Story A	Story B	WPPSI	WISC-R	WPPSI	WISC-R
Helping	0.14 (p = 0.10)	0.32 (p = 0.00)	0.12 (n.s.)	0.15 (n.s.)	−0.15 (n.s.)	−0.00 (n.s.)	−0.07 (n.s.)
Resistance to transgression	—	0.26 (p = 0.07)	0.30 (p = 0.04)	0.38 (p = 0.01)	0.02 (p = 0.94)	0.20 (p = 0.21)	−0.01 (p = 0.96)
Guilt (Story A)		—	0.43 (p = 0.00)	0.56 (p = 0.00)	−0.23 (n.s.)	0.40 (p = 0.00)	−0.037 (n.s.)
Guilt (Story B)			—	0.66 (p = 0.00)	0.59 (p = 0.01)	0.39 (p = 0.00)	0.375 (p = 0.08)

point of view, this test on a child's actual behaviour in terms of obedience to rules really may give us some indications on the development of superego functions. However, we observed that many of the children who refrained from touching the forbidden toy were the same ones who, faced with story B on sense of guilt, which dealt with a violation similar to the one implied in the "resistance to transgression" test (i.e., eating ice cream when this was forbidden), reported a "score 2" (i.e., "fear of parental punishment") rather than "score 3" ("uneasiness, guilt"). Therefore, many of these children probably did not touch the forbidden toy more for fear of the interviever who had just asked them not to touch it and had just left the room, rather than because they really meant not to (internalization of rules). Now, many of these same children, consistently with the theory (in the sense that they had not developed their superego completely), reported simple dreams, which might explain the lack of correlations with dream bizarreness measures. On the other hand, the group of "infringing" children (fifteen) who did touch the "forbidden toy" (scores 1–3), consistently with our hypotheses, reported a greater frequency of simple dreams, free from bizarreness (60%, according to Colace, Violani, & Solano's [1993] scale).

The lack of correlation between the measure of "readiness to help" (i.e., "helping") and dream bizarreness measures is *apparently* contradictory with respect to the data above. On the other hand, this test is the only one not correlated with the other indices of superego functions (see Table 8.4). The only correlation observed was with the measure of guilt, Story A ($rho = 0.32$, $p = 0.01$), probably due to the fact that this story could also detect the interviewee's readiness to help the other child who had been pushed (see above, Story A).

Two indications from the table above are worthy of further insight. In the first place, the concept of superego can include different subsets of functions, some of which are not necessarily correlated: from this point of view it may be appropriate to distinguish at least between a group of functions inherent to the aspects of *moral prohibition and self-criticism*, and a group of functions related more to the *positive aspirations* of the individual towards ideal ethical models of behaviour.

In the second place, if we assume the concept of superego as a series of functions, we may observe that those implied in *dream censorship* could be selectively those pertaining to *moral prohibition and self-criticism* (i.e, moral conscience). What I am trying to say is that *"dream censorship" functions might require the development of only one given subset of superego functions, and not of all.* There might be specific functions that, where developed, would lead to the possibility and necessity of intervening by censoring and deforming the latent material of the dream and causing its bizarre aspect.

Study III was conducted with the purpose of replicating these findings through the analysis of more reliable dream reports. In this study, we compared the level of dream bizarreness with the scores obtained from the stories about sense of guilt and from the comprehension subtest (WPPSI). As in Study II, the answers to the stories on guilt were classified according to three levels of development by two independent judges who did not know either the exact age of children or the score on dream bizarreness (percentage agreement between the judges was 80% for Story A and 90% for Story B).

Table 8.5 shows the Spearman's rho correlations between dream bizareness measure (ie., percentage of bizarre dreams) and the ability to experience sense of guilt (Story A & B).

As we may see in detail for scores on Story B (Table 8.6), a greater percentage of bizarre dreams is coupled with a more complete development of the ability to experience sense of guilt (scores 2 and 3). Conversely, those children who have a low percentage of bizarre dreams, or even none, show an incomplete development of that function (score 1).

The positive correlation between the measure of dream bizarreness and the measure of the ability to experience sense of guilt appears greater than the one observed in Studies I and II, and

Table 8.5.   Study III: Spearman's *rho* correlations between dream bizareness (percentage of bizarre dreams, scores "2" and "3")* and development of the ability to experience guilt (Story A, Story B).

	Ability to experience sense of guilt	
	Story A	Story B
Dream bizareness	0.72 ($p = 0.03$)	0.90 ($p = 0.00$)

*Dream bizarreness scale (Colace, Violani, & Solano, 1993).

Table 8.6.   Study III: percentage of bizarre dreams and development of
the ability to experience guilt feelings (Story B) in each child.

% of bizarre dreams (scores "2" and "3")*	Ability to experience sense of guilt (score range: 1–3), Story B
0	1 (no uneasiness)
100 %	2 (fear of parental punishment)
0	1 (no uneasiness)
0	1 (no uneasiness)
40%	2 (fear of parental punishment)
0	1 (no uneasiness)
60%	2 (fear of parental punishment)
100%	3 (uneasiness, guilt)
25%	2 (fear of parental punishment)
66%	3 (uneasiness, guilt)

confirms a clear relationship between dream bizarreness and superego development.

Also, the relationship between the percentage of bizarre dreams
of each child and the raw score of the comprehension subtest and
of the selection of its "moral items" was replicated in Study III
(although with some children, it was not possible to administer
WPPSI). In the case of the scores for the selection of its "moral
items", the correlation did not reach a clear statistical significance
(see Table 8.7).

As in the first two studies, we found that the scores for the
comprehension test and for the selection of "moral items" are
clearly correlated with the scores of both stories on guilt (Table 8.8).

From this point of view, we may consider, in further studies, the
comprehension subtest score as a good indicator of the "ability to
experience sense of guilt", with advantages in its administration
and score evaluation in children.

The role of cognitive abilities in dream bizarreness

The studies presented here were not focused on investigating the
cognitive correlations of the dreaming process; nevertheless, in
order to understand which cognitive factors may affect the production of dream bizarreness, in the first study, and above all in Studies

Table 8.7.   Study III: Spearman's *rho* correlations between measure of percentage of bizarre dreams and raw score of comprehension subtest and of the selection of its "moral items".

% of bizarre dreams (scores "2" and "3")*	Raw scores from comprehension subtest WPPSI	
	Comprehension	Comprehension *selection of "moral items"*
0	9	2
100 %	14	2
0	5	0
0	11	0
40%	11	0
0	7	1
0	12	1
25%	22	3
66%	19	3
	$rho = 0.67$ ($p = 0.02$)	$rho = 0.47$ ($p = 0.10$)

*Dream bizarreness scale (Colace, Violani, & Solano, 1993).

Table 8.8.   Study III. Spearman's *rho* correlations between the measures of the ability to experience sense of guilt and raw scores for the comprehension subtest (WPPSI) and the selected "moral items" of it.

	Guilt (Story B)	Comprehension	Comprehension selection of "moral items"
Guilt (Story A)	0.67 (p 0.07)	0.86 (p 0.02)	0.91 (p 0.01)
Guilt (Story B)		0.82 (p 0.00)	0.58 (p 0.06)

II and III, we considered the measures of different cognitive abilities (Table 8.9).

In the first study, we used a descriptive ability test, in which we asked each child to describe a visual stimulus (pictures no. 3, the lion, and no. 8, the monkeys of the Children Apperception Test [CAT]) and then to describe the same picture without having it in sight (after about one minute from the previous test) (memory test) and another test on imaginative ability, or the inclination to develop a story from a visual stimulus (two pictures) (Colace & Violani, 1993).

Table 8.9.   The cognitive ability tests administered.

Tests	Studies
• Descriptive ability test (two pictures, no. of details)	I
• Short-term recall of the details in two pictures (no. of details)	I
• Ability/inclination to imagination (two pictures)	I
• Descriptive ability test, "realistic" picture (no. of details)	II, III
• Descriptive ability test, "bizarre" picture (no. of details)	II, III
• Memory test (interval 7–8 days) of a "realistic" picture (no. of details)	II
• Memory test (interval 7–8 days) of a "bizarre" picture (no. of details)	II
• Wechsler Intelligence Scale for Children tests (WPPSI/WISC-R)	II,III

In the second study, the descriptive ability test presents two variations. In one situation, children were invited to describe two pictures: a "realistic" picture (a group of men playing bowls) and a "bizarre" picture (a village of houses set in a vase). (For the realistic picture we used a scaled-down copy of the painting "The bowls game", by Ruggero Focardi; for the bizarre picture we used a scaled-down copy of the painting "My world", by Ivan Rabuzin.) In a second situation, after an interval of 7–8 days, the children were asked to remember what was in the two pictures (memory test). Then, in both situations, we counted the number of details noticed by the children in the pictures. The purpose of this type of test was to simulate, and at the same time to measure, a form of cognitive ability probably similar to the one that may be required in children when attempting to remember their dreams, or to describe the details of their dreams, be they simple or bizarre.

As we may see in Table 8.10, dream bizarreness (three different scales) is not correlated with descriptive abilities (both realistic and bizarre picture), short-term and long-term memory of details, and imaginative ability.

These preliminary data seem to suggest that the measure of bizarreness of dream reports is not necessarily related to the ability to describe the dream, to remember its details, or with the propensity to take time in its reporting (i.e., loquacity of the child). From

Table 8.10.   Spearman's *rho* correlations between the measures of dream bizarreness, descriptive abilities, memory abilities, and imaginative ability/inclination.

	Study	Bizarreness[1]	Bizarreness[2]	Bizarreness[3]
Ability to describe two pictures	I	0.08 (n.s.)	0.01 (n.s.)	
Ability to describe a "realistic" picture	II	0.07 (n.s.)	—	0.08 (n.s.)
	III	0.39 (n.s.)	—	—
Ability to describe a "bizarre" picture	II	−0.10 (n.s.)	—	0.04 (n.s.)
	III	0.57 (n.s.)	—	—
Memory of a "realistic" picture	II	0.27 (n.s.)	—	0.20 (n.s.)
Memory of a "bizarre" picture	II	0.13 (n.s.).	—	0.26 (n.s.)
Short-term recall of the details in two pictures	I	0.16 (n.s.)	0.08 (n.s.)	—
Ability/inclination to imagination I	I	0.19 (n.s.)	−0.03 (n.s.)	—
Ability/inclination to imagination II	I	0.12 (n.s.)	−0.04 (n.s.)	—

[1] Colace, Violani, & Solano's scale (1993); [2] Zepelin's scale (1979);
[3] Domhoff & Kamiya's scale (1964).

this viewpoint, dream bizarreness might be a matter that concerns more the process of production of the dream, rather than of its recall and analytical descriptive abilities in its report.

In the second and third study, in addition to the cognitive ability test described above, we administered all the subtests of the Wechsler Tests (WPPSI, Wechsler Preschool and Primary Scale of Intelligence or WISCR, Wechsler Intelligence Scale for Children Revised). We applied the WPPSI to the majority of children, as it is a scale more appropriate for children aged 3–4 and up to six and a half. So, we obtained the most important indications from the larger group of children. A smaller group formed by older children, to whom we applied the WISC-R, could only give certain indications that need to be confirmed.

The administration of the WPPSI or WISC-R tests allowed us to analyse in greater detail the possible impact of other cognitive abilities on dream bizarreness. From the correlations that emerged between the raw scores for the WPPSI subtests and the measures of dream bizarreness with a global (Colace, Violani, & Solano, 1993) and analytical scale (Domhoff & Kamiya, 1964), we are able to outline a picture of those cognitive abilities that may represent a basic potential requirement for younger children in order to be able to start having and recalling bizarre dreams.

In Study II, the correlations between dream bizarreness and the raw scores from WPPSI subtests suggest that the possibility of having/reporting a bizarre dream may be influenced by linguistic skills, verbal ability, categorization ability, attention and discrimination ability, perceptive organization ability, and symbolizing ability (Table 8.11).

Also in older children, according to WISC-R raw scores, the cognitive abilities that influence dream bizarreness are, again, attention and discrimination ability, perceptive organization ability, and, here more clearly compared to younger children, also visual–spatial ability seems to be important (Table 8.12).

Study III has confirmed the picture delineated above; it also underlined the role of the child's background knowledge (historical memory), and the role played by visual–spatial ability (Table 8.13).

In brief, the cognitive abilities involved in dream bizarreness seem to be those that may concern its *process of production* (discrimination, symbolization, categorization, visual–spatial ability) and its *expression/narration* (linguistic skills, verbal ability). However, dream bizarreness does not seem to be affected by the development of those cognitive abilities that relate to *recalling* the dream, including its details (short and long-term memory and visual–spatial memory).

Conclusions

The results of the studies presented here clearly suggest that dream bizarreness is influenced by the development of the superego functions of children. Bizarreness in dreams becomes more probable only in those children who show a more complete development of the superego, evidenced by the appearance of the ability to experience a sense of guilt. There are, in these children, those intrapsychic conditions that enable the possibility/necessity of disguising the dream's latent content. Conversely, where these

Table 8.11. Study II: Spearman's *rho* correlations between cognitive abilities (WPPSI) and dream bizarreness.

WPPSI *Verbal tests – Measured ability* raw scores		Dream bizarreness	
		Global scale*	Analytical scale[†]
Information	General knowledge, long-term memory	0.18 (n.s.)	0.26 (p 0.07)
Vocabulary	Linguistic skills, verbal ability	0.30 (p 0.03)	0.42 (p 0.00)
Arithmetic	Mental agility, symbolization ability	0.11 (n.s.)	0.28 ($p = 0.05$)
Similarities	Concept formation and categorization ability	0.19 (n.s.)	0.30 (p 0.04)
Comprehension	Internalization of social rules, development of moral sense	0.26 (p 0.04)	0.37 (p 0.00)
Sentences	Auditive attention, short-term memory	0.00 (n.s.)	0.01 (n.s.)
Performance tests			
Animal pegs	Attention, concentration	0.20 (n.s.)	0.30 (p 0.04)
Picture contemplation	Attention, concentration, ability to discriminate	0.24 (n.s.)	0.40 (p 0.00)
Mazes	Visual–motor memory	0.23 (n.s.)	0.26 (n.s.)
Geometric design	Perceptive and visual-motor organization, inductive reasoning	0.14 (n.s.)	0.29 (p 0.05.)
Block design	Perception and visual–spatial ability	0.04 (n.s.)	0.27 (p 0.06)

* Scale of bizarreness (Colace, Violani, & Solarno, 1993); [†] Bizarre elements (Domhoff & Kamiya, 1964).

intrapsychic conditions are not present (i.e., children who have not yet fully developed the superego functions), the dream reports we have observed were more simple than bizarre.

These results are consistent with the Freudian disguise–censorship model that ascribed the bizarreness of dreams (in general) to the result of a defensive transformation of latent dream contents by request of the superego agency in the dreamer's ego.

Table 8.12. Study II. Spearman's *rho* correlations between cognitive abilities (WISC-R) and dream bizarreness.

WISCR		Dream bizarreness measures	
Verbal subtests – Measured ability *Raw scores*		Global measure	Analytic measure
Information	General knowledge, long-term memory	−0.28 (n.s.)	0.15 (n.s)
Vocabulary	Linguistic skills, verbal ability	0.03 (n.s)	0.29 (n.s)
Arithmetic	Mental agility, symbolization ability	−0.10 (n.s.)	0.30 (n.s.)
Similarities	Concept formation and categorization ability	−0.02 (n.s.)	0.09 (n.s.)
Comprehension	Internalization of social rules, development of moral sense	−0.01 (n.s.)	0.25 (n.s.)
Digit span	Auditive attention, short-term memory	−0.36 (n.s.)	−0.17 (n.s.)
Performance subtests			
Coding	Attention, concentration	−0.04 (n.s.)	0.27 (n.s)
Picture contemplation	Attention, concentration, ability to discriminate	−0.58 (*p* 0.01)	−0.37 (n.s.)
Mazes	Visual–spatial memory	0.05 (n.s.)	−0.07 (n.s.)
Object assembly	Perceptive and inductive visual–motor organization, reasoning	−0.50 (*p* 0.05)	−0.17 (n.s.)
Block design	Perception and visual–spatial ability	0.58 (*p* 0.01)	0.49 (0.05)
Picture arrangement	Understanding of social situations, ability to plan	−0.11 (n.s.)	0.00 (n.s.)

A new and unexpected indication coming from these studies is that *not all the functions that fall within the concept of superego might be involved in the dream censorship mechanism*. The superego functions that are activated in the dream censorship process may be seen as a group of more specific sub-sets of these. In other words, *the development of dream censorship functions may require selectively only the development of those pertaining to the moral conscience functions of the*

Table 8.13.   Study III. Spearman's *rho* correlation between cognitive abilities (WPPSI) and dream bizarreness.

WPPSI Verbal tests - P. Grezzi	Measured ability	Global bizarreness measurement
Information	General knowledge, long-term memory	0.80 (p 0.00)
Vocabulary	Linguistic skills, verbal ability	0.62 (p 0.03)
Arithmetic	Mental agility, symbolization ability	0.70 (p 0.01)
Similarities	Concept formation and categorization ability	0.29 (n.s.)
Comprehension	Internalization of social rules, development of moral sense	0.67 ($p = 0.02$)
Sentences	Auditive attention, short-term memory	0.25 (n.s.)
Performance subtests		
Animal pegs	Attention, concentration	0.45 (p 0.10.)
Picture contemplation	Attention, concentration, ability to discriminate	0.55 (p 0.06)
Mazes	Visual–spatial memory	0.05 (n.s.)
Geometric design	Perceptive and visual–motor organization, inductive reasoning	0.57 (p 0.05)
Block design	Perception and visual–spatial ability	0.83 (p 0.00)

superego. From this point of view, a study intended as a continuation of the Freudian model would imply a gradual precise statement and redefinition of the concept of dream censorship functions as a more restricted subset of functions within the broader range of superego functions.

These studies also replicate Foulkes's findings about a clear positive correlation between "distortion" in REM dreams and the raw scores of comprehension (WPPSI) (Foulkes, 1982). Now, since the comprehension subtest is indicative of the "level of adaptation to reality and to the social environment" and of the "level of aquisition of moral rules", and, furthermore, here we have found it to be correlated with the development of the ability to experience a sense of guilt, we interpreted the correlations between comprehension and dream bizarreness as a result consistent with the hypothesis of a relationship between dream bizarreness and superego functions.

In Foulkes's view, the appearance of "dream distortion" (i.e., unfamiliar character and setting) is due to cognitive factors. He found that "dream distortion" was correlated with the child's descriptive abilities and symbolic intelligence; thus, the possibility of having dreams with distorted "characters" and "settings" only appears at the age of 5–7, when children develop the ability to imagine unfamiliar characters and settings. Foulkes did not share Freud's theory, according to which deformation is the result of psychological conflict or of a defensive disguise (Foulkes, 1999, pp. 82–83). He supported this by asserting that the measure of anxiety during the period of wakefulness before sleep (in young children) was negatively correlated with "characters' distortion".

In my view, the positions of Foulkes and Freud are not conflicting. The findings from my studies suggest that dream bizarreness production may require certain cognitive prerequisites, but also that dream bizarreness is clearly affected by the level of development of the superego functions of personality, as Freud thought. From this point of view, both the cognitive and personality aspects do have their importance for dream bizarreness. We may view cognitive abilities as a necessary minimum requirement to generate dream bizarreness (i.e., a cognitive background); however, cognitive abilities would be implemented only when the development of the superego makes the defensive distortion of certain latent dream materials *necessary* and *possible*. When both factors (cognitive and personality) are developed, there is the possibility to find the most bizarre dreams. Of course, in adults, where the cognitive prerequisite is fully developed, the superego aspect might predominate in determining dream bizarreness. From this point of view, the correlation between dream bizarreness and cognitive abilities is not at all in contrast with Freud's view on the genesis of dream bizarreness.

Children, unlike adults, provide certain natural conditions for observing qualitative and quantitative differences in the development of the superego functions and in the level of dream bizarreness. From this point of view, the study of children's dreams will certainly allow the systematic investigation of the disguise–censorship model of bizarreness. I think that one aspect of this research may be to consider in detail which forms of bizarreness start to appear in the dreams of children, and what their relationship is with the different aspects of the superego functions and with the different types of defence mechanisms of the child's ego.

CHAPTER NINE

Wish-fulfilment in children's dreams

Observations on the frequency of wish-fulfilment dreams

A s we have seen in the first part of the book, Freud often used children's dreams as easy evidence of his general thesis that "a dream is a (disguised) fulfilment of a (suppressed or repressed) wish" (Freud 1900a, p. 160). Children's dreams, unlike those of adults, should show the fulfilment of wish in a direct and undisguised form with no need of interpretation or deduction of the dream content. From this point of view, in principle, the wish-fulfilment theory could be empirically tested more easily than in the case of adults, whose dreams require interpretation (disguised wish-fulfilment). Despite these favourable conditions, more than a century after these statements, the lack of systematic studies in literature conducted with the explicit purpose of verifying the frequency of wish-fulfilment dreams in children is surprising. I have found only a few anecdotal and clinical studies (e.g., Coriat, 1920; A. Freud, 1927, 1965; see Chapter Five).

In his classical description of children's REM dreams, Foulkes and his collaborators (Foulkes, 1982, 1999; Foulkes, Larson,

Swanson, & Rardin, 1969; Foulkes, Pivik, Steadman, Spear, & Symonds, 1967) considered various aspects of the children's behaviour, including common daytime situations such as play and interaction with teachers and peers; however, Foulkes himself admitted that an empirical test of Freud's thesis on the dream samples collected would have required "more information about the Ss' dream days than was generally at the authors' disposal" (Foulkes, Pivik, Steadman, Spear, & Symonds, 1967, p. 465). In reality, we have seen that Freud considered this information crucial in order to perceive the presence of the fulfilment of a wish in children's dreams. Foulkes (1982), however, concluded, probably based on his general impression, that dreams by children of preschool age did not show a fulfilment of everyday wishes (pp. 295–296).

When I began studying children's dreams, I did not think I could develop a test of Freud's hypothesis on children's dreams as direct wish-fulfilment. I considered the issue too complex to be approached at a methodological level. For instance, it would have involved asking parents to comment on the dreams and provide detailed information on the children's daytime experiences, especially on the day before a dream. Although these conditions were present in the home based study (Study III), when I planned this research my objective was only to try to replicate the results found in school-based studies on the formal aspects of dreams and on the relationship between dream bizarreness and development of superego functions on the basis of dream reports that were more reliable from a methodological point of view. Also, the mothers' comments on the dreams of their child scheduled in this study were aimed more at clarifying the possible bizarre and unclear aspects of the dream (i.e., measuring dream bizarreness) than at finding a wish-fulfilment situation. Despite this, when I started transcribing and reading the dreams collected, together with the comments and information provided by the mothers, I could not help noticing that there were several dreams that clearly and easily referred to children's wishes. At this point, I re-read with curiosity the dreams collected in the second study conducted at schools, the one that included a detailed interview on each dream with reference to the daytime experiences of children. I realized, from a more accurate reading, that in this case, too, there were clear examples of these wish-fulfilment dreams.

I decided to classify the children's dream reports from Study II (school) and those collected at home according to the presence/absence of the representation of a clear fulfilment of a wish (Colace, 1997a, 1998b). In order to classify the dreams, we used the information on the daytime experience of each child. In the second study, we could obtain this information only from what we were able to learn from the children themselves. In these cases, as soon as the child finished telling his/her dream, there was a standard interview targeting the details of the dream reports (i.e., questions on familiarity of characters, settings, actions, and objects in the daytime experience of the dreamer) that allowed us indirectly to gather certain aspects of the child's daytime experiences. For instance, if a child reported that he/she was riding a bicycle in his/her dream, we asked when he/she had used a bicycle the last time (during the day) (see Chapter Six). In the home based study, we obtained from the mother more accurate information about dream contents and their possible relation to daytime experience of the young dreamer (see Chapter Six). This classification of dreams allowed us to identify four categories of dreams denominated as listed below.

1. Dreams representing a direct wish-fulfilment.
2. Dreams representing a possible wish-fulfilment.
3. Dreams representing a wish-fulfilment attempt.
4. Dreams not representing any wish-fulfilment.

Direct wish-fulfilment dreams

These dreams clearly show the fulfilment, in the present time, of a (known) wish of the child. The dreams we have included in this category are easily comprehensible and only very rarely contain unclear elements apart from the direct fulfilment of a wish. As we will see later on, these dreams may be classified subsequently by type of relationship between the wish appearing in the dream and the daytime experience (affective state or event) the dream seems to refer to. Different examples of these dreams are given in the following pages. These dreams appear as in the example below, with comments or questions by the interviewer in square parentheses.

Dream 65: child aged seven years and two months (Study II)
A girl, E, is sorry because her beloved grandfather is in hospital; in her dream, grandpa leaves the hospital and they are going to celebrate this with a party.

> "Today I dreamed that it happened that grandpa had to go to the hospital and so he was feeling ill and then I went to see him, and then they made transfusions to him and then grandpa said, 'E, are you happy if I get out of here?' I say yes, and the next day grandpa left the hospital so we were all happy and had a party at home and then mummy woke me up."

> [How was this dream, a good one or a bad one?] "This was a good one. Yes, I think it was good, because if grandpa goes out a dream like this is good for me. So I called loud, I mean with my real voice, I called grandpa, grandpa, grandpa!! And I woke my sister up." [Were you worried?] "Yes, a bit, about grandpa's health, however afterwards he went out."

> The girl says she loves her grandfather very much. On the same morning in which the girl reported the dream her grandfather was actually discharged from hospital. About this event the girl said, "But I think the dream has come true because he went out today, mummy told me grandpa went out!"

Dreams representing a possible wish-fulfilment

This category includes dreams with pleasant contents that children define as "good dreams". In these dreams, wish-fulfilment can be read even if there is not enough information to establish this with certainty. We did not classify dreams like the one below as wish-fulfilment dreams only out of excessive scruple.

Dream 58: child aged six years and four months (Study II)

> "Tonight I dreamed I was driving an airplane, then I meet ... I can't remember what was there. . . . Ah, I also remember I had landed, only this."

> [Was this a good dream or a bad one?] "A good dream". [So what were you doing, were you piloting that plane?] "Yes." [Where were you seated in the dream?] "In the plane." [But did you really see this plane

also during the day?] "No! I dreamed it!" [But have you ever been on a plane while awake?] "No, never." [Have you ever been in an airport?] "Yes, I've been there to fetch someone . . . but not aboard." [And when did you go there?] "Eh . . . a long time ago . . . we went to fetch my uncle and aunt, they had landed, I saw them, they were too distant . . ."

We may assume this new experience left the child with regret for not having been able to board a plane, and the fantasy to even pilot one some day!

Dreams representing a wish-fulfilment attempt

In these dreams, the fulfilment of a wish is only initiated (or attempted) but not concluded. The dream has an unpleasant result.

Dream 48: child aged five years and eleven months (Study II)
A girl dreams she is in a toy shop and playing, but then it is time to go home and the toys have vanished.

> "So, I dreamed I was in a toyery [toy shop] and there were plenty of dolls, all Barbies, all bicycles, all toys and then I went back home and the toys were not there and that's it."

> [Was this dream good or bad?] "Bad." [But were you there in the dream?] "Yes." [Were you doing something in the dream or were you only watching what happened?] "I was doing something, I was playing dolls, I unpacked them and when I went home they had disappeared . . ." [What kind of toys were there?] "Now, there was one Barbie, one doll, a lot of kitchen pots, a sewing machine, and a Barbie house . . ."

Dream 7: child aged four years and six months (Study III)

> "I was at the kindergarten and mummy was supposed to come and fetch me at 2 but she did not come and she came at 4 and I cried."

> Mother's remark: It is a wish of Lisa to leave the kindergarten at 2 rather than at 4 in the afternoon.

Dream 80: child aged four years and nine months (Study IV)

> "My baby asked for apple pie, I gave it to him but when he was about to eat it the pie had disappeared."

Dreams not representing any wish-fulfilment

All dreams in which no wish-fulfilment is apparent. Some of these are "bad dreams" and have an unpleasant content, others have a pleasant content and are defined as "good dreams" by children; then there are those with neutral content or with pleasant and unpleasant aspects together. Examples are shown below.

Dream 30: child aged six years (Study II)

> "I dreamed that my mother was cooking and there was a man who wanted to kill her and then my father woke up from bed and caught that man with the knife who wanted to kill my mother."

Dream 02: child aged six years and eleven months (Study II)

> "I dreamed a ship that crashed on the reef and then dogs climbed on the ship and that's it."
>
> [Do you think this dream was a good one ore a bad one?] "Good." [But were you there in the dream?] "No . . ." [And these dogs that were in the ship, are they dogs you know?] "No . . ." [And do you know the ship? Have you ever been on a ship?] "No . . ."

The frequencies and percentages of dreams found for each category are shown in Table 9.1. In the young children group (3–5 years) altogether (Studies II and III), the dreams that have clear wish-fulfilment nature (type 1) in our classification are 61%; among older children (5–7 years) these dreams are noticeably less frequent (35%) (see Table 9.1).

In the young children interviewed in the school setting (Study II), wish-fulfilment dreams (type 1) were 57% (17/30), and dreams not falling in this category (types 2–4) were 43% (13/30); among older children (5–7 years) wish-fulfilment dreams were 35% (12/34), while others (types 2–4) were 65% (22/34): the differences between age groups are close to statistical significance ($\chi^2 = 2.93$, df 1, $p = 0.08$) (see Table 9.1). Equally, in dream reports of young children in the home-based study, wish-fulfilment dreams were 67 % (14/21 dreams), and dreams not falling in this category (types 2–4) were 33% (7/21); among older children (5–7 years) wish-fulfilment dreams were 35% (9/26), while others (types 2–4) were 65%

Table 9.1. Frequencies and percentages of child dream categories.

Age group	Study	Dreams	Type 1	Type 2	Type 3	Type 4
3–5		30	57% (17)	10% (3)	3.% (1)	30% (9)
5–7	II (school)	34	35% (12)	20% (7)	9% (3)	35% (12)
3–5		21	67% (14)	19% (4)	9% (2)	5% (1)
5–7	III (home)	26	35% (9)	23% (6)	7% (2)	35% (9)

(17/26): the difference between age groups are statistically signifi-cant ($\chi^2 = 4.77$, df 1, $p = 0.02$). We have observed that *the quantity of information available on the daytime experiences of children is essential for understanding the wish-fulfilment nature of the dreams*. We may notice that, in the sample of dreams collected in the school setting (young children), the percentage of dreams that do not seem to be of wish-fulfilment nature (category 4) is greater than that encountered for the same dream category among the dreams collected in the home-based study. The useful information given by the mothers was an essential evaluation tool. Therefore, future studies should include their co-operation. I also believe that a further refinement of the methodologies used to collect the daytime experience preceding the dream would further increase the percentage of dreams of clear wish-fulfilment nature. For instance, among the dreams classified as "pleasant" (category 2), where information is not enough to determine with certainty if they refer to desires (about 18% of all dreams), we would have greater probabilities of detecting those that actually represent the fulfilment of a wish.

The method of collecting information on child daytime experi-ence has not always allowed us to find a precise reference to the daytime event to which the dream seemed to refer. For example, at times, even if we had information about a wish that remained unsat-isfied during the daytime, we could not establish whether it actually referred to the day before the dream, or to several days before.

Unfortunately, these data on the frequency of wish-fulfilment dreams cannot be compared with other studies because, as I have said above, to the best of my knowledge there are no studies that have systematically investigated this aspect of children's dreams. These data must be considered as preliminary, a starting point for future investigations.

In the QDEA study, we lacked detailed information on the children's daytime experiences and, above all, we could not interview the children and their parents on the contents of the dream. The only information was represented by the fact that parents, after writing down the latest dream reported by their child, were asked to note down in the questionnaire form the daytime reference of the dream they believed they had identified (see Chapter Six, pp. 98–99). Despite these adverse methodological conditions, when reviewing these dream stories we could immediately observe different examples of clear wish-fulfilment dreams (77/325, 24%).

Below are a few examples of these dreams, from which readers may judge for themselves.

Dream 10: child aged seven years and ten months (Study IV)

He was playing football with his friends, took a free kick and scored a goal.

Diurnal experience noted by the mother. He had played a game and they had won; in the dream he won the game again, scoring another goal.

Dream 70: child aged five years and two months (Study IV)

F dreamed he was in our garden, and there were plenty of nests on the pine tree, with many little birds, and on top of the tree there was the mother of all those little birds.

Diurnal experience noted by the mother: I think F had this dream because a few days ago we had seen a nest with newborn birds inside.

Dream 189: child aged four years and four months (Study IV)

The boy dreamed that his father, coming home, hugged and kissed him, read a tale to him or in any case played with him.

Diurnal experience noted by the mother. The evening before the boy's father had actually gone out. However, when he came back V was already asleep; as he did not like that unexpected leaving, when the boy woke up he believed his dream was real.

Dream 300: child aged seven years and eight months (Study IV)

M dreamed her grandfather F, who died recently, was with all the relatives at her mother and father's home. Grandpa F went for groceries in the car, so they could have a big party with M and her cousins. The party was celebrated the evening, with all the relatives, and at midnight they all went to sleep in their respective homes, happy.

Diurnal experience noted by the mother. It happened recently, F's grandfather died; however, she recalled him alive, when he took her shopping with him in the car and she had great fun.

Dream 536: child aged eight years and four months (Study IV)

She dreams of her ex-swimming trainer, who she was very fond of. In the dream the trainer gave her advice.

Diurnal experience noted by the mother. That trainer does not work at the pool any more, but she had met her recently and was very pleased about it.

Dream 293: child aged six years and eight months (Study IV)

She dreams of the birth of her little brother, he is beautiful, blond with blue eyes.

Diurnal experience noted by the mother. I, her mother, am pregnant and J is happy and always dreams about her parents together with her and her little brother; she is a peaceful and happy girl at home.

Dream 271: child aged eight years and two months (Study IV)

He dreams of a schoolmate who is very fond of him.

Diurnal experience noted by the mother. That girl had come visit us at home and they had played together with other schoolmates.

Dream 225: child aged six years and seven months (Study IV)

My son told he dreamed he went fishing at an artificial pond with his uncle. He caught many small fish with his rod.

Diurnal experience noted by the mother. He would like to go fishing so much, he always says this at home, nearly every day.

Dream 36: child aged six years and eleven months (Study IV)

My son's dream is about him riding on horseback in the country, he feeds the horses and tidies the horse's stable.

Diurnal experience noted by the mother. My son often goes into the countryside with his father; we keep a horse there—he follows all the movements his father makes.

Dream 46: child aged six years and four months (Study IV)

The boy said he dreamed of his father and grandfather working, one on a tractor and one on a scraper.

Diurnal experience noted by the mother. Since he was very young, the boy has always had a feeling for trucks and tractors, and a few days ago he had seen a scraper at work near our home.

Dream 04: child aged seven years and ten months (Study IV)

My son was in a fantasy environment (which he knows is one of the Nintendo 64 game settings [Super Mario]). He was at Super Mario's place and challenged the course in a snowy mountain setting, trying to overcome the various obstacles in order to get a yellow star, the award Mario usually receives.

Diurnal experience noted by the mother. My son likes to play with Nintendo 64 and in the dream he lived the experiences of the Super Mario, the protagonist of the game.

Dream 02: child aged four years and nine months (Study IV)

His (deceased) grandfather had come to see him, and they talked together.

Diurnal experience noted by the mother. The boy liked to go to see his grandfather, he was very fond of him.

While waiting for further data on the frequency of children's wish-fulfilment dreams, an in-depth study of this type of dream may be represented by a *qualitative analysis of the nature of the wishes* appearing in these dreams, focusing in particular on their *diurnal origin*, that is, the experience they seem to derive from, and on the *scope and type of these wishes*. Also, analysing *how wishes are fulfilled in dreams* may be useful, cross-referencing the different types of wish-fulfilment to *the relationships between fulfilment (hallucinatory) and daytime experience*. These qualitative analyses were done considering all dreams (Studies II, III, IV) previously classified as clear wish-fulfilment dreams.

Nature of the wishes appearing in children's dreams

Diurnal origin

The diurnal origin of the wishes that appear in these dreams is invariably represented by an intense emotional daytime experience of child. Sometimes, it is an objectively intense experience, such as, for instance, the loss of a loved one, or a subjectively important experience, such as, for instance, the loss of a favourite doll. In this latter case, we are witnessing purely personal wishes, I would dare to say almost "egoistic" wishes that derive from absolutely ordinary daytime situations but that have their own importance from the point of view of the children, although they may seem banal to adults. While I am writing this, I have in mind children who have dreamed of eating their favourite dish, of going skating with new roller skates, or of rescuing their doll from an attempted theft. Some of these wishes refer to daytime situations in which a child has encountered new experiences that raised his/her interest: for example, seeing the snow for the first time, or taking a long trip by car with his/her parents. Table 9.2 provides a brief summary of a few diurnal experiences and the dreams that followed them.

Scope and type of wishes

The wishes appearing in the dreams refer to different aspects of a child's daily life. These wishes are about play or recreational activities, affective and social relationships, and the imaginary world of children (e.g., favourite characters, cartoons, etc.), more rarely about primary needs (e.g., food). Play/recreational activities appear in more than 50% of dreams, the presence of social and affective relationships is also frequent (34%). Table 9.3 shows a list of examples of wishes observed in the dreams reported. These wishes are portrayed as satisfied at the present time in the dream scenario.

Even in those dreams in which the child does not succeed in fulfilling the wish (dreams of the third category, wish-fulfilment

Table 9.2. Daytime origin of children's wish-fulfilment dreams.

Objectively intense emotional experiences

- Loss of elder brother →   Dream of talking to brother
- Repeated request to have→   Dream that mother has a baby
  a little sister
- Father goes out unexpectedly → Dream of father returning and
  embracing him
- Doctor gives an injection →   Dream that no doctor gives
  injections any more
- Pet cat is lost →   Dream of playing with cat that has
  come back

Subjectively important emotional experiences

- Missed purchase of →   Dream of purchasing the toy
  favourite toy
- Regrets not having new →   Dream of skating with new skates
  roller skates
- First time child sees the →   Dream of making a snowman
  snow
- Trip to the seaside →   Dream of being at the seaside with
  children
- Won football game →   Dream of playing football and
  scoring a goal   scoring a goal

Table 9.3. Types of wishes observed in children's dreams.

I would like to find the doll I lost
I would like to ride the bicycle without having to wait for sunny days
I would like to see my favourite cartoon
I would like to eat my favourite dish
I would like to be the protagonist of the fairy tale
I would like to be a cartoon hero
I would like to see that my friend's health has improved
I would like to kiss mummy and daddy
I would like to see grandpa returning home from the hospital
I would like to have a new toy
I would like to play with my friend again
I would like to go to the swimming pool again
I would like to see the film about the dinosaurs
I would like my birthday to come at once so I would get the presents
I would like to play ball and score a goal again
I would like to see my swimming trainer (who isn't there any more)
I would like to see my puppy again (dog has died recently)
I would like to eat more chocolate
I would like mummy to have my little sister soon (mother is pregnant)

attempt), the wishes are of the same type of those above. Apart from these wishes, we have observed dreams that seem to be simple achievements of daytime fantasies or repetitions of symbolic child games. These dreams are based on the identification with the characters of the child's favourite cartoons seen on television. The children, in their dreams, may wear the clothes of their favourite hero and repeat his feats in an oneiric adventurous plot. For example, children may dream of being Spiderman, or one of the Power Rangers or the Ninja Turtles. One child reported that in his dream he was Spiderman, and saved his best girlfriend from the villains. Another child, in his dream, played fighting with his friends (as he does in daytime), imitating the Power Rangers. We may think that these dreams are similar to the example brought by Freud of his son, Martin, who dreamed that "he was driving in a chariot with Achilles and that Diomedes was charioteer" (Freud, 1900a, p. 129).

A privileged perspective for the analysis of the wishes and the pleasant themes that appear in childish dream could be offered by the drawings of the dreams. Below I present some examples of dream drawings collected in a subgroup of children from Study II (see Chapter Six, p. 100). These drawings easily show the presence of pleasant contents, such as, for instance, the television characters loved by the child, or daily situations of play. As we can see, these themes are very similar to those that emerged in the verbal reports of wish-fulfilment dreams. The pleasantness of these themes is evident in the smiling expression on the face of the sleeping child and in those of the dream characters. However, in the case of these dreams "reported" through drawings, no interviews were arranged to review the details of dream contents and their daytime origin; therefore, it is difficult to understand with certainty whether the content of these dreams was a direct fulfilment of a wish. Nevertheless, it is certain that these drawings can help us to study the phenomenology of childish dreams. Examples are shown below.

Example 1. Child 73: A girl aged six years and eleven months). "*I was playing with Daniel*" [her cousin]." In the drawing, we observed the smiling expression on the face of the dreamer while she is sleeping and in the dream scenario (Figure 9.1a,b,c).

Figure 9.1(a,b,c). (Top) Drawing of dream "Playing with Daniel"; (bottom left) detail showing the smile of the dreamer; (bottom right) detail showing the smile of the dream image. Above the heads of her dream characters she wrote "I" and the name of her cousin, "Daniel".

Example 2. Child 63: A boy aged six years and seven months draws the dream *"I went skateboarding and I was fine"* with evident satisfaction (Figure 9.2a,b).

Figure 9.2(a,b). (Left) Drawing of dream "I went skateboarding . . ."; (right) detail of the same drawing.

Example 3: Child 12: A boy aged six years and five months. *The dream of Peter Pan and Tin Tin* (the favourite hero) (Figure 9.3a,b).

Figure 9.3(a,b). (Left) Drawing of "The dream of Peter Pan and Tin Tin"; (right) detail of the same drawing.

Example 4. Child 30: A boy aged six years. *"I dreamt Superman and Captain Flame"* (Figure 9.4a,b,c).

Figure 9.4(a,b,c). (Top) Drawing of "I dreamt Superman and Captain Flame"; (bottom left and right); details from the same drawings.

Example 5. Child 65: A girl aged seven years and two months. *"The dream that I became a fairy"*.

Figure 9.5.   Drawing of "The dream that I became a fairy".

Example 6. Child 69: A girl aged six years and two months. Two dreams: *"The dream of the paperella"* and *"The dream of Christmas"*.

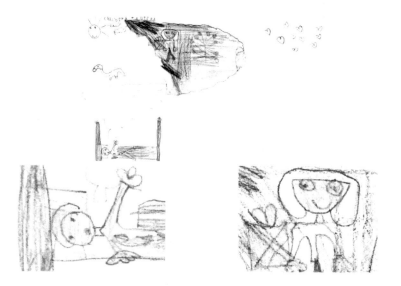

Figure 9.6(a,b,c).   (Top) Drawing of the dreams "Paperella" and "Christmas"; (bottom left and right) details from the same drawing.

Example 7. Child 57: A boy aged six years and ten months. *"A dream that I played ball with my cousin"* (Figure 9.7a,b).

Figure 9.7(a,b). (Top) Drawing of the dream "Playing ball with my cousin"; (bottom) detail from the same drawing.

Example 8. Child 14: A boy aged six years and two months. *"I dreamt Peter Pan"* (Figure 9.8a,b,c).

Figure 9.8(a,b,c). (Left) Drawing of the dream of "Peter Pan"; (right) details of the same drawing.

Example 9. Child 8: A girl aged six years and eight months. *"I was in the garden and there was a swallow."*

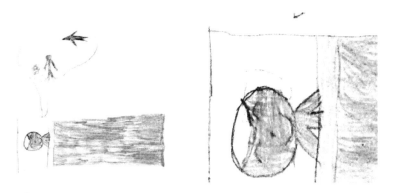

Figure 9.9(a,b).   (Left) Drawing of the dream ". . . there was a swallow"; (right) detail of the same drawing.

Types of wish-fulfilment in children's dreams

If we observed the relationship existing between wish-fulfilment in dreams and diurnal experience (affective state or event) the dream apparently refers to, we may notice that *child wish-fulfilment dreams differ from one another as expressions of different demands.* I believe that these differences deserve further investigation and are more likely to give information on the role of wishes in the dreaming processes than any study on the mere frequency of wish-fulfilment dreams. We have observed at least three types of wish-fulfilment dreams that are denominated as follows:

1.   "Compensation" dreams.
2.   "Continuation" dreams.
3.   "Anticipation" dreams.

Compensation dreams

These dreams have, as daytime background, a negative affective state and/or experience, such as, for example, the loss of a dear person or another negative situation. The wish that is represented as satisfied in the dream consists of the occurrence of the opposite of what happened in daytime (i.e., the negative situation). There-fore, in these dreams, wish-fulfilment represents a sort of compen-sation for a diurnal experience; in other words, the dream follows a real-life unpleasant situation and "stages" its opposite.

Examples are given below.

Dream 24: child aged three years and nine months (Study II)
A boy dreams of seeing his loved grandmother, who has actually died, "disguised" as a soft toy.

> "I dreamed the bunny and the she-bunny, now the she-bunny was grannie, and she was with C [the boy's little sister] and the blue bunny was with me . . ."
>
> *Information*: The boy reports spontaneously, "Grannie is dead. Now it is over, they gave her an injection . . . You know, grannie used to buy me sweets and chocolate . . ."

Dream 72: child aged six years and ten months (Study II)
A girl dreams of happily hugging her aunt, who is leaving the hospital: actually, her aunt died the day before the dream. The girl also draws her dream, where the smiles on the faces of the charac-ters drawn express happiness (see Figure 9.10).

> "My aunt, daddy and mummy and I, and uncle and aunt, for aunt had come home from the hospital and we ran to hug her, because we were happy" [and then?] "then . . . then I woke up" [laughs]. [How was this dream, a good or a bad one?] "Good." [Were you there in the dream?] "Yes." [But were you doing something in the dream or were you only watching what happened?] "I was watching aunt." [But is this aunt in the dream really your aunt?] "Yes." [Where were you in the dream?] "I was in the house of an old woman who is my mummy's mother." [But is your aunt still at the hospital now?] "She is dead." [I see.] "She died the day, the day before the night I dreamed of her, in the hospital."

In the examples that follow, too, children seem to "compensate" for a negative daytime experience by reversing the events in the dream.

Dream 94: child aged three years and ten months (Study II)
A girl dreams of playing with a bear-shaped golden charm and a soft toy dog that her mother did not allow her to play with during the day.

Figure 9.10 (a,b,c). (Top) Drawing of the dream about aunt leaving hospital; (bottom left and right) details of the same drawing.

"A toy, a toy bear, I was playing with it, I wanted to feed it".

[How was this bear in the dream, nice or ugly?] "Nice, I was also playing with a dog." [Where were you, while you were playing with the bear?] "In the kitchen . . ." [Do you really have that bear or did you only dream it?] "She hid it from me." [She hid it away?] "Yes." [Who hid it away?] "Mummy." [Why did she hide it from you?] "Because my friends will come and break it . . . All my friends who come over!" [Could you play with it?] "No . . ." [And what about the dog, do you really have it?] "She put it on top of the washing machine" [with a sad tone]. [And do you take it during the day?] "Yes." And you play with it? "Yes . . ." [In dream, how did you feel, sad or happy?] "Happy." [Why did you feel happy?] "Because I was playing with the bear."

Dream 251: child aged nine years and four months (Study IV)
A boy, after witnessing the defeat of his favourite football team, takes a kind of revenge by changing the outcome of the game in his dream.

> He was playing in his favourite football team and scored three goals against INTER, so when he went back to school his mates hailed him like a hero.

Dream 345: child aged five years and eleven months (Study IV)
A boy was reproached by the teacher for being too vivacious and noisy, so much so that apart from being distracted himself, he distracted the others. Things change a lot in his dream!

> The child was at the nursery school and, with me (i.e., the mother) present, asked the teacher whether he had behaved well and whether the teacher liked his drawings and his games and the teacher answered yes, that he had been a good boy, so the boy went home happy with his mother.

Continuation dreams

In these dreams, the fulfilment of a wish consists in the continuation of the—generally pleasant—daytime experience that was only partially satisfied. In other words, these are wishes that in the real life were not completely fulfilled. The daytime experience may have been interrupted, in which case the dream sort of continues it (i.e., starts from when it was interrupted), or may have finished, but too soon in the light of the child's expectations, in which case the dream perpetuates the pleasant daytime experience. Also, in continuation dreams we may notice a sort of "compensation"; however, in these dreams, unlike in compensation dreams, there has been at least one initial pleasant situation in the daytime experience, and the partial fulfilment of a wish, while in compensation dreams the dreamer passes from an unpleasant (daytime) situation to a pleasant (dream) one, in prosecution dreams the dreamer remains in a pleasant situation. A few examples are given below.

Dream 567: child aged four years and 2 months (Study IV)
A boy, after visiting the country farm of his grandparents, in which there are several animals, resumes the pleasant experience in a dream.

"The boy dreamed of farm animals, like hens, rabbits and chicks running about around him."

Dream 13: child aged six years and three months (Study II)
A girl who visited a castle during the day dreams of going there with (her) Prince Charming (a schoolmate).

"I dreamed I was the princess, and then I did like Cinderella I lost my slipper and then, then . . . then came Prince Charming" [laughs].

[Where were you in this dream?] "In the castle." [But do you really know this castle or not?] "Yes." [And where is this castle?] "The castle is in Rome. I saw it and then dreamed of it. Because daddy once took us to see it and then afterwards I dreamed it." [And who was the Prince Charming?] "He was a kid at the nursery school that I like." [How was this dream?] "Beautiful. I was happy."

Anticipation dreams

These dreams represent the fulfilment of a wish that has as background a daytime experience of eagerness for a pleasant event that will occur in the future. These dreams anticipate the event by making it happen in the present time. This type of dream includes those dreams that feature a wish that will be fulfilled in the day following the dream (dreams of impatience). See the examples below.

Dream 55: child aged five years and two months (Study II)
A boy is sorry because, even though he has received a bicycle as a present, for the moment he cannot use it: he dreams that he is riding the bicycle in the gardens.

"The Befana brought me the bicycle and my father took me to ride the bicycle, [I was riding it] in the park of C [initial of the town where the child lives], I made the tyres squeal!"

[How was this dream, good or bad?] "Good . . ." [Who was riding the bicycle, you and daddy or you alone?] "No, daddy held it from behind and I was riding." [But do you have this bicycle for real? Did Santa bring it to you?] "He brought it to me for Christmas." [When did you have this dream?] "Yesterday." [But did you really ride the bicycle already at some time?] "No, but now as Spring comes I will, I will!" [Did you ride it yesterday?] "No, yesterday I didn't . . ."

Dream 65: child aged seven years and two months (Study II)
A girl, E. is sorry because her beloved grandfather is in hospital; in her dream grandpa leaves the hospital and they are going to celebrate this with a party.

> "Today I dreamed that it happened that grandpa had to go to the hospital . . . and so he was feeling ill and then I went to see him . . . and then they gave him transfusions and then grandpa said, 'E. are you happy if I get out of here?' I say yes—and the next day grandpa left the hospital so we were all happy and had a party at home and then mummy woke me up."

> [How was this dream, a good one or a bad one?] "This was a good one . . . Yes, I think it was good, because if grandpa comes out a dream like this is good for me. . . . So I called out loud, I mean with my real voice, I called grandpa, grandpa, grandpa!! And I woke my sister up . . ." [Were you worried?] "Yes, a bit, about grandpa's health, however afterwards he came out."

> The girl says she loves her grandfather very much. On the same morning in which the girl reported the dream her grandfather was actually discharged from hospital. About this event the girl said, "But I think the dream has come true because he came out today, mummy told me grandpa came out!"

In both these dreams we noticed the fulfilment of a wish that refers to the anticipation of a desired event that comes true. Both desires derive from a real-life situation, referable to a recent period of wakefulness.

Some dreams in this category seemed to us similar to the "dreams of impatience" reported by Freud (see Chapter Three, p. 24).

An example is reported below.

Dream 32: child aged four years and nine months (Study II)
On 2 December, after seeing Santa Claus in town, a boy reported the following dream.

> "I dreamed that Santa brought me the present [and then?] and then came to my bedside." [Listen, how was this dream, good or bad?] "Good." [Were you there in the dream?] "Yes." [Where were you in the dream?] "In my bed." [But did you really meet Santa?] "Yes." [Where did you meet him?] "I went to the Pincio [a park in Rome] by car . . ." [So you saw him in the streets?] "Yes." [Listen, what did Santa bring you in the dream? What present did he have for you?] "The scraper."

All these types of dreams seem to have in common intense and partially or totally unfulfilled daytime wishes, in which the child is therefore strongly interested.

We may assume that the module of generation of these dreams includes different steps, as the wishes fulfilled in them derive from substantially different daytime situations. The generation of *compensation dreams* apparently includes one stage more compared to *continuation dreams*, since, in the *compensation dream*, the wish-fulfilled is in itself a reaction to a negative daytime event, while in the *continuation dreams* the wish dreamed derives directly from the daytime event.

As a preliminary indication, we have observed that both *compensation dreams* and *continuation dreams* are more frequent than *anticipation dreams*, and this distribution is similar between three and eight years of age. This might suggest a hierarchy of emotional experiences that enter dreams, regardless of child age and affecting mostly the nature of the wishes and dynamics of the dreaming process itself.

Based on the foregoing, we may develop a rough hypothesis about the function of wish-fulfilment dreams in children. The assignment of these dreams might be that of counterbalancing a sorrow, continuing an interrupted or incomplete pleasant experience, or anticipating a pleasant experience that still has to occur. Thus, *wish-fulfilment children's dreams appear as a solution of a state of affective uneasiness (sorrow, dissatisfaction, impatience) (i.e., affective re-establishment) during the day.*

The study of the various forms in which wish-fulfilment is achieved with respect to the different daytime situations may give useful clues for future investigation on the role of wishes in dream generation processes. I am inclined to consider the presence of this plurality of forms of wish-fulfilment in dreams as a meaningful indication of the importance of the role of wishes and of motivations in dream processes and contents, equally meaningful as the high frequency of wish-fulfilment dreams in childhood age.

A few methodology issues

The comparison between the study conducted in the school setting and the one conducted in the home setting with the co-operation of mothers succeeded in showing the need to have detailed information on the children's daytime experiences (including their emotional experience) in order to notice the fulfilment of a wish. While this may have been predictable, I would like to point out other, less obvious methodological points that should be taken into account in future studies.

In the first place, we should consider that mothers are not always able to give complete information on the children's previous day experiences, since there are periods of the day in which they are not with their children. The most common case is that of dreams that refer to situations related to the morning spent in school (or nursery school). But there may also be dreams that refer to daytime experiences in which only grandparents, or only one of the parents were present (e.g., in the case of separated parents). In these and other circumstances, the mothers who comment on the dream cannot see the possible connections with the daytime experience because they are not aware of them. For example, in the QDEA study, when we asked the parents if they could identify any certain connection in their child's dream to a recent daytime experience, 45% answered "no" and another 11% were uncertain (Colace, 2006a).

In the second place, quite unexpectedly, I often noticed cases in which mothers, while commenting on the dreams and reporting the daytime experiences of their child, may show a sort of "resistance" to reporting certain details. The nature of these details leads me to think that, in these cases, the mother fears the judgement of the interviewer on aspects that she-rightfully—considers private. This may prevent the interviewer from obtaining important information for understanding the dream. I remember the following case. A child had dreamed of spending a day at the sea, at a swimming pool. The details given by the mother did not fully explain the dream, because the child had indeed been to the sea, but the particular detail of the swimming pool seemed incongruous. In the end, after a remark by the child, who was present while his mother was explaining, this was cleared up. While they were driving to the sea, the boy had expressed the wish to go to a bathing establishment that required a fee for admission (probably the reason why his parents had made a different choice) and that had a swimming pool (the boy practises swimming and likes to go to swimming pools). It could be that the mother was somehow unwilling to give this information because the decision to go to the free beach instead of the establishment may be considered a family (and financial) question the interviewer is not supposed to know. In other words, in the collection of information on the children's daytime experiences, we may encounter the normal (and obvious) resistance against imparting certain details to the interviewer that, at times, may prevent the dream from being understood in full. This aspect will have to be kept in mind in future studies in order to refine the methodology. I believe it would be useful, for instance, to consider the information on the children's daytime experience that may be obtained from teachers and / or grandparents, at least in applicable circumstances. Parents will also have to be reassured about the confidential nature of the information collected and about the purpose of the study, which is not to cast any possible judgement on the family's habits.

Conclusions

The results shown here on the frequency and nature of wish-fulfilment dreams have at least two limits in their eligibility as general reference. In the first place, there are no similar studies that may be used for comparing the observed frequency of wish-fulfilment dreams, let alone their nature, so other studies would be required to confirm these suggestions. In the second place, unlike in the case of the formal aspect of dreams (e.g., dream bizarreness), we could not compare our results with the child dreams collected in the sleep laboratory (REM dreams): in fact, Foulkes's study (1982) does not provide for the tabulation of wish-fulfilment dreams. Also from this point of view, I believe that the data presented here are, at best, pioneering, and in any case insufficient to draw any general conclusion.

These preliminary results on the frequency of wish-fulfilment dreams are consistent with Freud's observations on children's dreams. More than half the dreams observed clearly show the fulfilment of a child's wish. The occurrence of these dreams, as the psychoanalytic theory predicts, decreases in older children. Undoubtedly, it must be said that the dream samples collected in these studies include several dreams that do not lend themselves to being classified as wish-fulfilment dreams. Further studies might show whether the percentage of these dreams is an actual datum, or is due to the lack of information on the dreamer's state of wakful experience.

From a methodological point of view, a collection of children's dreams that systematically includes also detailed information on the children's daytime experience, with the help of mothers, may be considered a good research design for carrying on an investigation of this kind: in the end, different studies will allow us to define more general indications on the frequency of this type of dream and a more consistent evaluation of Freud's hypothesis.

These studies could not give a certain indication on an important point raised by Freud, which is that dreams always refer to situations that occurred the day before (i.e., day-dream). The methodology used in the study conducted in a home setting might, in part, be adequate to assess this point: at times this was true, at times not. This will also require further studies and, above all, a refinement of the methodology that will allow for a systematic collection of the experiences lived the day before the dream. However, in many cases, we had the impression that the real-life event to which the wish-fulfilment dream referred had occurred a few days before. This is also evidenced by the fact that certain wishes appeared in multiple dreams had on different days (see Chapter Ten).

In the third chapter, we saw how Freud started to outline the nature of the wishes that appear in child dreams. The opportunity to analyse a significant group of children's wish-fulfilment dreams allowed us to investigate this in more detail, in regard to which, and particularly regarding the phenomenology of these dreams, I would say that our findings are absolutely consistent with Freud's observations and I believe they represent an insight in that direction.

The wish-fulfilment dreams presented here and their relationship with daytime experiences are similar to the examples reported by Freud. When Freud suggested that dreams represent wishes that were active during daytime but remained unfulfilled, he refers both to wishes entirely unfulfilled and to wishes fulfilled in an insufficient way, that is, ending sooner than expected (see Chapter Three). An example reported by Freud that is close to the ones we have called *continuation dreams* here is that of the "trip on the lake" (1901a, p. 644) and also that of "driving in a chariot with Achilles" (*ibid.*, p. 645). In both these dreams, the daytime situations that engendered the dream are represented by wishes whose fulfilment was interrupted. Freud also reported children's dreams of the *compensation type*, as, for instance, the dream of ". . . climbed up the Danchstein" (Freud, 1901a, p. 644). Besides, there is also another evident point in the examples of dreams reported by Freud: two forms of wish-fulfilment may appear in the same dream, one as "continuation" and the other as "anticipation" (see, for example, the dream of a six-year-old girl of a walk with her father, Freud, 1901a, p. 644).

In my opinion, a close examination of the type of wishes that appear in these dreams will give, in the long term, valuable information on the role played by wishes and motivations in the dream production process. A sort of map of dream wishes, their scope and type, will have to be defined. The same may apply to the real-life affective states that serve as background for these dreams (i.e., dissatisfaction, impatience, disappointment). I think this could be a prosecution of Freud's work: a study on the phenomenology of dream wishes as these may be observed directly with reference to the diurnal experience (affective state or event) that generate them. This study might define a hierarchy of the emotional experiences that enter the process of dream production.

For these dreams we have outlined the hypothesis, still to be confirmed, of an *affective re-establishment* or *affective resolution function* based on the hallucinatory fulfilment of a wish. This function is in line with the other dream functions hypothesized by Freud: the protection of the sleep state and the "safety-valve" for the excitation of the *Ucs.* (Freud, 1900a).

The wish-fulfilment dreams collected here are undoubtedly sensed and significant mental acts. These dreams are clearly understandable through information about the children's daytime experiences. They represent in an intelligible manner a scene of daytime life and do not show in their construction any sign of degradation of psychic faculties. This picture is in line with Freud's description of children's dreams as "significant and not puzzling" (Freud, 1901a, p. 643) or as "intelligible, completely valid mental acts" (Freud, 1916–1917, p. 127).

To observe systematically if, and with what frequency, children's dreams represent an undisguised wish-fulfilment, and to observe their nature and daytime origin, is not irrelevant for the purposes of an empirical judgement of Freud's general assumption that "a dream is a (disguised) fulfilment of a (suppressed or repressed) wish" (Freud, 1900a, p. 160). Freud suggested that children's dreams are the easiest way to test his assumption because, in these dreams, wish-fulfilment appears in a direct form. In other words, in the case of children it is supposed to be easier to recognize whether a dream represents a wish-fulfilment or not. From this standpoint, children's dreams are also useful to critics wishing to show the groundlessness of Freud's dream theory. *If empirical studies showed that even young children's dreams (with information on the dreamers' daytime experiences) lack frequent wish-fulfilment dreams, this would represent an "unambiguous" fact contrary to Freud's general thesis, for why should wish-fulfilment dreams be observed in adults, but not in children?*

We must say that having observed that young children's dreams frequently represent, or "stage", a direct wish-fulfilment says little about the "strong" version of the Freudian hypothesis whereby (a) wish is the motivational cause of the dream, and (b) the dream occurs with the explicit purpose of satisfying wishes (Freud, 1900a). The declared observational and correlative design of the studies presented here does not allow one to verify this version of Freud's hypothesis. In any case, we have observed that wish-fulfilment dreams are constantly and significantly associated with the daytime situation in which the wish remained unfulfilled or unresolved, and that, in the dream, the wish is not merely represented (in different ways), but selectively represented as satisfied. About this point, I have to say that I still consider valid and full of theoretical and experimental implications the reasoning brought by Freud in support of his main thesis, according to which, if we accept that daydreaming is a variation of night dreaming, we know that ". . . day-dreaming too is an activity bound up with satisfaction and is only practised, indeed, on that account" (1916–1917, p. 130).

However, other data on "infantile" dreams of adults are consistent with the correlation between wish-fulfilment in dreams and wishes remaining unfulfilled or unresolved in daytime experience observed here. There are at least two experimental results in literature that are not contrary to the concept that "childish" wish-fulfilment dreams actually occur with the precise purpose of fulfilling a desire. Subjects deprived of liquids who dream of drinking, drink less and rate themselves less thirsty in the period of wakefulness following the dream than thirsty persons who have not had those dreams (Bokert, 1968). Drug-addict patients who dream of using the drug they are addicted to (i.e., drug dreams) gratify their drug craving so much that they can abstain from drugs during the state of wakefulness for a longer period than patients who do not have drug dreams (e.g., Choi, 1973; for a review see Colace, 2004a).

For the time being, I think we do not need to approach the issue of whether wishes are the cause of these dreams and whether we should hold these dreams as occurring with the explicit purpose of satisfying the wish represented in them. The answers to these questions will probably come later on, as we achieve a greater knowledge on the phenomenology of this kind of dream.

The mere findings that (a) children's dreams are frequently of a wish-fulfilment kind and (b) children's wish-fulfilment dreams are constantly associated with a daytime situation in which these wishes were unresolved is, in my opinion, meaningful enough to justify any future attempt to investigate on the role of wishes in dream formation processes, leaving any other question aside. In fact, while on the one hand the studies on the frequency of wish-fulfilment dreams try to provide a conclusive evaluation of the validity of Freud's observations, at the same time they also represent the point of departure and the prosecution of empirical investigations in that direction.

CHAPTER TEN

Child dream development:
a longitudinal observation

The home-based study allowed the collection of dream reports from one child in two separate sessions at one year's distance. Lisa (not her real name) was interviewed in the first session when she was four years and six months old, and later at five years and six months of age. Lisa was a good dream recaller. Apart from reporting, at the request of her mother, twelve dreams (five in the first dream week session and seven in the second), she spontaneously reported additional dreams on certain mornings. Lisa's mother was co-operative during both observation periods. This allowed to us optimize the collection of the child's dream reports and the mother's comments about them.

The case of young Lisa allows me to describe in greater detail the changes that intervene in dream processes during development stage, which I covered in Chapters Seven and Nine. However, I cannot report the differences concerning the development of super-ego functions, because the relevant tests could not be administered in the second period of observation.

The following interviews on dreams are not reported entirely for reasons of space. Nevertheless, the part I am reporting is the verbatim transcription of tape-recorded interviews. The child's answers are between quotation marks. The interviewer's questions, when not necessary to understand the child's answers, are omitted. Where they have been included, they are in square parentheses. The number at the beginning of each dream report indicates their time sequence within the dream week session (e.g., 1, first dream reported in the week).

Lisa's dreams in the first period of observation

The dreams recalled by Lisa in the first period clearly show characteristics that we have observed in other children of this age group (3–5 years).

1. "We were, me, mummy, B and E [children known to Lisa] in the garden, then M [Lisa's little boyfriend] arrived and was walking and then I got lost and then I kissed him on the mouth and went home."

Mother's information: The child describes a common scene of her daytime experiences. In fact, M is really her sweetheart friend, and sometimes she actually happens to kiss him.

2. "I was at the kindergarten and mummy was supposed to come and fetch me at 2 but she did not come and she came at 4 and I cried."

Mother's information: It is Lisa's wish to leave the kindergarten at 2 rather than at 4 in the afternoon.

Both these dreams are very brief and show an elementary narration. The dream scenario directly refers to two familiar settings for the child, the gardens and the kindergarten. These dreams are understandable and do not show bizarre elements. Only in the first one is there an unclear situation, "I got lost."

In the first dream report, the situation described is a gesture of affection of the child towards her little boyfriend, as is commonly practised during the day. This dream is probably the representation of the fulfilment of a wish. In particular, in her dream, the child continues a pleasant situation probably not satisfied enough in her daytime experience (i.e., "prosecution dream").

The second dream report represents the wish to leave the kindergarten before the usual time, contrary to her parents' arrangements. However, in this case the wish is not satisfied, the dream has an unpleasant result, and the exit from kindergarten is confirmed, as happens in reality, at 4 p.m.!

However, on the same morning, the child spontaneously reported also the following dream, where that same wish seems to be satisfied.

Spontaneous dream

> "I was playing with M [her little boyfriend], F [her cousin], F [a friend] and A [a friend] at school, and mummy came to fetch me at 2 and I was happy."

This wish is so present to Lisa that it remains the object of her interest, together with other wishes, in the dream reported on the next early-morning awakening.

> 3. "I was at the kindergarten and mummy had come to fetch me at 2 and we had gone home. My cousin F had come over, we first played with the films, at school, and then we had dinner at home. F slept here at my house."

> *Mother's information*: The evening before, F had wanted to stay here with Lisa, and they both had cried desperately. Lisa wants F to sleep with her, and it often happens that they cry because they want to stay together. F and Lisa always play together (they live in the same building).

If we are prepared to admit that children's dreams often represent their wishes and if, as we have seen, these wishes always refer to important experiences of the dreamer (Chapter Nine), we should not wonder that the wishes of Lisa are not exhausted within a dream but, on the contrary, appear again in more than one dream (had the same night or the subsequent one). The same wish may appear satisfied, with certain variations, in different dreams, or in the form of a failed attempted fulfilment in one dream and as succeeded fulfilment in another (see also dreams no. 4 and 5, p. 186, and those of the second period no. 1 and the spontaneous dream, pp. 187–188).

In dream no. 3, we note that the narration is more articulated: there are two scenarios, the kindergarten and the house. The child, besides resuming the theme of leaving the kindergarten earlier, stages another wish-fulfilment: to play with her cousin. Here, the wish-fulfilment appears to be of the "compensation" type: in fact, the child reverses unpleasant daytime situations, where she does not leave kindergarten at two and where the time spent playing with her cousin is evidently always too short.

Lisa's wishes shown in dream no. 1 (to be with her little boyfriend) and in dream no. 3 (to be with her cousin) also appear in the following dream, with certain variations representing very pleasant situations for the child,

> 4. "I was with F [her cousin] here at home, first we had played and F was staying at our house, here, and then M (Lisa's little boyfriend) had bruschetta [a typical Italian snack made with bread toasted on charcoals] and we ate grapes and the dog barked [the neighbour's dog] and M went downstairs to see the dog."
>
> *Mother's information*: In reality, M does not play with Lisa here at home. The bruschetta is Lisa's favourite dish, she complains when I prepare it in the oven and not on the fireplace, as she would like it. Lisa also loves grapes, she often complains that I never buy grapes.

In this dream, another wish that is represented as fulfilled is the wish to eat the favourite dish (the bruschetta). This case shows how information about daytime life is essential to understand the dream. In fact, it is interesting to notice the detail that the bruschetta, as it is usually prepared by the mother (i.e., in the oven) does not fully satisfy Lisa, who would like it prepared in another way, that is, directly on the fire, which is certainly better for the taste but requires more attention by her mother and requires more cleaning afterwards. Also, the grapes that her mother regularly buys are not considered enough by the child. This is what we call a "compensation" wish-fulfilment dream: Lisa's wishes are satisfied through the realization of the opposite of daytime situations.

The dream that follows, no. 5, shows a narrative development. The dream plot develops across multiple time planes, evidently evoking a more articulated dream scenario.

> 5. "I and M [Lisa's boyfriend] had a little child called Ma, he jumped on the bed, then he fell from the bed and got hurt and then we were worried, we put oil on the bruise, then M went to work, but he arrived late and they sent him back home. It was a house with a fireplace."

Mother's information: Lisa says she is going to marry M and that they will have children.

Here, we noticed another case in which the same wish appears in more than one dream. In fact, in this dream, it is worth noting the detail that, in imagining the house in which she lives with her little boyfriend [object of desire already reported in the dreams no. 1 and 4], the child considered *the presence of a fireplace*: does this not make us think about the fact that, according to her mother's information, Lisa clearly said that she likes her favourite dish, the bruschetta, prepared on the fireplace? (See dream no. 4.)

These dreams also seem to show another element, that, on the basis of the few data available, may be considered only an hypothesis, but that I am determined to analyse in my next studies: these dreams often present more than one wish, and dream processes seems to be, from a motivational point of view, over-influenced.

Lisa's dreams in the second period of observation

Lisa's dream reports collected one year later, when she was 5–6 years old, show the changes described for children of this age. In fact, her dream reports are longer and show a more elaborate narration. They also present certain elements of bizarreness that were not present before. Some of these elements of bizarreness, such as sudden changes of scene or elements intrinsically inconsistent, are similar to those that appear in adults' dreams. Finally, in these dreams, it is more difficult to perceive a clear wish-fulfilment, even where daytime information about the child is available.

1. "I was at the kindergarten with the teacher and I was making artwork for Christmas with the teacher and an older child arrived and pushed me, I pushed him back and the teacher said I had done well."

Mother's information: They are making some artwork for Christmas at the kindergarten, preparing things for the Nativity and the Christmas tree. It actually happened that a child pushed her while they were going to the bathroom, I can't remember if it was the day before. However, Lisa said that the child she saw in her dream was a stranger.

In this dream, although there is a dream scenario on a common daytime experience of Lisa's, there is also an "unexpected" element of bizarreness: the child who appears in the dream is not known to Lisa as he could well be, as long as the dream refers to the kindergarten environment. Should we think that the dreamer, while reporting her dream, does not want to reveal the identity of the child that pushed her? If it is so, we have to notice that this is the first example of bizarreness in Lisa's dreams: in this specific case, it consists of an *omission*. On other occasions, I had the chance to observe similar "omissions" in dream content that prevent the dream from being understood with a minimum action of disguise. This may happen when, after noticing an anomaly in the dream content, one has the opportunity (and is lucky enough!) to clarify it through related information. (See, for instance, dream no. 13 on p. 174). In that case the child had omitted to say, for embarrassment, the name of her own Prince Charming, but a smile gave her away. However, later in the interview she decided she could reveal his identity.) Another bizarre aspect of this dream is that the teacher apparently acts in a scarcely plausible way, as she tells Lisa that she did a good thing in pushing another child.

On the same morning, Lisa spontaneously reported another dream in which a child appeared, quite probably the same one as in the first dream, but this time the identity is revealed (A) and the dream assumes a clear meaning: Lisa stages the punishment of that child who, in reality, is naughty to her. It is a clear example of "compensation dream".

Spontaneous dream

> "A was pinching me and the teacher punished him, then teacher M took him and sent him out of the classroom."
>
> *Mother's information*: These are things that happen at school, they annoy one another, give pinches, pull their hair, lift the girls' skirts up. The teachers punish them—now, I don't know if they really send them out, but they do punish. These are things that happen every day.

This dream, besides telling us the identity of the child (A) of the first dream, might also explain the fact that the teacher in the first dream says that she has done well to push him: it could be the fulfilment of a wish of Lisa's, that is, the transformation in a real-life experience of the desire "Oh, how I'd like the teacher to tell me 'well done!' when I push that naughty boy!"

The following dream shows how dream bizarreness starts to appear. This dream stages a common life experience that we know well because it is the same that appeared in Lisa's dreams of the first period, (i.e., the presence of her little boyfriend, M), but with a few incongruous elements here. We can notice, besides, that when the dream introduces bizarre elements, the mother's comments are longer and more articulated, because she cannot find at once a connection with Lisa's daytime experience. Other incongruous elements of the dream are also noticed by the mother herself.

2. "M [the boyfriend of the first period] was near me, he had come to my house, and then we had started playing then he did not want to play any more, then he wanted to play with the toys of E [cousin]. However, E was not born yet, but you [the mother] had already bought the toys for him, then M started playing with the toys. Then M said to me, 'Shall we go and buy some pizza?' and we went for the pizza. We went to M's home and started to play."

Mother's information: Lisa plays with M only at school, M has never come to our house. Even at school they do not play together very often. M is the child that appeared in the dreams reported last year (first period of observation) when she said that they were engaged, that she was in love. However, she said she is no longer engaged to him because he does not want to play with her. Lisa would like to play with him very much. E was not born yet, but I had bought him toys, she was very specific about this. This seemed really strange to me. I asked her if those toys were the ones E really has, she said yes, so these are the toys she plays with every day. Lisa said she was sad during the dream. This seemed strange to me because the dream was not about anything sad. Then I thought she was happy to play with M because she likes him. It seemed strange to me.

The same morning, Lisa also spontaneously recalled the following dream.

Spontaneous dream

"M [boyfriend] was at home. After a while a certificate arrives at grandma's house, then the doctor came, because I had a fever. The doctor, without asking for permission, sat on a chair, then when the doctor was there, you [the mother] started taking my temperature, then the doctor visited me and sent me to the kindergarten, with the fever and all."

Mother's information: She had been ill a few days before, but the doctor did not come over, he said it was ordinary influenza, we only spoke by telephone. . . . She had to stay home a few days. The doctor usually takes a seat when he comes. He knocks and comes in, he is polite. And also this fact that he sends her to school with the fever seems strange, as is the fact that M was in our house. This has never happened. And the certificate that arrives at grandmother's house is something I can't explain. No, nothing comes to my mind. But it's a fact that Lisa had had a fever the week before.

We may already see from the first two dreams (no. 1, p. 187 and no. 2, p. 189) that, contrary to what happened in the dreams of the first period, there is not a clear wish-fulfilment present. In these dreams, two situations are observed: dream no. 2, seems to contain a wish-fulfilment, but there are also other unexplainable elements; in dream no. 1, we may notice the wish that the teacher does not reproach the child any more, but, nevertheless, we need to proceed with a preliminary interpretation of dream content. Actually, when the dream is no longer the mere clear fulfilment of wish, it starts turning in two directions: on the one hand, it may show elements that disguise the fulfilment of a wish; on the other, it may happen that, together with the clear fulfilment of a wish, there other elements that make the dream strange and bizarre overall. Also, in the above spontaneous dream we notice that, notwithstanding the presence of Lisa's boyfriend, there are several different bizarre and incomprehensible aspects.

3. "I was here at home and I was married to A [current little boyfriend] and then all of a sudden M appeared [the boyfriend in the prior period of observation], he was my son, then he climbed on the bed because I was at the hospital because I was having a baby then I went back home and climbed on the bed and then A in bed moved his feet like this [imitates the movement of feet as is done by the character in a famous Italian television series] and I felt sick, then I felt better and went to the park."

Mother's information: A has really asked Lisa a while ago to become his fiancée. A made a true declaration of love. He said he really liked her.

However, now I don't know how things are with M, they are sort of rivals because she likes both A and M, but with M she said she is not going to be engaged because he will not play with her. So she and A are engaged because A plays with her. Lisa was at the hospital twenty or so days ago. She banged her head so we had to have X-rays. As to the movement of the feet, it could be because she used to watch *Casa Vianello* (a television situation comedy), where the main actress really moves her feet like that. Lisa really enjoys that feet joke. She goes to the park very often, and asks to go there also very often. She often plays "mother and children". She plays with A at the kindergarten, but that's the only place where they meet. He is a schoolmate.

The dream above represents very well the typical dreams of this age. Compared to the dreams of the earlier period it is remarkably longer, has a more detailed narration with some amount of discontinuity, and presents a typical element of bizarreness (e.g., boyfriend M who suddenly becomes her son, or M's sudden appearance while Lisa is marrying another boy, A). This dream also presents the fulfilment of a wish, but accompanied by and blurred into unclear elements.

4. "I, F and B were playing 'getting married', then all of a sudden it all ended and I found again—for I was lost—I found mummy again, who was B [while playing, B had the role of her mother]. Lisa was F [the girl reporting the dream was F in the play] and her father (a toy), I found my parents and my older sister again. And then suddenly I heard a noise and ran away, all of us ran away except F because she didn't see us going away. Then we went to dinner and we had gone away. Then at a certain moment, then F came looking for us in the room, then she said, 'What are you doing in our house? Run, run!' and then she left the door open, then B got her mask off, and the dream ended."

Mother's information: The dream might relate to something that had happened a few days before. She was playing in her room with B and F, then B said that there were ghosts and they ran out of the room frightened and came here. They were playing Smurfs. Lisa calls this play "getting married" or "mother and daughter", she uses those terms. About the mask, I don't know—it might be the cartoons, she always watches cartoons where the characters wear masks. Or Carnival. We had been talking about Carnival a few days before, about the costume she is going to wear at the Carnival parade. There was even a meeting at school about this. On Monday I had told the girls about the school meeting for the Carnival parade. There was another meeting on this matter at Lisa's kindergarten and I talked to the girls about Carnival again. They even play games about Carnival.

In this dream and in others, such as the following one, we may notice the presence of the primary symbols described by Piaget. These are symbols used knowingly by the child that, apart from being used in play, are also used in dream.

Example. Dream 72, child aged three years and five months (Study I).

> "I dreamed of a mother who—whom I figured out was a mother, but was not a mother, she was only someone playing, it was a toy."

(See also Chapter Nine, p. 171, the dream (24) of the bunny that was the deceased grandmother). Also, Piaget described a dream of a child aged three years and seven months in which Mamchat and Bebchat (i.e., the cat and its kitten, the house's pets) are grandmother and mother (Piaget, 1945).

Dream 4, above, is particularly long. It introduces sudden changes of scene and the plot is uncertain and confused. From the information given by the mother, the various daytime sources of the dream can be perceived; nevertheless state-of-wakefulness situations appear in the dream in an indirect way. The dream is barely understandable and does not seem to show a direct wish-fulfilment.

> 5. "So F had come here [to Lisa's house], we went to play and she didn't want to play with me and therefore she started to cry. But I hadn't done anything to her and she started crying all the same, then went to tell her mother. You [i.e., the mother] went to her, you said 'F, come here! Why are you crying?! F, come here!' She did not come and you went to get her and brought her here because her mother wasn't there, and you hit her. [Me? (the mother speaking) Did I hit her?] Yes. Then she hit me—no, I hit her, then you told me—Lisa, don't hit F!—then I slapped her and she went to her mother and the dream ended."

Mother's information: Lisa plays with F every day. A few days before it did happen that F hit Lisa. Also their quarrels are a common occurrence. And also F crying, or that she is at F's place and then she starts to cry and comes back home; these are things that happen every day. And it also happened the day before the dream that F had hit Lisa. I recall one day when they quarrelled rather heavily (in the same week in which the dream was reported), they had quarrelled and teased each other all day long.

This is what I call a typical "intermediary dream", between the simple forms of dream of the earlier period and more complex dreams. It presents a certain length and an articulated narration, yet it is not particularly bizarre because it maintains a rather sound narration consistency and reports directly enough certain common daytime experiences of Lisa. However, it contains certain implausible elements (e.g., Lisa's mother hitting another child, F).

6. "B was telling me a story but then F came here and we started to hit each other, then you said 'Why are you fighting?' (and the child)—it was her who started it! Send her back to her house! Then you arrived, because aunt had put on the mask, then we were all sleeping because it was night and the day after we got up and I remained here alone and prepared my breakfast, watched television, did some cleaning, tidied up, then I dressed up, took the clothes I had to take, then you arrived and said, 'You tidied up? Good girl, did you have breakfast?' (mother said) and I said yes. 'Did you turn the TV on?' Yes. 'Did you tidy up?' Yes. 'Did you put everything in its place?' Yes. 'Are you dressed?' Yes. Then aunt arrived and asked, 'Who is she?' And who is she supposed to be, she's your niece! What niece? Lisa. And who is Lisa? (aunt asked). Your niece, who else do you think she is! and the dream ended."

Mother's information: In this dream there are things the child usually does, except she does not prepare breakfast herself and does not tidy things up. I don't know why she has reported this. She had not seen the mask her aunt was wearing.

7. "I had to go to the kindergarten, we had gone downstairs than went back up because I wanted to play, I wanted to bring the toy to play with at kindergarten, and we went to buy a toy and mummy asked me, 'Do you like this one?' I said yes, and the dream ended."

Mother's information: She brings toys to school every Monday (the dream was reported on a Monday morning). On that same morning, after reporting the dream, she hurried to get her toys ready.

Dream no. 6 is complex and articulated, while no. 7 seems a dream report of the earlier period (one year ago), as it is shorter, clearly relating to common experiences and showing a clear wish-fulfilment. It is the only dream of the second period in which there is a clear wish-fulfilment, probably a "dream of impatience".

During this second period, Lisa spontaneously reported other dreams characterized by a certain narration complexity, a greater length, and different elements of bizarreness that make them difficult to understand.

The case of Lisa offers an opportunity to study in depth and support the observations on development of dream bizarreness and on the matter of wish-fulfilment. Certainly, in Lisa's dreams wishes seems to play a central role. One aspect noticed here is that some wishes may not be satisfied in one dream alone. These are wishes that Lisa cannot withdraw her interest from. It is really in this strong interest that the strength of such desires resides and stimulates the dream.

CHAPTER ELEVEN

Implications for dream research and theory

Systematic research on Freud's dream theory has been frequently hindered by the conviction that its hypothesis cannot be tested empirically. Actually, the studies on children's dreams that I am presenting here are evidence of the contrary. These studies point out that it is possible to test empirically Freud's hypotheses on the early forms of dreaming and that these tests are not irrelevant for an empirical judgement of certain more general statements of Freud's dream theory. This methodological result is the most important one to me. Certainly, from a theoretical and methodological standpoint, I have developed the belief that without an appropriate study and systematization of the Freudian dream theory, identifying research hypotheses correctly derived from the original ones is a difficult task. However, considering the vastness and complexity of Freud's work, this is not surprising. The studies that I have presented here also allowed us to find a first empirical support of certain Freudian observations and hypotheses on children's dreams. Particularly, the characteristics observed by Freud on the dreams of his children (i.e., brevity, lack of bizarreness, direct wish-fulfilment, etc.) received confirmation through the analysis of larger samples of dream reports collected in a more systematic way. The same hypothesized relationship between the increase of dream bizarreness and the development of the superego functions of the personality received substantial support, which encourages a more in-depth study of the disguise–censorship model. This second, empirical result, I believe represents an interesting point of departure. My purpose was to try to define a methodological way to test Freud's hypotheses on children's dreams and, at same time, to collect some preliminary data to begin to appraise the empirical value of these hypotheses. Therefore, I regard this work as a project in progress, which will require further development through additional studies. My hope is that other authors will be able to appraise in further studies the reliability of the characteristics of children's dreams found here.

The "discovery" that important portions of the Freudian theory of dream, such as the hypotheses on children's dreams, on the genesis of dream bizarreness, and on wish-fulfilment hypotheses, can be scientifically tested implies, I believe, a new responsibility for the community of dream researchers in the analysis of this model, which will have to be based more on empirical grounds rather than on dogmatic and factious positions. What I wish for the Freudian model of dream is not a "special treatment", but a normal treatment of empirical evaluation, as for those reserved for other theoretical models in psychology, and I believe that this is both possible and necessary.

As a dream researcher, I find that Freud's observations and hypotheses on children's dreams have an extraordinary heuristic value. Many results found in the studies presented here could be explicitly predicted only on the basis of these. If, as I believe, the heuristic and empirical value of a theoretical model is valued by its ability to make statistically significant predictions that provide reasonable, however tentative, interpretations of the facts observed, the hypotheses on child dreaming of the Freudian dream model have proved applicable.

The studies on children's dreams presented here highlight a number of useful points for the current dream research and theory that I am discussing here.

Theory of dream bizarreness

The study of bizarreness in dreams of children has several implications for the current debate on dream bizarreness (see Colace, 1997b, 2003, 2006d; Boag, 2006a,b; Domhoff, 2001, 2005; Hobson, 2002, 2004, 2005; Hobson, Pace-Schott, & Stickgold, 2000a,b). Dream bizarreness has been studied from the 1960s until the 1980s, based exclusively on the analysis of REM dreams of adults, which are bizarre in about 70% of cases (e.g., see Colace & Natale, 1997; McCarley & Hoffman, 1981; Natale & Esposito, 2001). Different theoretical models, also based on these data, are inclined to consider bizarreness as an invariant characteristic of dreams and intrinsic to the neurophysiological processes underlying the production of REM dreams (Crick and Mitchison, 1983, 1986; Gottesman, 2006; Hobson, 1988, 2002; Hobson, Pace-Schott, & Stickgold, 2000a; Mamelack & Hobson, 1989; Resnick, Stickgold, Rittenhouse, & Hobson, 1994; Seligman & Yellen, 1987). Elsewhere, from an extensive review of the literature, I have suggested that there is evidence that dream bizarreness cannot be considered either an invariant characteristic or a peculiarity of REM dream (i.e., of its neurobiological substrate), since bizarreness also appears in NREM dreams and even in daytime fantasies (i.e., day-dreaming) (Colace, 1997b, 2003). Now, the dreams of children provide a confirmation in this sense. Children's dreams show unmistakably that the early forms of dream are not bizarre and, therefore, that bizarreness cannot be considered an intrinsic property of dreams. These dreams reject the assumption that the underlying neurobiological substratum of dream may be considered in itself a sufficient condition for the generation of dream bizarreness. Actually, the children's dreams collected in my studies very rarely show signs of random processes; nor does their content show any signs of a degraded or lacking cognitive activity. These dreams appeared, in their contents and the more so in their meaning, perfectly understandable and logical with respect to the daytime events that were their background. From this standpoint, I believe that the formal properties of younger children's dreams represent a new significant datum for any theory about the nature of dream bizarreness. Furthermore, as children's dreams show dream bizarreness in a gradual manner, they may represent a methodology tool to observe, in nature, the possible development factors (cognitive and personality) that affect its appearance. At the same time, child dreams offer an opportunity to identify qualitatively the early forms of bizarreness that appear in the dreaming processes.

Debate on the disguise–censorship model

With regard to dream bizarreness, the "disguise–censorship" theory has frequently been at the centre of dream debates. While certain authors consider this model superfluous and misleading, with serious implications for the validity of the entire Freudian dream theory (Domhoff, 2001; Hobson, 1986, 1999, 2006; Hobson & Pace-Schott, 1999), others have tried to review it more closely (see Boag, 2006a,b; Colace, 2006d) and have investigated the neuro-anatomical correlate of its components (i.e., censorship functions) (Solms, 1999, 2000; Yu, 2001, 2003, 2006). I have frequently had the impression that the criticism of the disguise–censorship model is attracted by, and focused on, its exterior rather than material aspects. Terms like "censor" or "censorship" have eased the way for malevolent critics of Freud's model. However, it is too often forgotten that those terms were used by Freud as mere theoretical postulates to describe tangible clinical phenomena, such as, for instance, the patients' resistance to the interpretation of their dream (Colace, 2006d). Freud himself would have wanted to change them, having become aware at once that these terms would have been prone to critics (see Freud, 1916–1917, p. 140). Besides, when Freud started to develop his second theory of the mind, he replaced the "dream censor" with the superego functions as a separate agency in the ego (Freud, 1923b). From this point of view, the terms "censor of the dream" and "dream censorship" are completely replaceable, without any implication for the validity of the theory: the essence of the disguise–censorship model remains the assumption that a substantial portion of dream bizarreness has a motivational–conflictive origin (Colace, 2006d; Yu, 2006) (Freud [1900a] himself predicted that part of dream bizarreness might have a non-defensive origin.) Now, the significant correlation between dream bizarreness and the indices of superegoic functions found here is consistent with this assumption and encourages further analysis of this model. This correlation, which is predictable only on the basis of the disguise–censorship model, suggests that this model can still be useful in the explanation of dream bizarreness and should not be abandoned by the scientific community.

Neuropsycological perspective

The recent research on the neuroanatomical correlations of dream, apart from supporting the assumption of a motivational activation of dreams, which is central and peculiar to Freud's dream model, has tried to investigate the possible neuroanatomical correlations of the "censorship activity" (Kaplan-Solms & Solms, 1996, 2000; Solms, 1998; Yu, 2001, 2003, 2006). Nevertheless, so far there are no sufficient indications. According to Solms and Turnbull (2002), the experimental evidence that frontal lobes are partially inactive during sleep with dreams may respond to the Freudian hypothesis that our defences are partly disarmed, that is, more permissive, during sleep, which might let psychic material incompatible with our conscience emerge. However, the same authors, with reference to neuro-anatomical studies, have concluded that it not yet clear whether the discrepancy between latent and manifest content of dreams has a motivational origin. At present, it can be individual-ized as some inherent anatomical structures that include abilities theoretically involved in the superegoic functions and, therefore, in the "censor" of dreams. Yu (2006), in his overview of literature on this topic, underlined some of these abilities, such as the "ability to interpret nonverbal emotional expression" and the "decision-making abilities" (p. 55), which neurological evidence has shown to be impaired in patients with lesions involving the ventromesial prefrontal region (regions implicated in the moral functioning). I believe that the study of the relationships between dream bizarre-ness and superegoic functions in children may contribute to a pro-gressive definition and individualization of those functions that may be actively involved in dream censorship. This may yield profit both for the purposes of updating the "disguise–censorship" model and for the research on the neuro-anatomical correlations of these functions (Boag, 2006a,b; Kaplan-Solms & Solms, 2000; Solms, 1999, 2000; Yu, 2001, 2003, 2006).

Towards a motivational approach to dreaming

Dream research has recently shown a new interest in studying the influence of motivations on dreaming processes, also thanks to the contribution of some areas of research. The functional neuro-imaging studies that employ such techniques as PET (position emitting tomography) and NMR (nuclear magnetic resonance) have allowed us, on the one hand, to improve our knowledge on the neuro-anatomical and neuro-physiological substratum of basic motivations and emotions (i.e., "affective neuroscience") (Damasio, 1994; LeDoux, 1996; Panksepp, 1998), and, on the other, to start drawing a map of those cerebral areas that are active during dreaming processes (see Braun et al., 1997; Maquet et al., 1996; Nofzinger, Mintun, Wiseman, Kupfer, & Moore, 1997). During the same period, the neuropsychoanalytical approach (Solms, 1997, 2000) highlighted the involvement in dream generation of the mesolimbic–mesocortical dopaminergic system, that to which affective neurosciences attribute a role in the activation of motivated behaviours, that is, the system whose activation mediates our appetitive behaviours, curiosity, and expectations towards the external world (i.e., the "seeking" or "wanting" system) (Berridge, 2001; Berridge & Robinson, 1998; Ikemoto & Panksepp, 1999; Panksepp, 1998). This system is active, for instance, during goal-seeking behaviours and appetitive interactions with the world (including hunger, sexual drives, or desire for drugs). It has recently been said that a contribution to the study of the role of the dopaminergic system in dreaming processes may be the one given by the study of the dream reports in drug-addict subjects, where the system in question is altered due to a prolonged exposure to drug abuse (i.e., drug craving) (Colace, 2000, 2004a, 2006e, 2009b, 2010; Colace et al., 2009; Johnson, 2001; Shevrin, 2001). It may be worth noting that the focus on the motivational aspects of dreaming was channelled from this type of approach (clinico–anatomical) rather than from psychological studies on the dream. Dream researchers needed an anatomical basis for the motivational fact issue in order to get interested in their role in dream processes; psychoanalytic findings were not enough to arouse their interest! For instance, we cannot refrain from pointing out that authors certainly not close to the psychoanalytic tradition have recently stressed the importance of studying emotions and motivations in the dreaming processes (Antrobus, 2001; Smith, et al., 2004).

I believe that all this is the signal of a new approach, a *motivational* one, to dreaming. I consider as pioneers of this present trend those authors who were interested in the emotional and motivational factors of dream at a time when many others focused only on the physiological or purely cognitive aspects of dreaming. I am referring to those studies which gave life to the various forms of "adaptive theories of dreaming" (Breger, 1967; Breger, Hunter, & Lane, 1971; Cartwright, 1991; Cartwright, Newell, & Mercer, 2001; Fiss, 1980; Hartmann, 1996; Kramer, 1993; Lavie & Kaminer, 1991). However, when the research starts studying in more detail the motivational aspects of dream, in one way or another, it will have to cope with the Freudian model, the only systematic theoretical dream model that makes motivational factors its strength. In this, the scientific community has a new opportunity to analyse what is actually and empirically valid in this model. The research on children's dreams, and particularly on those forms of dreams in which wish-fulfilment is evident, may represent a valid research benchmark capable of providing useful information for studying dreams from a motivational point of view. In a wider sense, a similar contribution may also come from a revaluation of the study of infantile forms of dreams in adults, in particular, the study of dreams under the effects of deprivation from vital needs (Colace, 2004a, 2009a). If we are interested in determining if and how wishes and motivations enter dreams, we need to study exactly those forms of dreams where wishes and their fulfilment are clear, leaving aside, for the time being, the more complex and ambitious question of whether, theoretically, all dreams should be intended as the fulfilment (or attempted fulfilment) of an (unconscious) wish. By reconsidering the motivational aspects of dreaming under a neutral perspective that draws inspiration from the psychoanalytic theory in an attempt to preserve its most effective assumption is, in my view, a good opportunity for those dream theorists who want to oppose the assumption that dreams are mere epiphenomena of neurobiological facts. Children's clear wish-fulfilment dreams, apart from psychoanalysis, are examples of motivationally direct dreams that represent a piece of evidence against all the reductionist neurobiological assumptions that, as in the nineteenth century, still consider dreams and dream contents as the result of random processes. The dreams that I have reported in this book prove to be sensible acts with a meaning, and understandable within the context of the child dreamer's life and experiences.

In conclusion, the study of children's dreams, although still at a preliminary stage and subject to planning, has shown its advantages for the understanding of different aspects of dreaming. Here, I have tried to highlight the profitable use of the study of these dreams in the evaluation of the empirical credentials of Freud's observations on children's dreams and of other parts of the Freudian dream model and in relation to certain main themes of contemporary dream research and theory. I have underlined the advantages for the understanding of the motivational and defensive origin, at least in part, of dream bizarreness, and for the observation of which types of wishes enter the dreams, and how: information that is needed in order to identify the possible functions of these dreams. The gradual refinement of the methodologies for the collection and evaluation of children's dreams is, therefore, an objective of great strategic importance for dream research and theory. Dream research has done very little to use knowingly the information available on children's dreams, and there have been very few research programmes on children's dreams in sleep laboratories. Filling this gap would be desirable in the future. An important part of this research will have to deal with the comparison of the characteristics of child dreams collected with different methods as the only way of achieving standardization of the results.

REFERENCES

Ablon, S. L., & Mack, J. E. (1980). Children's dreams reconsidered. *Psychoanalytic Study of the Child, 35*: 170–217.

Altschuler, K. Z. (1966). Comments on recent sleep research related to psychoanalytic theory. *Archives of General Psychiatry, 15*: 235–239.

Amerio, P., Bosotti, E., & Amione, F. (1978). Cognitive dissonance and internalization of social norms: effects of threat severity on children. *International Journal of Behavioral Development, 1*: 355–362.

Andersson, O. (1962). *Studies in the Prehistory of Psychoanalysis*. Stockholm: Esselte Studium AB.

Antrobus, J. S. (1977). The dream as metaphor: an information processing and learning model. *Journal of Mental Imagery, 2*: 327–338.

Antrobus, J. S. (1978). Dreaming for cognition. In: A. M. Arkin , J. Antrobus, & S. J. Ellman (Eds.), *The Mind in Sleep: Psychology and Psychophysiology* (pp. 569–581). Hillsdale, NJ: Lawrence Erlbaum Associates Publisher.

Antrobus, J. S. (1983). REM and NREM sleep reports: comparison of word frequencies by cognitive classes. *Psychophysiology, 20*: 562–568.

Antrobus, J. S. (1986). Dreaming:cortical activation and perceptual thresholds. *Journal of Mind and Behavior, 7*: 193–212.

Antrobus, J. S. (1991). Dreaming: cognitive processes during cortical activation and high afferent thresholds. *Psychological Review, 98*: 96–121.

Antrobus, J. S. (2001). Rethinking the fundamental processes of dream and sleep mentation production: defining new questions, that avoid the distraction of REM versus NREM comparison. *Sleep and Hypnosis, 3*: 1–3.

Aserinsky, E., & Kleitman, N. (1953). Regularly occurring periods of eye motility and concurrent phenomena during sleep. *Science, 118*: 273–274.

Avila-White, D., Schneider, A., & Domhoff, G. W. (1999). The most recent dreams of 12–13 year-old boys and girls: a methodological contribution to the study of dream content in teenagers. *Dreaming, 9*: 163–171.

Becker, T. E. (1978). Dream analysis in child analysis. In: J. Klen (Ed.), *Child Analysis and Therapy* (355–374). New York: Jason Aronson.

Berkowitz, L. (1964). *The Development of Motives and Values in the Child*. New York: Basic Book.

Berridge, K. C. (2001). Reward learning: reinforcement, incentives, and expectations. *Psychology of Learning and Motivation, 40*: 223–278.

Berridge, K. C., & Robinson, T. E. (1998). What is the role of dopamine in reward: hedonic impact, reward learning, or incentive salience? *Brain Research Reviews, 28*: 309–369.

Blasi, A. (1980). Bringing moral cognition and moral action: a critical review of the literature. *Psychological Bulletin, 88*: 1–45.

Boag, S. (2006a). Freudian dream theory, dream bizarreness, and the disguise–censor controversy. *Neuropsychoanalysis, 8*(1): 5–17.

Boag, S. (2006b). Freudian dream theory, dream bizarreness, and the disguise–censor controversy. response to commentaries. *Neuropsychoanalysis, 8*(1): 59–68.

Bokert, E. G. (1968). The effects of thirst and related verbal stimulus on dream reports. *Dissertation Abstracts, 28*: 4753b.

Bosinelli, M., & Cicogna, P. (1989). Sonno e sogno. In: M. W. Battacchi (Ed.), *Trattato Enciclopedico di Psicologia dell'Età Evolutiva* (Vol. II, pp. 1319–1342). Padova: Piccin.

Bosinelli, M., & Molinari, S. (1968). Contributo alle interpretazioni psicodinamiche dell'addormentamento. *Rivista di Psicologia, 62*(3): 369–393.

Braun, A. R, Balkin, T. J., Wesenten, N. J., Carson, R. E., Varga, M., Baldwin, P., Selbie, S., Belenky, G., & Herscovitch, P. (1997). Regional cerebral blood flow throughout the sleep-wake cycle—an (H_2O)-O-15-PET study. *Brain, 120*: 1173–97.

Breger, L. (1967). *Function of Dreams. Journal of Abnormal Psychology,* Monograph 641.

Breger, L., Hunter, R. W., & Lane, I. (1971). The effect of stress on dreams. *Psychological Issues, 7*: 3.

Burton, R. V., Allinsmith, W., & Maccoby, E. E. (1966). Resistance to temptation to sex of child, sex of experimenter, and withdrawal of attention. *Journal of Personality and Social Psychology, 3*: 253–258.

Canestrari, R., & Ricci Bitti, P. E. (Eds.) (1993). *Freud e la ricerca psicologica.* Bologna: Il Mulino.

Cartwright, R. (1991). Dream that work: the relation of dream incorporation to adaptation to stressful events. *Dreaming, 1*: 3–9.

Cartwright, R., Lloyd, S., Knight, S., & Trenholme, I. (1984). Broken dreams: a study of the effect of the divorce and depression on dream content. *Psychiatry, 47*: 251–259.

Cartwright, R., Newell, P., & Mercer, P. (2001). Dream incorporation of sentinel life event and its relation to waking adaptation. *Sleep and Hypnosis, 3*(1): 25–32.

Cassi, V., Pinto, G., & Salzarulo, P. (1999). Developmental changes of children's about sleep and dreaming. *Sleep Research Online,* 2(Suppl.1): 194.

Cavallero, C., Cicogna, P., Natale, V., Occhionero, M., & Zito, A. (1992). Slow wave sleep dreaming. *Sleep, 15*(6): 562–566.

Choi, S. Y. (1973). Dreams as a prognostic factor in alcoholism. *American Journal of Psychiatry, 130*: 699–702.

Cicogna, P. (1991). Il sogno in età evolutiva. In: M. Bosinelli, P. Cicogna (Eds.), *Sogni: figli d'un cervello ozioso* (pp. 328–346). Turin: Bollati Boringhieri.

Cicogna, P., Cavallero, C., & Bosinelli, M. (1991). Cognitive aspects of mental activity during sleep. *American Journal of Psychology, 104*(3): 413–425.

Cicogna, P., Natale, V., Occhionero, M., & Bosinelli, M. (2000). Slow wave and REM sleep mentation. *Sleep Research Online, 3*: 67–72.

Colace, C. (1991). *Studio sulla teoria freudiana del sogno.* M.D. thesis. Università degli Studi di Roma "La Sapienza".

Colace, C. (1997a). I sogni dei bambini nella teoria psicodinamica: un contributo teorico e sperimentale. PhD Dissertation. Department of Psychology, Università degli Studi di Bologna.

Colace, C. (1997b). Perchè i nostri sogni sono così strani? Un esame della letteratura sul tema della bizzarria onirica. *Archivio di Psicologia, Neurologia e Psichiatria, 58*(5–6): 498–563.

Colace, C. (1998a). Sulla valutazione della credibilità dei sogni raccontati dai bambini: uno studio preliminare. *Psichiatria dell'infanzia e dell'adolescenza*, *65*(1): 5–18.

Colace, C. (1998b). I sogni di "appagamento di desiderio" nei bambini dai 3 ai 5 anni di età. *3° Riunione della Società Italiana di Ricerca sul Sonno (S.I.R.S.)*, Trento, Italy, 29–30 May 1998. Abstract Book, pp. 13–14.

Colace, C. (1998c). Wish-fulfillment in dream reports of young children. *Sleep*, *21*(3 Suppl.): 286.

Colace, C. (2000). Dreams in abstinent opiate drug addicts: four case reports. *Sleep and Hypnosis*, *4*: 160–163.

Colace, C. (2003). Dream bizarreness reconsidered. *Sleep and Hypnosis*, *5*(3): 105–128.

Colace, C. (2004a). Dreaming in addiction. A study on the motivational bases of dreaming processes. *Neuro-psychoanalysis*, *6*(2): 167–181.

Colace, C. (2004b). Dreaming in young children and dream bizarreness. *Sleep*, *27*: 136, A61.

Colace, C. (2004c). Dreaming in childhood. *Sleep*, *27*: 139, A62.

Colace, C. (2005). L'appagamento di desiderio nel sogno infantile: un'analisi descrittiva. *10° Riunione della Società Italiana di Ricerca sul Sonno (S.I.R.S.)*, Roma, 26–27 November 2005, abstract book, 33.

Colace, C. (2006a). Children's dreaming: a study based on questionnaire completed by parents. *Sleep and Hypnosis*, *8*(1): 19–32.

Colace, C. (2006b). A content analysis of young children's dreams collected in school setting. *Sleep*, *29*: 0152: A51.

Colace, C. (2006c). Nota sulle idee prescientifiche sul tema della bizzarria onirica. *Psychofenia*, *IX*(15): 15–36.

Colace, C. (2006d). Commentary on "Freudian dream theory, dream bizarreness, and the disguise-censor controversy (S. Boag)". *Neuro-psychoanalysis*, *8*(1): 24–27.

Colace, C. (2006e). Drug dreams in cocaine addiction. *Alcohol & Drug Review*, *25*(2): 177.

Colace, C. (2009a). Gli studi sull'effetto della frustrazione dei bisogni primari sul sognare e la recente ricerca e teoria sui processi onirici. *Psycofenia*, *XII*(20): 49–72.

Colace, C. (2009b). Drug dreams, drug craving e misura dell'attività del sistema limbico attraverso il Limbic System Checklist (LSCL-33): un studio pilota su un caso clinico. Salute & Prevenzione. *La Rassegna Italiana sulle Tossicodipendenze*, *52*: 85–91.

Colace, C. (2010) Drug dreams in mescaline and lsd addiction. *The American Journal on Addictions*, in press.

Colace, C., & Natale, V. (1997). Bizarreness in REM and SWS dreams. *Sleep Research, 26:* 240.

Colace, C., & Tuci, B. (1995). A content analysis of children's dreams at ages 4–6: preliminary data. *Sleep Research, 24:* 68.

Colace, C., & Tuci, B. (1996a). Early children's dreams are not bizarre. *Sleep Research, 25:* 147.

Colace, C., & Tuci, B. (1996b). Caratteristiche di semplicità dei primi sogni di bambini e implicazioni per la teoria neurobiologica della bizzarria onirica. *AIP, Congresso Nazionale della Sezione di Psicologia Sperimentale*, Capri (Italy). Summary of communications, pp. 248–250.

Colace, C., & Violani, C. (1993). La bizzarria del sogno infantile come correlato della capacità di provare sensi di colpa. *Psichiatria dell'infanzia e dell'adolescenza, 60*(4–5): 367–376.

Colace, C., Claps, M., Antognoli, A., Sperandio, R., Sardi, D., & Benedetti, A. (2009). Measure of limbic system activity and drug dreams in drug addicted patients: a preliminary study. *Poster presentation, 10th International Congress of Neuropsychoanalysis*, Paris, 26–29 June.

Colace, C., Dichiacchio, C., & Violani, C. (2004). Tempo trascorso davanti alla TV e caratteristiche del sonno infantile. *9° Riunione della Società Italiana di Ricerca sul Sonno (S.I.R.S.)*, Napoli, 24–26 giugno 2004.

Colace, C., Dichiacchio, C., & Violani, C. (2006a). Effects of television viewing on sleep habits and dream contents in children at ages 3–8. *Sleep, 29*(1035): A354–355.

Colace, C., Dichiacchio, C., & Violani, C. (2006b). Effetti della televisione della TV sul sonno e sognare nei bambini dai 3 agli 8 anni di età. *Psichiatria dell'Infanzia e dell'adolescenza, 73*(1): 31–40.

Colace, C., Doricchi, F., Di Loreto E., & Violani, C. (1993). Developmental qualitative and quantitative aspects of bizarreness in dream reports of children. *Sleep Research, 22:* 57.

Colace, C., Ferendeles, R., Tuci, B., & Celani, G. (2000). Children's dreaming: a study based on questionnaire compiled by parents. *Sleep (Abstract supplement 2), 23:* A175-A176, 1196.D.

Colace, C., Tuci, B., & Ferendeles, R. (1997). Bizarreness in early children's dreams collected in the home setting: preliminary data. *Sleep Research, 26:* 241.

Colace, C., Tuci, B., & Ferendeles, R. (2000). Self-representation in young children's dream reports. *Sleep (Abstract supplement 2), 23:* A176-A177, 1198.D.

Colace C., Tuci, B., Ferendeles, R., Testa, A., Celani, G., & Gasparini, S. (2000). Uno studio sul sognare in età evolutiva attraverso un questionario compilato dai genitori: dati preliminari. *Psichiatria dell' Infanzia e dell'adolescenza*, 67(4–5): 559–570.

Colace, C., Tuci, B., Ferendeles, R., Testa, A., Celani, G., Gasparini, S., & Violani, C. (1999). Uno studio sul sognare in età evolutiva: dati preliminari. *4° Riunione della Società Italiana di Ricerca sul Sonno (S.I.R.S.)*, Isola d Elba (Italy), 4–6 giugno 1999.

Colace, C., Violani, C., & Solano, L. (1993). La deformazione-bizzarria onirica nella teoria freudiana del sogno: indicazioni teoriche e verifica di due ipotesi di ricerca in un campione di 50 sogni di bambini. *Archivio di Psicologia, Neurologia e Psichiatria*, 54(3): 380–401.

Colace, C., Violani, C., & Tuci, B. (1995). Self-representation in dreams reported from young children at school. *Sleep Research*, 24: 69.

Conte, M., & Dazzi, N. (Eds.) (1988). *La verifica empirica in psicoanalisi.* Bologna, Il Mulino.

Coriat, I. H. (1920). *The Meaning of Dreams.* Boston: Little, Brown.

Crick, F., & Mitchison, G. (1983). The function of REM sleep. *Nature*, 304: 111–114.

Crick, F., & Mitchison, G. (1986). REM sleep and neural nets. *Journal of Mind Behaviour*, 7: 229–249.

Damasio, A. R. (1994). *Descartes' Error: Emotion, Reason, and the Human Brain.* New York: Avon.

De Martino, F. (1955). A review of literature on children's dreams. *Psychiatric Quarterly (Suppl.)*, 1: 1–12.

Dement, W. (1960). The effect of dream deprivation. *Science*, 131: 1705–1707.

Despert, J. L. (1949). Dreams in children of preschool age. *The Psychoanalytic Study of Child*, 3–4: 141- 180.

Diatkine, R. (1975). Ontogenesis of sleep and dream in psychoanalytical theory. In: G. C. Lairy & P. Salzarulo (Eds.), *The Experimental Study of Human Sleep. Methodological Problems* (pp. 217–222). Amsterdam: Elsevier.

Domhoff, B., & Kamiya, J. (1964). Problem in dream content study with objective indicators. *Archives of General Psychiatry*, 11: 519–532.

Domhoff, G. W. (1996). *Finding Meaning in Dreams: A Quantitative Approach.* New York: Plenum.

Domhoff, G. W. (2001). Why did empirical dream researchers reject Freud? A critique of historical claims by Mark Solms. *Dreaming, 14*: 3–17.

Domhoff, G. W. (2005). Refocusing the neurocognitive approach to dreams: a critique of the Hobson versus Solms debate. *Dreaming, 15*: 3–20.

Doricchi, F., & Violani, C. (1992). Dream recall in brain-damaged patients: a contribution to the neuropsychology of dreaming through a review of the litterature. In: J. S. Antrobus & M. Bertini (Eds.), *The Neuropsychology of Sleep and Dreaming* (pp. 99–140). Hillsdale, NJ: Lawrence Erlbaum.

Erdelyi, M. H. (1985). Psychoanalysis: Freud's cognitive psychology. New York: W. H. Freeman and Company.

Eysenk, H. J. (1953). *Uses and Abuses of Psychology*. Harmondsworth: Penguin.

Ferenczi, S. (1925). Psychoanalysis of sexual habits, J. L. Sottie (Trans.). In: J. Rickman (Ed.), *Further Contribution to the Theory and Technique of Psycho-Analysis* (pp. 259–297). London: Maresfield (1980).

Fisher, S., & Greenberg, R. P. (1977). *The Scientific Credibility of Freud's Theories and Therapy*. New York: Basic Books.

Fiss, H. (1980). Dream content and response to withdrawal from alcohol. *Sleep Research, 9*: 152.

Foulkes, D. (1962). Dreams report from different stages of sleep. *Journal of Abnormal and Social Psychology, 65*: 14–25.

Foulkes, D. (1978). *A Grammar of Dreams*. New York: Basic Books.

Foulkes, D. (1979). Home and laboratory dreams: four empirical studies and conceptual revaluation. *Sleep, 2*: 233–251.

Foulkes, D. (1982). *Children's Dreams, Longitudinal Studies*. New York: Wiley-Interscience.

Foulkes, D. (1985). *Dreaming: A Cognitive-Psychological Approach*. Hillsdale, NJ: Lawrence Erlbaum.

Foulkes, D. (1993a). Freud e la psicologia del sogno. In: R. Canestrari, & P. E. Ricci Bitti (Eds.), *Freud e la ricerca psicologica* (pp. 241–253). Bologna: Il Mulino.

Foulkes, D. (1993b). Children's dreaming. In: C. Cavallero & D. Foulkes (Eds.), *Dreaming as Cognition* (pp. 114–132). New York: Harvester Wheatsheaf.

Foulkes, D. (1996). Dream research: 1953–1993. *Sleep, 19*(8): 609–624.

Foulkes, D. (1999). *Children's Dreaming and the Development of Consciousness*. Cambridge, MA: Harvard University Press.

Foulkes, D., & Rechtschaffen, A. (1964). Presleep determinants of dreams content: the effects of two films. *Percep. Motor Skills, 19*: 983–1005.

Foulkes, D., & Vogel, G. (1965). Mental activity at sleep onset. *Journal of Abnormal Psychology, 20*: 231–240.

Foulkes, D., Hollifield, M., Sullivan, B., Bradley, L., & Terry, R. (1990). REM dreaming and cognitive skills at ages 5–8: a cross-sectional study. *International Journal of Behavioral Development, 13*(4): 447–465.

Foulkes, D., Larson, J., Swanson, E., & Rardin, M. (1969). Two studies of childhood dreaming. *American Journal of Orthopsychiatry, 39*: 627–643.

Foulkes, D., Pivik, T., Steadman, H. S., Spear, P. S., & Symonds, J. D. (1967). Dreams of the male child: an EEG study. *Journal of Abnormal Psychology, 72*: 457–467.

Fraiberg, S. (1950). Sleep disturbances of early childhood. *Psychoanalytic Study of the Child, 5*: 285–309.

Fraiberg, S (1959). *The Magic Years.* New York: Charles Scribner's Sons, p. 79.

Frank, G. (1999). Freud's concept of the superego. Review and assessment. *Psychoanalytic Psychology, 16*(3): 448–463.

Freud, A. (1927). Four lectures on child analysis. *The Writings of Anna Freud*, Vol. 1. New York: International Universities Press.

Freud, A. (1965). *Normality and Pathology in Childhood.* New York: International Universities Press.

Freud, S. (1900a). *The Interpretation of Dreams. S.E., 4–5.* London: Hogarth Press.

Freud, S. (1901a). *On Dreams. S.E., 5.* London: Hogarth Press.

Freud, S. (1905c). *Jokes and their Relation to the Unconscious. S.E., 8.* London: Hogarth Press.

Freud, S. (1909b). *Analysis of a Phobia in a Five-year-old Boy. S.E., 10.* London: Hogarth Press.

Freud, S. (1910a). *Five Lectures on Psycho-analysis. S.E., 11*: 3–55. London: Hogarth Press.

Freud, S. (1910c). *Leonardo da Vinci and a Memory of his Childhood. S.E., 11*: 59–137. London: Hogarth Press.

Freud, S. (1913d). *The Occurrence in Dreams of Material From Fairy Tales. S.E., 13*: 279–388. London: Hogarth.

Freud, S. (1914c). *On Narcissism: An Introduction. S.E., 14.* London: Hogarth Press.

Freud, S. (1915f). *A Case of Paranoia Running Counter to the Psychoanalytic Theory of the Disease. S.E., 14.* London: Hogarth Press.

Freud, S. (1916–1917). *Introductory Lectures on Psycho-Analysis. S.E., 15/16.* London: Hogarth Press.

Freud, S. (1917d). *A Metapsychological Supplement to the Theory of Dreams. S.E., 14.* London: Hogarth Press.

Freud, S. (1917e). *Mourning and Melancholia. S.E., 14.* London: Hogarth Press.

Freud, S. (1918b). *From the History of an Infantile Neurosis. S.E., 17.* London: Hogarth Press.

Freud, S. (1923b). *The Ego and the Id. S.E., 19.* London: Hogarth Press.

Freud, S. (1924d). *The Dissolution of the Oedipus Complex. S.E., 17.* London: Hogarth Press.

Freud, S. (1925d). *An Autobiographical Study. S.E., 20:* 3–70. London: Hogarth Press.

Freud, S. (1925i). *Some Additional Notes on Dream-interpretation as a Whole. S.E., 17.* London: Hogarth Press.

Freud, S. (1930a). *Civilization and Its Discontents. S.E., 21.* London: Hogarth Press.

Freud, S. (1933a). *New Introductory Lectures on Psychoanalysis. S.E., 22.* London: Hogarth Press.

Freud, S. (1985). *The Complete Letters of Sigmund Freud to Wilhelm Fliess: 1887–1904*, J. M. Masson (Ed. & Trans.). Cambridge, MA: Belknap Press of Harvard University Press.

Goodenough, D. R., Lewis, H., Shapiro, A., Jaret, L., & Sleser, I. (1965). Dream reporting following abrupt and gradual awakenings from different types of sleep. *Journal of Personal and Social Psychology, 2:* 170–179.

Gottesmann, C. (2006). Commentary on "Freudian dream theory, dream bizarreness, and the disguise–censor controversy". *Neuropsychoanalysis, 8*(1): 27–32.

Grinder, R. E. (1961). New techniques for research in children's temptation behavior. *Child Development, 32:* 679–688.

Grotjahn, M. (1938). Dream observation in two-year, four-months-old baby. *Psychoanalytic Quarterly, 7:* 507–513.

Grünbaum, A. (1984). *The Foundations of Psychoanalysis. A Philosophical Critique.* Los Angeles, CA: University of California Press.

Hall, C. S., & Domhoff, B. (1963a). A ubiquitous sex differences in dreams. *Journal of Abnormal and Social Psychology, 66:* 278–280.

Hall, C. S., & Domhoff, B. (1963b). Aggression in dreams. *International Journal of Social Psychiatry, 9:* 259–267.

Hall, C. S., & Domhoff, B. (1964). Friendliness in dreams. *Journal of Social Psychology, 62:* 309–314.

Hall, C., & Van de Castle, R. (1966). *The Content Analysis of Dreams*. New York: Appleton-Century-Crofts.

Hartmann, E. (1996). Outline for theory on the nature and function of dreaming. *Dreaming, 6*: 147–170.

Hill, J. C. (1926). *Dreams and Education*. London: Methuen & Co.

Hobson, J. A. (1986). Psychoanalysis on the couch. Encyclopedia Britannica. *Medicine and Health Journal, 74–91*.

Hobson, J. A. (1988). *The Dreaming Brain*. New York: Basic Books.

Hobson, J. A. (1999). The new neuropsychology of sleep: implications for psychoanalysis. *Neuro-Psychoanalysis, 1*: 157–183.

Hobson, J. A. (2000). The ghost of Sigmund Freud haunts Mark Solm's dream theory. *Behavioral and Brain Sciences, 23*: 951–952.

Hobson, J. A. (2002). *Dreaming: an Introduction to Science of Sleep*. New York: Oxford University Press.

Hobson, J. A. (2004). Freud returns? Like a bad dream. *Scientific American, 290*: 89.

Hobson, J. A. (2005). In bed with Mark Solms? What a nightmare! A reply to Domhoff (2005). *Dreaming, 15*: 21–29.

Hobson, J. A. (2006). Dream Debate. Should Freud's dream theory be abandoned? Hobson (yes) vs Solms (no). Presented to the *Conference "Toward a Science of Consciousness"*, Tucson, Arizona, April.

Hobson, J. A., & McCarley, R. W. (1977). The brain as a dream-state generator: activation-synthesis hypothesis of dream process. *American Journal of Psychiatry, 134*: 1335–1348.

Hobson, J. A., & Pace-Schott, E. F. (1999). Response to commentaries. *Neuro-Psychoanalysis, 1*: 206–224.

Hobson, J. A., Hoffman, S. A., Helfand, R., & Kostner, D. (1987). Dream bizarreness and the activation-synthesis hypothesis. *Human Neurobiology, 6*: 157–164.

Hobson, J. A., Pace-Schott, E. F., & Stickgold, R. (2000a). Dream science 2000: a response to commentaries on dreaming and the brain. *Behavioral and Brain Sciences, 23*(6): 1019–1035.

Hobson, J. A., Pace-Schott, E. F., & Stickgold, R. (2000b). Dreaming and the brain: toward a cognitive neuroscience of conscious states. *Behavioral and Brain Sciences, 23*(6): 793–842.

Hobson, J. A., Stickgold, R., & Pace-Schott, E. F. (1998). The neuropsychology of REM sleep dreaming. *Neuroreport, 9*(3): 1–14.

Hoffman, M. L. (1970). Conscience, personality and socialization techniques. *Human Development, 13*: 90–126.

Hoffman, M. L., & Saltzstein, H. D. (1967). Parent discipline and the child's moral development. *Journal of Personality and Social Psychology*, 5(1): 45–57.

Hug-Helmuth, H. (1919). *A Study of the Mental Life of the Child*. Washington, DC: Nervous and Mental Diseases Publishing.

Hunt, H. T. (1982). Forms of dreaming. *Perceptual and Motor Skills, 54*: 559–633.

Hunt, H. T. (1989). *The Multiplicity of Dreams*. New Haven, CT: Yale University Press.

Hunt, H. T., Ruzycki-Hunt, K., Pariak D., & Belicki K. (1993). The relationship between dream bizarreness and imagination: artifact or essence? *Dreaming, 3*(3): 179–199.

Ikemoto, S., & Panksepp, J. (1999). The role of nucleus accumbens dopamine in motivated behavior: unifying interpretation with special reference to reward-seeking. *Brain Research Reviews, 31*: 6–41.

Jersild, A., Markey, F. V., & Jersild, C. L. (1933). Children's fears, dreams, wishes, day-dreams and likes, dislikes, pleasant and unpleasant memories. *Child Development Monographs*, 12.

Johnson, B. (2001). Drug dreams: a neuropsychoanalytic hypothesis. *Journal of the American Psychoanalytic Association, 49*: 75–96.

Jouvet, M. (1962). Recherches sur le structures nerveuses et les mécanismes responsables des differents phases du sommeil physiologhique. *Archives of Italian Biology, 100*: 125–206.

Jouvet, M., & Delorme, F. (1965). Locus coeruleus et sommeil paradoxal. *Social Biology, 159*: 895.

Jung, C. G. (1910). Über Konflikte der kindlichen Seele. *Jb. psychoan. psychopath. Forsch, 2*: 33.

Kahn, D., Pace-Schott, E. F., & Hobson, J. A. (1997). Consciousness in waking and dreaming: the roles of neuronal oscilation and neuromodulation in determining similarities and differences. *Neuroscience, 78*(1): 13–38.

Kaplan-Solms, K., & Solms, M. (1996). Psychoanalytic observations on a case of frontal-limbic disease. *Journal of Clinical Psychoanalysis, 3*: 405–438.

Kaplan-Solms, K., & Solms, M (2000). *Clinical Studies in Neuro-Psychonalysis*. Madison CT: International Universities Press.

Kimmins, C. W. (1937). *Children's Dreams, an Unexplored Land*. Allen & Unwin.

Kinoshita T. (1994). Young children's understanding of mental representation: pretend and dream. *Psychologia: An International Journal Psychology in the Orient, 37*: 3–6.

Klein, M. (1932). *The Psychoanalysis of Children*. London: Hogarth.

Kohler, W. C., Coddington, R. D., & Agnew, H. W. (1968). Sleep patterns in 2-year-old children. *Journal of Pediatrics, LXXII*: 228–233.

Kramer, M. (1993). The selective mood regulatory function of dreaming: an update and revision. In: A. Moffitt, M. Kramer & R. Hoffman (Eds.), *The Functions of Dreaming*. State University of New York Press.

Laplanche, J., & Pontalis, J. B. (1967). *Vocabulaire de la psychanalyse*. Paris: Presses Universitaires de France.

Lavie, P., & Kaminer, H. (1991). Dreams that poison sleep: dreaming in holocaust survivors. *Dreaming, 1*: 11–21.

LeDoux, J. (1996). *The Emotional Brain. The Mysterious Underpinnings of Emotional Life*. New York: Simon & Schuster.

Levi, G., & Pompili, E. (1991). La narrazione del racconto del sogno in bambini in età prescolare. *Psichiatria dell'infanzia e dell'adolescenza, 58*: 517–525.

Lucart, L. (1977). An approach to mental space: drawing of dreams in children. *Journal the Psychologie Normale et Pathologique, 74*(4): 431–449.

Mack, J. E. (1965). Nightmares, conflicts and ego development in children. *International Journal of Psychoanalysis, 46*: 403–428.

Mamelak, A., & Hobson, J. A. (1989). Dream bizarreness as the cognitive correlate of altered neuronal behavior in REM sleep. *Journal of Cognitive Neuroscience, 1*: 843–849.

Maquet, P., Peters, J. M., Aerts, J., Delfiore, G. Degueldre, C., Luxen, A., & Franck, G. (1996). Functional neuroanatomy of human rapid-eye-movement sleep and dreaming. *Nature, 386*(6596): 163–166.

McCarley, R. W. & Hobson, J. A. (1977). The neurobiological origins of psychoanalytic dream theory. *American Journal of Psychiatry, 134*: 1211–1221.

McCarley, R. W., & Hoffman, E. (1981). REM sleep dreams and the activation–synthesis hypothesis. *American Journal of Psychiatry, 138*(7): 904–912.

Meyer, S., & Shore, C. (2001). Children's understanding of dreams as mental states. *Dreaming, 11*(4): 179–194.

Moruzzi, G., & Magoun, H. W. (1949). Brain stem reticular formation and activation of the EEG. *EEG Clinical Neurophysiology, 1*: 455–473.

Natale, V., & Esposito, M. J. (2001). Bizarreness across the first four cycles of sleep. *Sleep and Hypnosis, 3*(1): 18–24.

Niederland, W. G. (1957). The earliest dreams of a young child. *Psychoanalytic Study of Child, 12*: 190–208.

Nofzinger, E., Mintun, M., Wiseman, M., Kupfer, D., & Moore, R. (1997). Forebrain activation in REM sleep: an FDG PET study. *Brain Research, 770*: 192–201.

Panksepp, J. (1998). *Affective Neuroscience: The Foundations of Human and Animal Emotions*. Oxford: Oxford University Press.

Peterson, N. D., Henke, P. G., & Hayes, Z. (2002). Limbic system function and dream content in university students. *Journal of Neuropsychiatry & Clinical Neuroscience, 14*: 283–288.

Piaget, J. (1926). *Le représentation du monde chez l'enfant*. Paris: Alcan.

Piaget, J. (1945). *La formation du symbole chez l'enfant*. Neuchâtel: Delachaux et Niestlé.

Popper, K. (1959). *The Logic of Scientific Discovery*. London: Hutchinson.

Popper, K. (1963). *Conjectures and Refutations. The Growth of Scientific Knowledge*. London: Routledge.

Rapaport, D. (1960). *The Structure of Psychoanalytic Theory. A Systematizing Attempt*. New York: International Universities Press.

Reinsel, R., Antrobus, J., & Wollman, M. (1992). Bizarreness in dreams and waking fantasy. In: J. Antrobus & M. Bertini (Eds.), *The Neuropsychology of Sleep and Dreaming* (pp. 157–183). Hillsdale, NJ: Lawrence Erlbaum.

Reinsel, R., Wollman, M., & Antrobus, J. S. (1986). Effects of enviromental contex and cortical activation on thought. *Journal of Mind and Behavior, 7*: 259–275.

Resnick, J., Stickgold, R., Rittenhouse, C., & Hobson, J. A. (1994). Self-representation and bizarreness in children's dream reports collected in the home setting. *Consciousness and Cognition, 3*: 30–45.

Robert, W. (1886). *Der Traum als Naturnotwendigkeit erklart*. Amburgo.

Saline, S. (1999). The most recent dreams of children ages 8–11. *Dreaming, 9*: 173–181.

Schredl, M., & Heuser, I. (1999). Nightmares in children: correlation to personality and stress. *Sleep Research Online, 2*: 276.

Schwartz, D. G., Weinstein, L. N., & Arkin, A. M. (1978). Qualitative aspect of sleep mentation. In: A. M. Arkin, J. S. Antrobus, & S. J. Ellman (Eds.), *The Mind in Sleep: Psychology and Psychophysiology* (pp. 143–241). Hillsdale, NJ: Lawrence Erlbaum.

Seligman, M., & Yellen, A. (1987). What is a dreaming? *Behavior Research Therapy, 25*(1): 1–24.

Sharon, T., & Wolley, J. (2004). Do monsters dream? Young children's understanding of the fantasy/reality distinction. *British Journal of Developmental Psychology, 22*(2): 293–310.

Shevrin, H. (2001). Drug dreams: an introduction. *Journal of the American Psychoanalytic Association, 49*: 69–73.

Smith, M. R., Antrobus, J. S., Gordon, E., Tucker, M. A., Hirota, Y., Wamsley, E. J., Ross, L., Doan, T., Chaklader, A., & Emery, R. N. (2004). Motivation and affect in REM sleep and the mentation reporting process. *Consciousness and Cognition, 13*: 501–511.

Solms, M. (1995). New findings on the neurological organization of dreaming: implications for psychoanalysis. *Psychoanalytic Quarterly, 64*: 43–67.

Solms, M. (1997). *The Neuropsychology of Dreams: A Clinico-Anatomical Study*. Mahwah, NJ: Lawrence Erlbaum Associates Publishers.

Solms, M. (1998). Psychoanalytic observations on four cases of ventro-mesial frontal lobe damage. *Psyche, 52*: 919–962.

Solms, M. (1999). Commentary on "The New Neuropsychology of Sleep: Implications for Psychoanalysis". *Neuro-Psychoanalysis, 1*: 183-195.

Solms, M. (2000). Dreaming and REM sleep are controlled by different brain mechanisms. *Behavioral Brain Science, 23*(6): 843–850.

Solms, M. (2004). Freud returns. *Scientific American, 290*: 83–88.

Solms, M. (2006). Dream debate. Should Freud's dream theory be abandoned? Hobson (yes) vs Solms (no). Presented to the *Conference "Toward a Science of Consciousness"*, held in April at Tucson, Arizona.

Solms, M., & Turnbull, O. (2002). *The Brain and the Inner World: An Introduction to the Neuroscience of Subjective Experience*. New York: Other Press.

Spitz, R. (1958). On the genesis of superego components. *Psychoanalytic Study of the Child, XIII*: 375–404.

Strauch, I., & Meier, B. (1996). *In Search of Dreams: Results of Experimental Dream Research*. Albany: State University of New York Press.

Thompson, R. A., & Hoffman, M. L. (1980). Empathy and the development of guilty in children. *Developmental Psychology, 16*(2): 155–156.

Trosman, H. (1963). Dream research and the psychoanalytic theory of dreams. *Archives of General Psychiatry, 9*: 9–18.

Van de Castle, R. L. (1970). Animal figures in fantasy and dreams. In: A. H. Katcher & A. M. Beck (Eds.), *New Perspectives in Our Lives With Companion Animals*. University of Pennsylvania Press.

Van de Castle, R. L. (1983). *The Psychology of Dreaming*. General Learning Press.

Van de Castle, R. L. (1994). *Our Dreaming Mind*. New York: Ballantine.

Vogel, G. W. (2000). Critique of current dream theories. *Behavioral and Brain Sciences, 23*: 1014–1016.

Wiggam, A. (1909). A contribution to the data of dream psychology. *Ped. Sem. J. Genet. Psycholo., 16*: 250.

Winget, C., & Kramer, M. (1979). *Dimension of Dream*. Gainesville: Presses of Florida.

Wollman, M., & Antrobus, J. S. (1986). Sleeping and waking thought-:effects of external stimulation. *Sleep, 9*: 438–448.

Woolley, J. D., & Boerger, E. A. (2002). Development of belief about the origins and controllability of dreams. *Developmental Psychology, 38*(1): 24–41.

Woolley, J. D., & Wellman H. M. (1992). Children's conceptions of dreams. *Cognitive Development, 7*: 365–380.

Yarrow, M. R., & Waxler, C. Z. (1976). Dimension and correlates of prosocial behavior in young children. *Child Development, 47*: 118–125.

Yu, C. K.-C. (2001). Neuroanatomical correlates of dreaming: the supra-marginal gyrus controversy (dream work). *Neuro-Psychoanalysis, 3*(1):47–59.

Yu, C. K.-C. (2003). Neuroanatomical correlates of dreaming, III: The frontal lobe controversy (dream censorship). *Neuro-Psychoanalysis, 5*(2): 159–169.

Yu, C. K.-C. (2006). Commentary on "Freudian dream theory, dream bizarreness, and the disguise–censor controversy". *Neuro-Psychoanalysis, 8*: 53–59.

Yu, C. K.-C. (2007a). Memory loss in not equal to loss of dream experience: a clinicoananatomical study of dreaming in patients with posterior brain lesions. *Neuro-Psychoanalysis, 8*: 191–198.

Yu, C. K.-C. (2007b). Cessation of dreaming and ventromesial frontal-region infarcts. *Neuro-Psychoanalysis, 9*: 83–90.

Zepelin, H. (1979). Dream distortion scale. In: C. Winget & M. Kramer (Eds.), *Dimension of Dream* (pp. 140–143). Gainesville, FL: Presses of Florida.

Zepelin, H. (1989). Bizarreness in REM dreams. *Sleep Research, 18*: 161.

Zito, A., Cicogna, P., & Cavallero, C. (1992). Sogni REM e sogni di addormentamento: in che termini è ancora legittimo parlare di differenze? *Ricerche di Psicologia, 2*: 7–18.